"All Scripture is given by inspiration of God, and is profitable for doctrine, for reproof, for correction, for instruction in righteousness, that the man of God may be complete, thoroughly equipped for every good work"
2 Timothy 3:16-17

Walnut Street Church of Christ

Manifesting the fruit of the Spirit...
Proclaiming Christ to the lost...
Serving mankind...
To the glory of God!

Walnut Street 2024 Devotional Book
© 2023 by Walnut Street Church of Christ
All rights reserved.

Published by Walnut Street Church of Christ
Center Avenue, Dickson, TN 37055, USA

Assembly times:
Sunday Worship: 9:00 AM & 5:00 PM
Sunday Bible Classes: 10:15 AM
Wednesday Bible Study: 7:00 PM

Author Index Included

From WSCOC Elders

The Walnut Street Church family was asked early in 2023 to write devotionals to be included in a devotional book for 2024. Many of our family responded resulting in this book. We hope it will be a blessing to our church family, our community, our friends and our neighbors.

The idea of making God's thoughts and plans a priority for a child of God is the goal of this book. These short devotionals should help focus our minds on spiritual insights that will make our day better. Many of them highlight only a few verses and some a single verse on which we can meditate throughout the day.

In addition to regular reading of the Bible, let's also begin our day by reading each day's devotional, valuing our time spent in prayer and cherishing our time with the Word of God. We must take the time to reflect on the spiritual implications of the things we have on our calendar each day. When we begin our day with God, it seems everything else goes better.

We are encouraged and pleased with these powerful devotionals and the writers are to be commended. It is our earnest prayer that this volume will be received with delight, read daily and shared freely.

Bob Spencer and Gary Brunett
(for the elders)
January 1, 2024

Introduction

"All Scripture is given by inspiration of God, and is profitable for doctrine, for reproof, for correction, for instruction in righteousness, that the man of God may be complete, thoroughly equipped for every good work" (2 Timothy 3:16-17). While no other source of instruction and insight provides the help and healing provided by the Word of God, the thoughts and insights of saints, young and old, regarding the application of the Word can bring us closer to a better understanding of God's will for our lives.

This Walnut Street 2024 Devotional Book offers Monday through Friday devotionals containing brief, easily readable devotionals, written by Christians from every point along the physical and spiritual spectrum. Each devotional is written for the purpose of stimulating the reader to meditate on the Scripture and dig deeper into the ever enriching Word of God.

Special appreciation is extended to: the Walnut Street elders who authorized that this work be undertaken, all who authored the devotionals, those talented individuals who carefully proofread each submission (Becky Cargile, Allee Hill, Richard Jones, LeAnn Polk, and Barbara Mangrum), Shawn Harmon who designed the cover, and to our entire staff who supported this effort in a variety of ways (Pamela Massie, Wanda Phillips, Barbara Mangrum, LeAnn Polk, Shawn Harmon, Chris Hedge, Kyle Dickerson, Chad Garrett, and Chris McCurley).

May God richly bless you as you read these devotionals, delve deeper into His Word, and grow as a child of God.

Steve Baggett
Associate Minister

Monday, January 1, 2024

The Best Dream

Alice Poole

Today's Scripture: Hebrews 4:15

When it comes to sleep, I've been blessed. I'm one of those lucky people who can go to sleep easily and sleep soundly. Seven to nine hours is typical for me. The flip side is that I rarely remember my dreams. A few years ago, I was blessed to awaken and remember the best dream. Details have faded, but I still remember the main parts. I was trying to tell someone about God's wonderful plan, the plan that was His even before creation.

I recounted that God created man and this amazing universe in which we live, our purpose being to glorify Him. He gave us free will; we are not robots. We worship and glorify Him willingly because we love Him. Creating us as human, He knew that we would sin. No human has ever been without sin except Christ. The Old Testament laws teach us about sin. Those many laws were impossible to keep completely; yearly sacrifices were required to roll sins forward. The Old Testament also teaches us about God's nature; He cannot abide sin. He is a loving God, as witnessed by His patience with mankind, but our sins keep us from His presence. When the time was right, it was His plan for Jesus Christ to come to earth and live as a man. He lived among us, teaching us with His words and His example, and finally gave Himself as the perfect sacrifice for our sins. He took all of our sins upon Himself when His blood was shed, and He died for us on the cross. He arose, took His place at God's right side, and is our high priest to God. "For we do not have a high priest who is unable to sympathize with our weaknesses, but one who in every respect has been tempted as we are, but without sin" (Heb. 4:15).

Application for the Day: Today I will remember God's wonderful, simple plan and His amazing grace, and I will continue to follow Christ's example, walking in His light and loving God supremely.

1

Tuesday, January 2, 2024

The Only Way Out Is Through

Andrea Beaubien

Today's Scripture: Romans 12:9-18

I love the phrase "The Only Way Out Is Through." I think about it practically every day!

Here are some scenarios where it seems to fit: exercise, difficult conversations, global pandemics, new learning, haunted houses, life, eliminating debt, escaping temptation, and getting through someone's devotional thoughts. To me the phrase means that going through something, which may or may not be unpleasant, has some sort of reward on the other side of the something.

Bryan McAlister once shared a list of ideas and suggestions to adopt when getting "through" seems too daunting. His thoughts came from Roman 12:9-18.

- Get sick and let people serve you.
- Believe that others are praying for you.
- Make a plan, regardless of how you feel, and carry it out.
- Wake up at the same time every day.
- Read THE book every day.
- Listen daily to what God says about you.
- Hear, discern, but don't believe what the world says about God.
- Read more than one book at a time.
- Be intentional with your speech.
- Daily tell your spouse, children, and those closest to you that they are valuable and loved.

When I looked up the original quotation of the phrase "the only way out is through," I learned that it is from Robert Frost's poem "Servant of Servants." Here is the excerpt: "Len says one steady pull more ought to do it. He says the best way out is always through." It seems to be saying that just one more row, one more push, one more prayer, and just steadily holding on will get us through to the other side. For Christians, the other side is Heaven and being in God's presence always.

I know you are going through something right now. And no one may know or understand. I hope these words can encourage your heart a little and help you hold on.

Application for the Day: Today I will remember that the best way out is always through and that Jesus makes it possible.

Wednesday, January 3, 2024

Slow to Anger

Anita Moore

Today's Scripture: Ephesians 4:26-27; 1 Corinthians 13:5

In 2012 during a Wednesday night Ladies Bible Class, a sweet friend shared a book by Lysa Terkeurst called <u>Unglued: Making Wise Choices in the Midst of Raw Emotions</u>. Courtney read an excerpt from the book, and I was convinced it was something I needed to read. I was struggling with anger – A LOT of anger. I was aware that my most important relationships with my husband and children were fraying, and I was causing them a lot of pain. I also noticed some relationships with my siblings were suffering; it seemed like every area of my life was being scorched by my uncontrolled anger. Thank God for calling me out and helping me seek counseling with Bud Lambert. It was the beginning of a healing journey that I am still on today.

I learned that anger is an action as well as a reaction. It is a secondary emotion that is really a symptom that something deeper is going on in your heart and soul. Anger is a poor coping mechanism and can become an addiction. You can wire your brain to respond to situations, even small ones, with anger. It becomes your go-to when things get stressful. Anger is a choice, a very poor one.

Throughout Scripture God encourages us to put away anger, and Paul tells us our anger will not achieve God's righteous will. As Lysa says in her book, "God gives us emotions to build relationships not to destroy them." I pray if you are struggling with anger, that you recognize how destructive it is and will reach out for help. As always God will provide a way to escape from this flesh response. He can make beauty from our ashes, and there can be true healing when we seek Him with our whole heart.

Application for Today: I will reach for God's help when angry. I will pray to be full of compassion and mercy for others, as well as myself. I will thank Him for His abounding love and faithfulness and seek His help and healing through His Word and His church.

Thursday, January 4, 2024

Anxiety and Worry

Written by Dr. B.J. Smith
Published Here In His Loving Memory
(January 17, 1934 – June 5, 2023)

Today's Scripture: Philippians 4: 6-7 - "Do not be anxious about anything, but in situation, by prayer and petition, with thanksgiving, present your requests to God. And the peace of God, which transcends all understanding, will guard your hearts and your minds in Christ Jesus."

Worry is a conscious choice to try to control life events, rather than believe that God is in control. Worry is a thief that robs us of joy, energy, peace of mind, and strength. Society is worrying itself to death. What are the major problems in our society today to God? God promises to guard our hearts and minds if we give everything to Him. Our bodies were not meant to carry these worries.

The antidote for worry is absolute faith in God, turning everything over to Him in prayer. During our prayers, God wants us to have an attitude of thanksgiving, not complaining. It seems there is always something to worry about. Overcoming anxiety and worry is a struggle for most people; very few seem truly carefree and optimistic about the future. Christians have a secure future, so we should be the happiest people on earth. Anxiety is a result of envisioning the future without God.

The best defense against worry is staying in communication with God. When your thoughts turn toward God, you think much more positively. Remember to listen as well as to speak, making your thoughts a talk with God.

If you must think about events that are troublesome, the following may be helpful.
1. Do not linger in the future, for anxieties sprout like mushrooms.
2. Remember the promise of God's continual presence; include God in any imagery that comes to mind. This mental imagery does not come easily because we are accustomed to being the gods of our own fantasies. However, the reality of God's presence with us, now and forevermore, outshines any fantasy we could ever imagine.

Application for the Day: Today I will remember to "Cast all your anxiety on Him because he cares for you" (1 Pet. 5:7).

Friday, January 5, 2024

We Are Not Always Okay

Barbara Mangrum

Today's Scripture: "And this is the confidence that we have toward him, that if we ask anything according to his will he hears us" (1 John 5:14).

Today's daily life gives us many challenges and disappointments to face. We should always remember that God doesn't expect us always to "Be Okay." We get wrapped up in being strong and staying "put together" or have been taught to just "suck it up." We don't allow ourselves to be vulnerable. We often hesitate to ask for assistance when we need it from others. Pride keeps us from admitting that we are not okay. We often fear that we may let friends or family down if we admit we need help. To admit we are "Not Okay" feels like we are admitting failure. God loves us and will forgive us for our weaknesses. The Bible teaches, "For all have sinned and fall short of the glory of God" (Rom. 3:23).

God understands that we may need to ask Him for strength, forgiveness, and guidance at times during our lives. Psalm 46:10 states, "Be still, and know that I am God." Being still means to stop striving or fighting, but to relax or put our hands down. We should stop putting our hands up to defend ourselves from all that life can bring our way. We should let God take care of our disappointments, heartaches, personal imperfections, and pain. If we lean on God for our strength, He will help us meet the challenges of life.

Proverbs 3:5-6 says, "Trust in the LORD with all your heart, and do not lean on your own understanding. In all your ways acknowledge him, and he will make straight your paths." With any challenge we might face, God will always be there when we need Him to guide us in the path that we need to follow.

Application for the Day: Today, if life hands me anything that makes me feel "Not Okay," I will admit that I need a place to rest my heart and spirit, and I will pray to God for His guidance and understanding.

5

Monday, January 8, 2024

A Gold Ring in a Pig's Snout

Becky Cargile

Today's Scripture: Proverbs 11:22 – "Like a gold ring in a pig's snout is a beautiful woman without discretion."

This is one of the more colorful proverbs in the Bible. It's what I like to refer to as a "visual oxymoron." You are probably familiar with oxymorons: jumbo shrimp, working vacation, silent scream, etc. But this is a picture of two things that don't go together: a gold ring and a pig's nose. As they are for many women today, nose rings were popular in Old Testament times. Abraham's servant presented Rebekah with bracelets and a nose ring when he was wooing her for Isaac (Gen. 24:47). God told unfaithful Jerusalem in Ezekiel 16:12, "And I put a ring on your nose and earrings in your ears and a beautiful crown on your head."

Pigs were also abundant in Old Testament times, but they were considered unclean for the Israelites. Leviticus 11:7-8 says that God's people could not eat pork or even touch a pig's carcass. No wonder the prodigal son's job in Luke 15 would have been such an embarrassment to him!

Who would dream of putting something so beautiful (like a gold ring) in the nose of something so detestable (like a pig)? No one. Not now—and certainly not then. But that is the image that the Bible paints here of a woman without discretion.

Who were such women in the Bible? Eve, Lot's wife, Potiphar's wife, Jezebel, Delilah, and certainly the "unworthy woman" of Proverbs 7. Conversely, who were some discretionary women in the Bible? Esther, Ruth, Mary (the mother of Jesus), Lydia, Priscilla, Lois and Eunice, and certainly the "worthy woman" of Proverbs 31.

While this devotional is written especially for women, it should apply to all children of God. We are supposed to be the image of Christ; let's be sure that we are living up to our calling.

Application for the Day: Today I will strive to present a lovely picture to the world of what a Christian should look and act like.

Tuesday, January 9, 2024

A Personal God

Becky Cargile

Today's Scripture: Psalm 139

Have you ever felt that you were just a speck in this world and that no one else knew what makes you tick or cares very much about you? If that's the case, please read Psalm 139. In this psalm, David says that the Creator of the universe knows you intimately and cares about what happens to you.

First, David says that God knows everything he does and every-thing he says, even before he says it. David reacts by saying that he cannot even comprehend this fact; it is "too wonderful for me" (vr. 6). Then he says that there is no place in this world that he might go but that God is already there—in the heavens, in Sheol (the place of the dead), in the depths of the sea, or in the blackest darkness. If such was true for David, it must be true for us as well. Wherever we go, God is there with us, offering His mercy and grace to help us through any trial.

Next, David says that God knew him basically from the time he was conceived—when his parts were still unformed in the womb. Jesus says in Matthew 10 that God cares about the sparrows that fall to the ground and that he cares for us even more. In verse 31, Jesus claims, "You are of more value than many sparrows." And in verse 30, Jesus assures us that "the hairs of your head are all numbered." That's a pretty powerful statement about a God who might some-times feel far from us.

Just remember that if God seems far from you today, He has not moved an inch. He is still loving you and looking out for your best interests. If you have moved away from Him, why don't you make the decision to rest in His arms once again? It's THE PLACE where you can find joy and peace.

Application for the Day: Today I will draw near to the One who is always available to me.

7

Wednesday, January 10, 2024

Listening to the Wrong Voices
Becky Cargile

Today's Scriptures: 1 Kings 22; 2 Chronicles 18

King Ahab (of Israel) had many strikes against him. He did not follow the ways of the Lord. 1 Kings 16:30 says that he "did evil in the sight of the Lord, more than all who were before him." Not only did he commit the sins of Jeroboam, but he also married Jezebel, a Sidonian, and began to worship her god, Baal. 1 Kings 16:33 says that Ahab "did more to provoke the Lord, the God of Israel, to anger than all the kings of Israel who were before him."

One day King Jehoshaphat (of Judah) and King Ahab got together and decided to go to war against Syria. First, however, Jehoshaphat wanted the Lord's blessing on this venture. At his insistence, Ahab called together 400 prophets—all bad guys. They told the two kings that they would surely be successful in this war. Jehoshaphat wasn't satisfied with their counsel, so he asked Ahab to call the prophet Michaiah for his advice. Ahab hesitated because he believed that Michaiah always prophesied evil against him. And Michaiah told the kings the truth—advice which caused Ahab to throw him in prison.

When the battle began, Ahab disguised himself as a soldier, and 1 Kings 22:34 says that "someone drew his bow **at random** and hit the king of Israel between the sections of his armor." Ahab died that day. Does that sound a bit like the David and Goliath story?

Sometimes we are tempted to seek advice from those who will tell us what we want to hear. Not only is such the case in our personal lives, but also in our religion. 2 Timothy 4:3 says, "For the time is coming when people will not endure sound teaching, but having itching ears they will accumulate for themselves teachers to suit their own passions." Let's be aware that God's will is going to be carried out—with OR without us.

Application for the Day: Today I will seek advice from the Word and from faithful Christians.

Thursday, January 11, 2024

Mature Christians
Becky Cargile

Today's Scripture: Psalm 92:12, 14

When my dad was in his 80s, he bought a lift chair and a motorcycle during the same week. With his arthritis, he needed the lift chair. At his age, however, he did **not** need the motorcycle. A small part of me was happy that he was so ambitious at his age. A much bigger part of me was afraid that he was going to kill himself—and possibly others. It wasn't long, fortunately, until Dad realized that the motorcycle was not in his best interest, so he traded it for a bright yellow tricycle (a three-wheeled motorcycle), which he rode around the neighborhood until he finally got tired of it.

There is a group of people in any congregation who are not as young as we used to be. That does not mean, however, that we cannot be active in the Lord's work. We may not be able figuratively to ride motorcycles, but we can fit comfortably on tricycles and ride to the glory of God. Translated into practical terms, we may not be able to continue to go on short-term foreign door-knocking mission trips, but we can support a young person with the financial load of such a trip. Especially in wintry weather, we may not be able to visit as much as we would like, but we can always pick up the phone or send a card to those who are sick, bereaved, or lonely. And we can always offer advice to those who are struggling and who seek our counsel.

Psalm 92:12, 14 says, "The righteous flourish like the palm tree and grow like a cedar in Lebanon . . . They still bear fruit in old age; they are ever full of sap and green." Remember that, while we may retire from secular work, we cannot retire as Christians. Let us resolve to be like the aged Paul, who "fought the good fight" and "finished the race" (2 Tim. 4:7-8).

Application for the Day: Today I will try to do something to bring glory to God—whatever my age.

Friday, January 12, 2024

Memorizing Scriptures
Becky Cargile

Today's Scriptures: Psalm 55:2a; Psalm 119:10b

When I was young, I went to Mid-South Youth Camp in Henderson every summer. One year I participated in a challenge at camp to memorize 100 Bible verses well enough to recite them all at once. For that feat, I was awarded a blue ribbon, but I also received much more. I can still recall many of those verses well enough to recite them today. And when I am discouraged by hardships or when I am tempted, I can receive strength from those scriptures. Psalm 55:2a says, "Cast your burden on the Lord, and he will sustain you." Psalm 119:10b says, "I have hidden your word in my heart that I might not sin against you."

I have a good friend in Sarasota, Florida, who has been legally blind for about two years. All her life, she has been a student of God's word, and when she lost her sight, one of her first thoughts was that she would not be able to read her Bible. She and I have a mutual friend in Jackson, Tennessee, who calls her several times a week. Not long ago, the two women formed a habit of memorizing scriptures together over the phone. Both friends have told me what a rewarding experience this practice has been for them. I would venture to say, further, that it is much easier for two women to refrain from gossip if they are busily committing scriptures to memory!

I still enjoy memorization. The older I get, though, the harder it is for me to learn new passages. I hope that all of our parents with children at home will encourage their little ones to memorize Bible verses. You could create your own system, or you might participate in the program of the Lads to Leaders organization. Either way, you and your children will be blessed. Psalm 119:97 says, "Oh how I love your law! It is my meditation all the day."

Application for the Day: Today I will spend time meditating on and memorizing a favorite passage from God's word.

Monday, January 15, 2024

The Very Best Adoption

Becky Cargile

Today's Scripture: Ephesians 1:5

One day in August 1975, my husband, a second-year family practice resident, just "happened" to be walking down the hall of the hospital when he was summoned by a fellow resident. The other resident was in delivery and sensed that he could not finish in time to assist another woman who was in labor across the hall. After my husband delivered a healthy, red-haired little girl, he noticed on her chart that she was going to be put up for adoption. Three days later, that little baby went home with us. And before long, she was legally and permanently "ours."

Ever since that time, Ephesians 1:5 has been special to me: "God decided in advance to adopt us into his own family by bringing us to himself through Jesus Christ. This is what he wanted to do, and it gave him great pleasure" (NLT). I can identify with that verse because we chose that little girl to be ours and our decision gave us great pleasure. I can even identify with the first part of Romans 8:17: "And since we are his children, we are his heirs." When we die, we plan for our daughter to inherit from us as though she were ours from conception.

Romans 8:17, however, continues: "In fact, together with Christ we are heirs of God's glory." The KJV calls us "joint heirs." That part is hard for me to identify with. I simply cannot imagine sharing our daughter's inheritance with the world. But an even harder verse for me is Romans 5:8, which says, "But God showed his great love for us by sending Christ to die for us while we were still sinners." It's impossible for me to fathom the deep love that my Father has for me. To be adopted into God's family and to be an heir of God and a joint heir with Jesus, whom God sacrificed for me, must be the very best kind of adoption.

Application for the Day: Today I will treasure my adoption into God's precious family.

Tuesday, January 16, 2024

Worse Than a She-Bear?

Becky Cargile

Today's Scripture: Proverbs 17:12

This summer Ken and I traveled with another couple to the Grand Tetons and Yellowstone National Park in Wyoming. Besides seeing hundreds (maybe thousands) of bison, as well as elk and moose, we took a wrong turn one afternoon and happened upon a mother grizzly with three healthy cubs. She literally ran across the highway, and her babies followed closely behind.

The incident happened so quickly that I could barely grab my camera and get a quick photo of the bear as she scampered in front of our car and a second photo of just one of her babies—the slowest one. Meanwhile, a park ranger several yards away was yelling for gawkers to get back in their vehicles because she realized how dangerous that mama bear could be if she felt that her babies were being threatened.

Ken sometimes watches TV shows about animals, and he related to the group incidents where bears ripped off car doors or attacked people. He said enough to make me glad that none of us ventured from our rented Ford Explorer that day. As far as I could tell, that grizzly mama seemed placid enough, but I knew that she had the potential for destruction—and I didn't want to upset her.

Coincidentally, one of the daily Bible readings while we were on the trip was Proverbs 17, and verse 12 reads this way: "Let a man meet a she-bear robbed of her cubs rather than a fool in his folly." It's hard to imagine that facing an enraged grizzly would be better than dealing with a fool, but that's just what this verse says. The book of Proverbs contains several reminders about fools (12:23, 13:20, 18:2, 23:9), and Paul describes those who "claiming to be wise . . . became fools" (Rom. 1:22). May we all realize the potential that we have for good, but may we also realize the harm we can cause if we do not live according to God's will.

Application for the Day: Today I will strive to make wise decisions and avoid foolish choices.

Wednesday, January 17, 2024

Blocked

Becky Cline

Today's Scripture: Matthew 6:13

Have you ever been about to cross a train track only to see flashing lights and arms going down to block your way? It's frustrating, but these hindrances provide safety. God provides roadblocks as well for our spiritual safety.

In 1 Samuel 25:2-42, we read the amazing story of Abigail. When her worthless husband, Nabal, offends David by refusing to provide food for him and his men, David prepares to kill every male in the household. When Abigail is alerted to the problem, she immediately loads donkeys with food and drink for David and his men. Then she bravely approaches them as they come ready to attack. Abigail falls on her face before David, taking the blame for Nabal's lack of hospitality. Obviously amazed, David says, "'Blessed is the Lord God of Israel, who sent you this day to meet me! And blessed is your advice and blessed are you, because you have kept me this day from coming to bloodshed" (1 Sam. 25:32-33a). David's plan is suddenly blocked by a beautiful, intelligent, courageous young woman, who will eventually become his wife.

In Acts 9, Saul is on his way to Damascus to persecute followers of the Way. When a light from heaven shines around him and a voice speaks to him, Saul falls to the ground terrified. "And he said, 'Who are you, Lord?' Then the Lord said, 'I am Jesus, whom you are persecuting. It is hard for you to kick against the goads'" (Acts 9:5). Saul never turns back. That roadblock leads him in a new direction for the rest of his life.

We may sometimes feel like mice in a maze experiment when the way we want to go is blocked, but I have actually learned to pray to be blocked when I am going the wrong way because it allows me to stop and consider what choice I am trying to make and what choice God wants me to make.

Application for the Day: Today I will pay attention to the roadblocks God puts in my path and trust in His will for my life.

Thursday, January 18, 2024

Comfort in a Traffic Light

Becky Cline

Today's Scripture: Psalm 5:11, 12

There are two things that cause me extreme anxiety - mice and traffic. The mice phobia dates back to childhood, but the traffic anxiety has evolved as traffic has gotten worse. That's why I love traffic lights! I hate merging, pulling into turning lanes with oncoming traffic, or having to pull out of store parking lots, and I usually refuse to turn left without an arrow!

I was sitting at a traffic light one afternoon when I realized traffic lights are calming. Sure, there are always those who take risks by running through red lights, but generally, people stop. Then, when the light turns green, everyone can go safely relying on the opposite side of the light to have once again stopped traffic.

God is our traffic light when He allows us to safely go or stop by obeying His will. A hymn I grew up with is <u>Trust and Obey,</u> and includes, "Trust and obey for there's no other way to be happy in Jesus but to trust and obey." Whether we like them or not, "rules" give us a sense of security when we understand the boundaries and how they protect us. We can acknowledge that with traffic lights, and we can accept and be grateful for the "soul safety measures" provided in His word. In fact, we show love for God when we submit to him (I John 5:3), and he then abides in us (I John 3:24).

To be conditioned to obey traffic lights, we must trust that they will work to make traffic flow properly and to reduce accidents. To be able to obey God, we need to trust just as the old hymn says (Psalm 5:11, 12). Trust takes faith, "so then faith comes by hearing, and hearing by the word of God" (Romans 10:17). So, then we're back to God's being like a traffic light for us by providing guidance and safety through his word

Application for Today: I will rely on the guidance and safety of God's word by trusting and obeying! Now to deal with mice!

Friday, January 19, 2024

Important Memories

Becky Cline

Today's Scripture: Deuteronomy 11:18-19

"It was a beautiful spring day in May, and I was out picking peas." That's how my mother always started the story of my birth. She would go on to describe what she and my dad were wearing and how her principal hadn't even known she was pregnant because she had disguised the fact all winter and spring. She wouldn't have been allowed to keep teaching back then.

The yearly birth memory used to annoy or embarrass me, but by the time my own children and grandchildren were born, I came not only to expect it, but to look forward to it. The last May of my mother's life found her failing both physically and mentally, and I had resigned myself to the fact that I would never hear my birth story again, but I did. It has never been written down until now, but I remembered it. Now I make it a point to tell my children their birth story and to encourage them to do the same for their children.

Passover was instituted to commemorate the saving of Israel from the death angel. Moses, on behalf of God, told the people always to remember that event (Ex. 12:23-27). Later, Moses instructed the people to make sure they continued to tell their children and grandchildren about the laws given to them (Deut. 11:18, 19). It wasn't enough for instructions to be written down; they were to be spoken as well.

In Luke 22:19, as Jesus instituted the Lord's Supper, He said, "This is my body which is given for you; do this in remembrance of me." Jesus didn't tell His apostles to run out and write everything down right then but to remember. Fortunately, for us, the command to remember was written down as Scripture through the guidance of the Holy Spirit. Spoken or written, memories are special!

Application for the Day: Today I will focus on the memories of Jesus: His life, His death, His burial, and His resurrection, not only as I take of the Lord's Supper each Sunday but also as part of my everyday life.

Just a Pinch

Becky Cline

Lesson Scripture: *I Corinthians 5:6-8*

I always let my children and grandchildren make a dessert request for their birthdays. Recently, one granddaughter requested a lemon meringue pie. I had never made meringue, but I was determined to tackle it. I followed the recipe carefully, but my egg whites were not whipping up like they should. After whipping them until my mixer was getting hot, I called my husband into the kitchen to see if he could find the problem. He asked if I had gotten anything into the egg whites before I started whipping them. I had gotten just a little bit of egg yolk into the egg whites. I had to pour out all the egg whites and start over. This time, the egg whites beat up beautifully, and I had made my first (and maybe my last!) meringue.

In Matthew 13:33, Jesus compared the kingdom of heaven to leaven in a positive manner. Leaven is a symbol of spreading from the inside out, foretelling the growth of the church through the Holy Spirit. In Matthew 16:5-12, however, Jesus cautioned His disciples against the leaven of the Pharisees and the Sadducees. The disciples didn't understand at first because they missed the meaning of Jesus' teachings, but they finally understand that Jesus was warning about false doctrines.

In I Corinthians 5:1-8, Paul reprimanded the church in Corinth for ignoring sexual immorality in an even boastful manner. He emphasized that allowing sin to reign in one situation will allow it to continue more and more just as leaven spreads. Paul gave a positive twist to discipline, however, by encouraging a "new lump" that would result in sincerity and truth.

If Paul were with us today, would he need to remind us to beware of certain leaven? Do we need to throw out old ways like I had to do with the egg whites?

Application for Today: Today I will be a reflection of the type of leaven Jesus describes as we strive to serve Him in the kingdom of heaven.

Tuesday, January 23, 2024

Makeup Armor

Becky Cline

Today's Scripture: Ephesians 6:10-18

When I was in the eighth grade, my parents gave me an ornate-looking makeup mirror for Christmas. Now, after more years than I care to mention, I still have and use that same mirror. I began to look at my makeup routine as a type of armor for the day. As I carefully apply each item, I think about the challenges ahead.

It occurred to me one day that my makeup "armor" was only a physical preparation for the day. It was actually useless spiritually, but then I began to reflect on one of my favorite passages, Ephesians 6:11-13, in which Paul gives the call to battle with the requirement for spiritual warfare: "Put on the whole armor of God, that you may be able to stand against the schemes of the devil. For we do not wrestle against flesh and blood, but against the rulers, against the authorities, against the cosmic powers over this present darkness, against the spiritual forces of evil in the heavenly places. Therefore, take up the whole armor of God, that you may be able to withstand in the evil day, and having done all, to stand firm."

I have always loved the idea of conquering an evil foe. My guidance office contained figures of Yoda from Star Wars and Gandalf from Lord of the Rings, along with a Precious Moments figurine of a soldier. The real foe, however, is neither Darth Vader nor Sauron, but Satan, as Peter well knew and warned against in I Peter 5:8: "Be sober-minded; be watchful. Your adversary the devil prowls around like a roaring lion, seeking someone to devour." For this reason, a daily inventory of our battle gear is necessary before we go to war, and it is all laid out for us to "put on" in Ephesians 6:14-17.

Makeup obviously isn't armor to rely upon. Money, power, popularity, jobs, education, etc. cannot make a dent in Satan's arsenal. We, however, have been given the secret weapon—Jesus Christ!

Application for the Day: Today I will pray for strength to continue to fight in the army of God!

Wednesday, January 24, 2024

Take a Load Off

Becky Cline

Today's Scripture: Matthew 11:28-30

Have you ever had something or someone weighing so heavily on you that you felt like you were sinking in emotional quicksand? Have your precious children ever worn you down to the point you felt like you had nothing left to give? Is your job sucking the life out of you? Have your commitments begun to close in on you? Well, guess what! You are not alone!

We like to think that we can handle everything life throws at us. Even Moses fell into that trap. While Moses dealt with Pharaoh and led the people out of Egypt, his wife and sons remained with Jethro, his father-in-law. When they journeyed into the wilderness to be with Moses again, Jethro noticed that Moses was spending day after day judging the people from morning until night and made an insightful suggestion: "Look for able men from all the people, men who fear God, who are trustworthy and hate a bribe, and place such men over the people as chiefs of thousands, of hundreds, of fifties, and of tens. And let them judge the people at all times. Every great matter they shall bring to you, but any small matter they shall decide themselves. So it will be easier for you, and they will bear the burden with you" (Exodus 18:21-22).

Jesus understood what it means to be weighed down. Choosing to leave the perfection of heaven for a world of sin, being rejected by his own family and friends, and knowing the horrors of the cross that ultimately awaited him, he still offered to take our burdens. "Come to me, all who labor and are heavy laden, and I will give you rest. Take my yoke upon you, and learn from me, for I am gentle and lowly in heart, and you will find rest for your souls. For my yoke is easy, and my burden is light" (Matthew 11:28-30).

Moses listened. Can we?

Application for the Day: Today I will be willing to accept help, whether from God or from those around me.

Thursday, January 25, 2024

Your Best vs. Mediocrity

Becky Cline

Today's Scripture: Colossians 3:17

When I started college, I already had nine years of public speaking training, including five years of theater. The required freshman speech class looked like a piece of cake to me, even though most of the other students were visibly trembling at the very thought of getting up in front of the class to make a speech. Many were seniors who had put this requirement off until the last quarter. (Yes, we were on a quarter schedule back then.)

After my first speech, the professor called me aside and said, "It's obvious that you have given speeches before. Can you imagine how it would be if you actually tried?" I was indignant and embarrassed that he had called me out on my first speech and had highlighted my mediocrity. After all, my other classes were extremely challenging, so having a speech class that I could basically float through seemed like a reasonable idea. The more I pondered his words, however, the more I realized that I had fallen into a mediocrity trap.

I think many of us try to slide by in our spiritual lives. My Daddy used to call it "tiptoeing into hell." That may sound harsh, but can you really "just get by" with God? The book of Colossians has quite a bit to say about how to be pleasing to God. Colossians 1:10 reads, "So as to walk in a manner worthy of the Lord, fully pleasing to him: bearing fruit in every good work and increasing in the knowledge of God," and in Colossians 3:17, Paul admonishes, "And whatever you do, in word or deed, do everything in the name of the Lord Jesus, giving thanks to God the Father through him." If I'm reading these verses correctly, mediocrity can't be part of our spiritual lives if we are to bear fruit, increase in the knowledge of God, and serve the Lord Christ through what we do!

Application for the Day: Today I will thank God for not being mediocre in His plan for me!

Friday, January 26, 2024

Feeding Our Fire
Bernadette Bullington

Today's Scripture: Hebrews 12:1

"I stand to praise You, but I fall to my knees. My spirit is willing, but my flesh is so weak. Light the fire in my soul. . ." ("Light the Fire" by Bill Maxwell). These words are often sung with great passion, but then what? What happens once the fire is lit in my soul? Hebrews contains some very practical suggestions to feeding our fire.

We can begin by rereading the stories of the faithful in Hebrews 11. People like Abraham, Jacob, or Moses: men who withstood fire, sword, scourging, imprisonment, and even death. Then we can renew our commitment to worship with the people of God and participate in Bible studies (Heb. 10:23-25). Remembering those of old who remained faithful, being with those who are faithful today, and encouraging others to be their best selves can help us feed our fire.

Then we must look "diligently lest any man fail of the grace of God" (Heb. 12:15). We have all sinned (Rom. 3:23), and all must repent. Then "being justified by faith, we have *peace* with God" (Rom. 5:1). With that inner peace, we can continue the race, running with patience, focusing on Jesus, so that "we may serve God acceptably with reverence and godly fear" (Heb. 12:28).

We may need to "reframe" an experience to remind ourselves of the Lord working in our lives. We read in Hebrews 12:2, "Jesus . . . who for the joy that was set before Him endured the cross." Christ "reframed" the horror of the cross and His impending death as "joy" because of the blessings He knew it would bring. We may not know why, but "we know that all things work together for good to them that love God, to them who are called according to his purpose" (Rom. 8:28).

Finally, in Philippians 4:4, Paul encourages us to "rejoice in the Lord always," and in Philippians 4:13, to remember, "I can do all things through Christ."

Application for Today: Today I will ask God to help me feed my fire to live for Him.

Monday, January 29, 2024

Imitation, Not Fake

Bernadette Bullington

Today's Scripture: Ephesians 5:1

A few years ago, I had the privilege of watching Alma Sagurit, a dressmaker in the Philippines, create one of the most beautiful dresses I had ever seen. She began her work by creating a pattern to ensure that her finished product was exactly as she envisioned. The result was not a fake, but a work of art created from a perfect pattern.

In Ephesians 5:1, we are commanded to "be imitators of God, as beloved children." God isn't asking us to be a fake, pretending to be something we are not. He is asking us to imitate, follow as a model, take on the same qualities that Christ exhibited, and reflect God to others. In 1 Peter 2:21-25, we are told that Christ left us a pattern that we should follow in His footsteps.

Paul had taken this command to heart and worked hard to imitate Christ, so much so that in 1 Corinthians 4:16 and 11:1, Paul encouraged those in Corinth to "imitate" him as he "imitates" Christ. In 2 Thessalonians 3:7, Paul encouraged the Thessalonians to imitate him and to keep their eyes on those who walked according to the example set by him.

How does one become an imitator of God? In Matthew 16:24-26, Christ tells us to deny ourselves and take up our cross. In Philippians 2:5, we are told to have the mind of Christ. In 2 Timothy 2:15, we are told to give diligence to be approved by God, "a workman who does not need to be ashamed." We must study all of God's word and the life of Christ in detail. We can't imitate or reflect what we don't know.

Just like the beautiful dress mentioned in the beginning of this devotional, Christians can only become the beautiful, finished products God has envisioned for them if they use Christ as their perfect pattern. 3 John 1:11 says, "Do not imitate what is evil, but what is good."

Application for Today: Today I will ask God to help me be a true imitation of Christ.

Tuesday, January 30, 2024

Pardon the Interruption

Bernadette Bullington

Today's Scripture: James 4:13-17

"God is in the interruptions in my life and seldom in my plans," says Gloria Gaither. At times I think we are all guilty of this mind-set. We have everything planned for the day, and then someone calls with a care, need, etc. We struggle between our plan and their need and fail to remember that God had a different plan for our day. He doesn't mind if I have my plans; He just doesn't mind interrupting them.

So often we read passages in the Bible about people with plans that begin with words like "he was on his way" and "as they went on," when God interrupted their plan for a much bigger one. In Genesis 32:1-2, Jacob was "on his way" when the angels of God met him and changed his life. In Exodus 3:1-4, while Moses was leading his flock, the angel of the Lord appeared to him in a burning bush and changed the course of history. In Matthew 4:18-20, while Peter and Andrew were fishing, Jesus walked by and called them to be fishers of men. They all had a plan, not a bad plan, just not God's plan for them.

There are many other examples of both men's and Christ's plans being interrupted for a much greater good: 2 Kings 2:11; Matthew 14:13-14; Matthew 15:21-22. Also another very notable one is in Acts 9:3 when Saul was traveling to Damascus to arrest Christians for imprisonment or slaughter.

"Sometimes you have to let go of the picture of what you thought life would be like and learn to find joy in the story you are actually living," says Rachel Marie Martin (*The Brave Art of Motherhood*). Proverbs 16:9 states, "A man's heart devises his way, but the Lord directs his steps."

Application for Today: Today I will consider this thought: if I knew then what I know now, would I have been frustrated when my plans were interrupted?

Wednesday, January 31, 2024

Respect
Bobby Cathey

Today's Scripture: Proverbs 22:1

At a very young age, I was taught respect: "yes ma'am, yes sir, no ma'am, no sir," and most of all to respect God's Holy Word. I was taught that we should have respect for authority: for our teachers, our police officers, our elders, as well as respect for others and for myself. I was taught the Bible and encouraged to practice it all the time. I was taught to love other people, regardless of race and ethnic differences. I was taught that a good name is better than gold or silver, that honesty is most important, and that I should be kind to others and have a kind heart.

A true story was told to me about a man who was to have an interview for a great job with good pay that he had been wanting for a long time. Well, as the story goes, his alarm clock didn't go off, and he was running late. On the way to the interview, he saw a woman stranded on the side of the road with a flat tire. Should he stop, or should he just pass on by? He was running late, but after all, it probably would not matter if he were any later. He had little chance of getting the job anyway, so he stopped to change the tire for the lady. After changing the flat, he set out still later for the interview with no chance at all of getting the job. When he was called into the office for the interview, he was amazed to see the lady behind the desk. It was the lady he had stopped to help with the flat tire! Guess who got the job he had wanted so badly!

What is lacking in today's world is teaching respect, kindness, honesty, love for others, love for self, and, most of all, respect for God's word. Teaching RESPECT would solve a lot of problems in today's world!

Application for the Day: Today I will respect others and exhibit kindness in my relationships.

Thursday, February 1, 2024

Dealing with Change

Brian Fortner

Today's Scripture: Jeremiah 29:11

I am sure we can all think of some type of change that has happened in our lives. It may have been last week, last month, or a year ago.

The truth is that things are always changing. It may be with our job, our family life, or our spiritual growth. There are good changes and bad changes, all of which bring on different feelings. We can have feelings of happiness, sadness, or anxiety. Sometimes just the anticipation of change can make us worried. Someone once told me that worrying is like a rocking chair: it gives you something to do, but it doesn't get you anywhere.

So what do we do when things happen? To whom do we turn for answers? Some will look to their friends, family members, or coworkers for the answers. Some will try to deal with it themselves, bearing their burdens alone. But the one sure answer to our troubles is Jesus! We can always count on Him because He never changes. Hebrews 13:8 states, "Jesus Christ is the same yesterday and today and forever."

When we live a Christian life, letting Him guide us, our first call for help will go to Him. This kind of faith doesn't come overnight. But, if we place our trust in Jesus, our lives will change. He will change the way we think, act, and speak. Everything in life is part of the perfect plan He has set in place for us.

Jeremiah 29:11 says, "'For I know the plans I have for you,' declares the Lord; 'plans to prosper you and not to harm you, plans to give you hope and a future.'"

We must remember that God is always going to give us the strength to get through whatever trials we face. He will always provide that plan of escape for us. He is never going to close one door without opening a new one.

Application for the Day: Today I will be faithful and trust in God because, in a world full of change and chaos, I have an unchanging and constant friend in Jesus!

Friday, February 2, 2024

Learning to Feed One Another

Brian Fortner

Today's Scripture: Philippians 2:3

A Parable – A man asked an angel the difference between Heaven and Hell. He was taken to two doors. Behind Door #1 he saw hungry people surrounding a large pot of soup. Each one had a long spoon attached to one arm. They each took their own scoop and tried to eat the soup with the long spoon. However, they could not eat. Everyone continued starving in pain. The angel said, "Now you have seen Hell."

Behind Door #2 was the same situation. Everyone was surrounding a large pot of soup, each given the same long spoon. However, everyone in this situation was full and satisfied. Why was this so? They had learned to use the long spoons to feed each other. The angel said, "Now you have seen Heaven."

Some people in our society today have the same thoughts as the people in Hell. Why should I feed the person around me? I am hungry myself. Besides, if I am kind to the person opposite me, will he be kind to me? Worst still, if I were to feed him, then there would be less soup in the pot for me. Why should I be so dumb?

The person who adopts a selfish mindset is living in a Hell within himself. Only if we pray for a selfless heart like Jesus can we live free from our own depression, loneliness, and selfishness. Life is full of routine. When we feel that life is meaningless and dull, it's because our life is centered on ourselves. We prioritize our own ambition, pride, benefits, advantage, and everything we call our own as more important than others. Whenever we are really caught up with ourselves, we tend to not notice the people around us in need. Just remember: It's not about you! The purpose of your life is far greater than your own personal fulfillment.

Application: Today I will make every effort to be sure that I am living my life in service to others.

Monday, February 5, 2024

A Good Listener

Brian Ragan

Today's Scripture: Proverbs 18:13

"He who gives an answer before he hears, It is folly and shame to him."

It can be hard to be a good listener, but it's a critical part of our mission to go and make disciples.

We want to fix things…to solve problems…to share information we know. It's easy to focus so intently on giving a response in a conversation that we miss the opportunity to make a connection and to "hear" and "know" the person.

I've failed in this area more times than I can count, and regret that I've missed opportunities because I was impatient and more focused on transmitting information than developing a relationship.

Being a good listener requires patience and time. As my friend, Mike Stroud, with the Timothy Network writes, "it's about being genuinely relational and never manipulative…disciples are handcrafted, one life at a time, not mass-produced…"

Application for Today To be "all-in" includes being a good listener.

Tuesday, February 6, 2024

Be Still

Brian Ragan

Today's Scripture: Genesis 22:6-9

"6 Abraham took the wood of the burnt offering and laid it on Isaac his son, and he took in his hand the fire and the knife. So the two of them walked on together. 7 Isaac spoke to Abraham his father and said, "My father!" And he said, "Here I am, my son." And he said, "Behold, the fire and the wood, but where is the lamb for the burnt offering?" 8 Abraham said, "God will provide for Himself the lamb for the burnt offering, my son." So the two of them walked on together. 9 Then they came to the place of which God had told him; and Abraham built the altar there and arranged the wood, and bound his son Isaac and laid him on the altar, on top of the wood."

Sometimes being "all-in" is about being still. Isaac did not fight it – he did not wrestle his way out of it. He submitted and waited.

David wrote in Psalm 46:10 - "10 Be still, and know that I am God: I will be exalted among the heathen, I will be exalted in the earth."

Chip Haslam once said of Romans 12:1 that the problem with being a "living sacrifice" is that we keep getting up and moving ourselves off of the altar.

Application for Today: Today's challenge is to find time to "be still."

Wednesday, February 7, 2024

Beyond What We Ask or Think

Brian Ragan

Today's Scripture: Ephesians 3:20-21

"Now to Him who is able to do far more abundantly beyond all that we ask or think, according to the power that works within us, to Him be the glory..."

BEYOND what we can "ask" or "think!"

That's hard to wrap my mind around. I've experienced pain in my life where I prayed for a certain outcome, and then watched as God answered with a different and better result...one that had not even occurred to me. It was humbling...I cried...it reminded me of the smallness of my "ask"...and the blind spots in my thinking.

Sometimes my "ask" is a shortcut to avoid pain, vulnerability, or being uncomfortable, but God can see the best path...the one that equips me for something better or blesses someone else in a way that may never be known to me.

I once heard an author speak on how we limit God....he challenged how we pray...to consider how we ask God to "help" instead of being bold and asking him to "do" whatever we are praying about.

Application for Today: Dream big today..."ask" and "think" boldly!

Thursday, February 8, 2024

Discipleship

Brian Ragan

Today's Scripture: Ephesian 2:10

"For we are God's handiwork, created in Christ Jesus to do good works, which God prepared in advance for us to do."

Former sports director for WSMV, Rudy Kalis', comments in an op-ed recently are perfect for our devotional thoughts.

Rudy has been working with inmates through the Men of Valor organization and shared these thoughts/insights.

Working in the news/sports business "little did I know, the Lord was preparing me and humbling my heart to serve men in prison…" helping them "reconcile…with their Creator…"

"Over the last 5 years, I've learned to become a good listener and ask the right questions. I've learned that one selfish crime or 5 seconds of anger affects countless people across several generations. I've learned that there are too many men in prison [longing] for hope, forgiveness, and wanting to believe that someone out there still loves them."

"I also learned that you can't con a con. They see right through you and know if you are holding back, unsure of yourself, and weak in your convictions."

"Inmates require authenticity and boldness in communication, and when it's sincere and heartfelt, it becomes contagious. Men ease into our meetings, starting to sit around the edge of the circle and just listen."

"They hear about a God who loves them despite all they may have done. It's a powerful and foreign concept for them. Hardened men slowly allow themselves to be vulnerable and after weeks or months of faithfully ministering to these incarcerated men, a bond and trust is developed."

Application for Today: Rudy has tapped into the key to reaching the hearts and minds of others – discipleship - being "all-in."

Friday, February 9, 2024

Image Bearers

Brian Ragan

Today's Scripture: Mark 6:34a

"When Jesus went ashore, He saw a large crowd, and He felt compassion for them…"

His first thought was not annoyance or frustration, but rather a tenderness of spirit toward them.

I read an article recently where the author asked the question "How do you know if you're looking at life from God's viewpoint?" and he answered the question by suggesting one gauge is to "think about how you see other people."

A few years ago at a fundraiser for the Crisis Pregnancy Center, the speaker talked about viewing everyone we meet as "image bearers." That's not always easy…and sometimes I find myself placing people into boxes.

As I think about how I view others, I'm reminded of the thief on the cross. What box would I have placed him in? What would I have focused on?

What did he steal? Who did he steal from?

Yet, in the midst of this chaos…Jesus saw beyond the pain…beyond the insults…He saw a person…an imperfect person…an image bearer…and had compassion on him.

How does God see me, and how does He see the people I interact with each day?

Application for Today Being "all-in" requires that my vision be corrected to bend "the Light" correctly so that I see others clearly.

Monday, February 12, 2024

Love Never Fails

Brian Ragan

Today's Scripture: 1 Corinthians 13:2b-3, 8a

"...if I have all faith, so as to remove mountains, but do not have love, I am nothing. And if I give all my possessions to feed the poor, and if I deliver my body to be burned, but do not have love, it profits me nothing."

"Love never fails..."

Being "all-in" begins and ends with love.

A few years ago, George Caudill said in one of his lessons:

"You see...love is not just action. Love is sacrificial action. Love always pays a price. Love always costs something. Love is expensive. When we love...benefits accrue to another's account. Love gives...it doesn't grab."

I love his description "it gives...it doesn't grab."

Love is the key that opens the door to the hearts of others. It's life-on-life. Not a rush to make some point or achieve some goal...but a relational approach to loving and caring about and for others.

We all need each other. We all have times when we are exhausted, distracted, preoccupied, or inwardly focused...and it's in these times that we need an Aaron and Hur in our lives to help hold up our hands and arms...to love us unconditionally.

Application for Today: I love each of you, and am thankful to be on this journey and in this battle with you!

Tuesday, February 13, 2024

The Power of One (October 2020)

R. W. McAlister

Submitted by Bryan McAlister (WSCOC Pulpit Minister 2018-2022), in honor of the late RW McAlister and WSCOC, whose love provokes a heart to "good works"

Today's Scripture: Hebrews 10:19-25

Do you remember the '80's TV show *Knight Rider*? What a show—beautiful women, a hero every boy wanted to emulate, and this incredible talking car! I can still remember the opening monologue, which included, "One man can make a difference." In so many areas of my life, especially my spiritual life, I've come to realize how true this statement is.

Many years ago, my father had drifted away from the church but saw the need to become faithful again. He was restored. Because of him, Mom, Bryan, and I are Christians. Thanks, Dad.

Every Sunday, I heard a sermon from John Shelton based squarely on the Bible and delivered with such precision that even a young boy could learn from it. Much of what I know about the Bible and preaching, I learned from him. Thanks, John.

Dave Smith was the only Sunday School teacher I had after I obeyed the gospel. Dave had significant influence over me as I struggled to mature as a teenage Christian. Near the end of my college years, his constant encouragement led me to become a Sunday School teacher. Thanks, Dave.

In June 2001, a close friend, Brent Miller from the Wetaug church of Christ, told me I was preaching at Wetaug next Sunday. I said, "No." He tried again six months later, and again I said, "No." He tried one more time, and I figured I'd do it so he'd shut up. Turns out, I'm the one who can't shut up! All these years later, I'm preaching every Sunday. Thanks, Brent.

We never know how much good can come from one person's actions. At various points of life, one person has made a difference. Often, we can see someone's potential before they do. Never doubt the power of your influence.

Application for the Day: Today I will strive to provoke someone to do a good work for the Lord.

Wednesday, February 14, 2024

This One Is Mine

Bryan McAlister (WSCOC Pulpit Minister 2018-2022)

Today's Scripture: Hebrews 2:10-14

Lisa Brennan was born in the spring of 1978. Her story is not unlike the story of many children. Caught in the turmoil of contested paternity lawsuits, her mother insisted the father own up to his responsibility and pay child support. The father denied the child was his. By the time Lisa was two years old, the district attorney fought to have Lisa and the supposed father undergo a relatively new procedure to determine paternity: DNA testing. The tests returned the highest probability measurable at 94.4 percent. In a rush by the father's lawyers to finalize the case, he was ordered to pay $385.00 per month in child support (which he increased to $500.00) in addition to her medical insurance until the age of eighteen. On December 8, 1980, with paternity confirmed, the payments owed to the young daughter were conferred. Four days later, the father's private company, Apple, began trading publicly. Lisa Brennan-Jobs's father, Steve, was instantly worth more than $200 million.

Never in the history of man has God been ashamed to call us His children (Heb. 2:10-14). God has grieved over our sin (Gen. 6:6) and even wept at the refusal of His children to see the forgiveness and provision He offers to escape sin (Luke 19:41-44). Still, His commitment to own us and call us out of darkness remains constant (1 Pet. 2:9).

Furthermore, God holds nothing back from His children. He has offered us keys to the kingdom; He invites us to wear His shoes, robe, and ring, and to dine at a feast in honor of the wayward child who has come home. He names us "joint heirs" and supplies all our needs "according to His riches in [not out of, but equal to] glory by Christ" (Matt. 16:13-20; Luke 15:11-32; Rom. 8:17). God's message of abundant love, immeasurable grace, and unending mercy stands separate from the world's lie of our lives being accidental or inconsequential.

Application for Today: Today I will pray, thanking God for unashamedly naming me to the world as His own child.

Thursday, February 15, 2024

None of It Is Mine

Caleb Boggs (2017 Summer Ministry Intern)

Today's Scripture: 1 Chronicles 29:10-14

Does it bring you joy to give your stuff away? You have worked hard for what you own, right? Why should someone else get what you have earned? It can be tough for us to let go of our money or our valued possessions. Sometimes, even when we give, we may share what we have just because God has told us to do so. When that happens, we are giving reluctantly. If you are not cheerful in your giving, take some inspiration from King David near the end of his life, as recorded in the final chapter of 1 Chronicles.

1 Chronicles 29 is about a time of great celebration! As King David was nearing the end of his life, he saw his son Solomon become king of Israel. Though David was forbidden to build the temple, he gathered the materials and gave Solomon the blueprints for its construction. In addition to the materials that he gathered from the nation, David contributed 225,000 pounds of gold and 525,000 pounds of silver from his own private treasury! Inspired by David's generosity, the leading men of Israel gave over ten million pounds of gold, silver, bronze, and iron as freewill offerings to God. I am not even going to try to calculate the modern-day value of all these contributions to the temple. If you find it hard to imagine such generosity, read what David declared as he praised God.

David said that EVERYTHING belongs to God. EVERY blessing that we have comes from God. King David didn't claim ownership of his kingdom; rather, he declared, "Yours is the kingdom, O LORD." Riches and honor come from God. Power and might come from God. NOTHING that we own is truly ours. That's stewardship! It's easy to give cheerfully when we remember that we are just stewards of what God has given us.

Application for the Day: Today I will happily give something to someone else: money, time, or maybe even a drink from Sonic.

Friday, February 16, 2024

Thanksgiving in My Heart

Caleb Boggs (2017 Summer Ministry Intern)

Today's Scripture: Luke 17:11-19

The earliest song I can remember singing is "He Has Made Me Glad," based on Psalm 100. It has yet to get old; it's one of my favorites.

> *I will enter his gates with thanksgiving in my heart.*
> *I will enter his courts with praise.*
> *I will say this is the day that the Lord has made.*
> *I will rejoice, for he has made me glad.*

Remember the story of the grateful Samaritan in Luke 17. Jesus met ten lepers, ten victims of a repulsive skin disease. He sent them to the priests, and they were miraculously healed as they went. Luke records, "Then one of them, when he saw that he was healed, turned back, praising God with a loud voice; and he fell on his face at Jesus' feet, giving him thanks. Now he was a Samaritan." The nine were changed on the outside; their leprous skin had been restored to health. The one was changed both outside and in; he had thanksgiving in his heart. His faith gave him complete wellness, and his good health was evidenced by his gratitude!

You may live by Christian general principles. You may be able to quote scripture. These are admirable qualities, but they are not unique to God's elect. They are only outward qualities. How can we know if we have been inwardly restored to spiritual health? One powerful evidence is thanksgiving in our hearts. Let's follow the example of grateful faith seen in the Samaritan!

How often do you reflect on the healing power of Christ? How often do you remember the badness of sin and the goodness of God's grace? How often do you thank God meaningfully? How often does your family hear you thank God? How often are your actions the overflow of a thankful heart (Col. 2:6-7; 3:15-17)? Let's be changed from the inside, remember the work of Jesus, and live with thanksgiving in our hearts.

Application for the Day: Today I will offer a prayer of thanks and tell a friend about the thankfulness in my heart towards God.

Monday, February 19, 2024

A Team Sport

Caleb Hammond (2023 Ministry Intern)

Today's Scripture: Philippians 1:27-28

In our text Paul said, "Only let your conduct be worthy of the gospel of Christ, so that whether I come and see you or am absent, I may hear of your affairs, that you stand fast in one spirit, with one mind striving together for the faith of the gospel, and not in any way terrified by your adversaries, which is to them a proof of perdition, but to you of salvation. and that from God."

Have you ever watched a great sports team win a championship? It's a lot of fun as long as they don't beat your favorite team to do it. Think for a moment about great teams. Are they usually made up of one outstanding player surrounded by a bunch of nobodies? Or are they typically composed of several players who, when working together, are capable of remarkable things? While there are some exceptions, I believe that the latter is more typical. Great sports teams are just that—a team! Their success is a collective effort.

The same is true of the church. It is a collective effort, not a "one-man show." That is why Paul commanded the Philippians to "stand fast in one spirit" and to strive together "with one mind." He wanted them to be unified. He wanted them to be firmly rooted in Christ. He wanted them to strive for the faith. How? Together! Paul did not want the best and most talented Christians to step into the spotlight, do all the work, and receive the glory. He wanted all Christians to work side by side and heart by heart to advance the gospel and bring glory to God. Why? Because the church is a team sport.

Let's work for Christ together. Let's be rooted in Christ together. Let's grow towards Christ together. Let's be the team that God has called us to be.

Application for the Day: Today I will ask God to help me be the member of His team that I ought to be, serving Him faithfully and working with my fellow Christians for His glory.

Tuesday, February 20, 2024

Come, Let Us Reason Together

Caleb Hammond (2023 Ministry Intern)

Today's Scripture: Isaiah 1:18-20

In the book of Isaiah, the prophet comes out of the gate swinging. The first chapter is a call to repentance, convicting the people of their sins and describing God's sadness and anger. They were sinful people who worshiped Him in vain, and He was tired of it.

That loosely summarizes verses 2-17. I encourage you to read it, really to feel the weight of the situation. Simply put, God was angry with a wicked nation. And that is why verses 18-20 are so powerful:

> "Come now, and let us reason together," Says the Lord, "Though your sins are like **scarlet**, They shall be as **white** as snow; Though they are **red** like crimson, They shall be as **wool**. If you are willing and obedient, You shall eat the good of the land; But if you refuse and rebel, You shall be devoured by the sword;" For the mouth of the Lord has spoken.

God was undoubtedly upset with His people. They were rebellious and iniquitous, making Him sorrowful and angry. However, notice what He called them to do—how He pleaded with them: "let us reason together." He did not want to destroy them; He wanted to save them!

The same is true for us. If we will turn to God and obey Him, He will wash us clean and forgive us completely. What a tremendous blessing! He does not want to vaporize us; rather, our Glorious, Holy, and Reverend God humbly and patiently asks us to listen to what He has to say, to think logically with Him, and to repent of our sins. Let's do just that, allowing him to make us "as white as snow."

Application for the Day: Today I will ask God to help me listen to Him, be logical like Him, and obey Him so that I can receive the forgiveness and salvation He offers; further, I will praise God for being patient with me and for wanting me to be saved.

On Your Tombstone: Leaving a Legacy That Matters

Caleb Hammond (2023 Ministry Intern)

Today's Scripture: Ecclesiastes 12:13-14

If you could have any phrase written on your tombstone, what would it be? In other words, for what do you want to be remembered? What kind of legacy do you want to leave?

If I were to hop in Dr. Emmett Brown's Delorean time machine, travel back in time, and pose this question to the writer of Ecclesiastes, the Preacher, what do you think he would say? What kind of legacy would he think was worth leaving? To determine his answer, let's notice what he wrote in Ecclesiastes 2:4-7:

> I **made my works great**, I built myself houses, and planted myself vineyards. I made myself gardens and orchards, and I planted all kinds of fruit trees in them. I made myself water pools from which to water the growing trees of the grove. I acquired male and female servants, and had servants born in my house. Yes, I had **greater possessions** of herds and flocks **than all who were in Jerusalem before me**.

He told us that he had tried to leave a legacy of fame and fortune, but when he had done all he could do, he said that "**all was vanity** and grasping for the wind" (2:11). The Preacher definitely felt that wealth and greatness constituted an unworthy and unfulfilling legacy—a life that was not well lived.

But what would the Preacher define as a good legacy? Let's read Ecclesiastes 12:13-14:

> Let us hear the **conclusion** of the whole matter: **Fear God** and **keep His commandments**, for this is man's **all**. For God will bring every work into judgment, Including every secret thing, Whether good or evil.

His answer to my question is very simple. A fulfilling legacy is being remembered for revering, honoring, adoring, and serving God, and a life well lived is defined by loving and submissive service to the King of Kings.

Application for the Day: Today I will pray that God will help me to put Him above everything and to love Him more than anything, leaving a legacy that matters.

Thursday, February 22, 2024

The Christian's Happy Place

Caleb Hammond (2023 Ministry Intern)

Today's Scripture: Psalm 84

What is your happy place? What is that one place where you can go just to get away, find peace, and have joy?

In Psalm 84, the writer communicates his desire to be in his happy place. Notice verse 2:

"My soul **longs**, yes, even **faints** for the **courts of the Lord**." The courts of the Lord captivate the writer's heart. In them he finds solace; for them he yearns; by them he is strengthened. They are truly his happy place. He goes on to say this in verse 10:

> For **a day** in Your courts is better than **a thousand**. I would rather be a **doorkeeper** in the house of my God Than **dwell** in the tents of wickedness.

The writer holds his happy place in such high regard that he prefers one day there to a thousand anywhere else. He prefers a life of service there than a life of rest anywhere else. The Lord's courts are that good. But why? What makes them so good? Let's read verses 11 and 12:

> For the **Lord God** is a sun and shield; The Lord will give grace and glory. . . . **O Lord of hosts**, Blessed is the man who trusts in **You**!

What makes the courts of the Lord so desirable? God is there. Why are the courts of the Lord the writer's happy place? God is there. What then should our happy place be? Where God is. Like the Psalmist, we need to love the Lord's courts because of how much we love the Lord. Let's orient our hearts to desire God's presence, approach Him, trust Him, and rest in Him. Let's spend our days in His presence, for He is our sun and shield. The Lord is our true happy place, so let's live in His light and thirst for Him daily.

Application for the Day: Today I will pray for God to orient my heart toward Him that I might long to be in His presence above all else.

Friday, February 23, 2024

The Mediator Job Wanted

Caleb Hammond (2023 Ministry Intern)

Today's Scripture: Hebrews 4:14-16

The book of Job is replete with theological truth. It is about much more than a man who lost everything; the majority of the text is a dialogue in which Job mourns, rationalizes, complains, and inquires about his situation. In verses 7-10 of chapter 9, Job says this about the Lord:

> He **commands the sun,** and it does not rise; He seals off the stars;
> He **alone** spreads out the heavens, And treads on the waves
> of the sea;
> He made the Bear, Orion, and the Pleiades, And the chambers of
> the south;
> He does great things **past finding out**, Yes, wonders
> without number.

Here, Job recognizes that God is awesome! He recognizes that God is supreme! That should be comforting, but in verses 32-35, he cries out in complaint, clearly upset:

> For He is **not a man**, as I am, That I may answer Him, And that
> we should **go to court together**,
> Nor is there any **mediator** between us, Who may lay his hand on
> us both.
> Let Him take His rod away from me, And do not let dread of
> Him terrify me.
> Then I would speak and not fear Him, But **it is not so** with me.

Job's problem was simple: there was no one to connect him to God. There was no one who understood them both. There was no one who could be on both of their levels. There was no one who could give Job the opportunity to speak boldly to God. There was no **mediator**.

But unlike Job, we **do** have a mediator—"Jesus the Son of God" (Heb. 4:14). And because He bridges the gap between us and the Father, laying His hand on us both, we can "come boldly to the throne of grace" (Heb. 4:16) and receive the mercy that our God offers. What a tremendous blessing!

Application for the Day: Today I will communicate with my God more often and more deeply, recognizing that it is a blessing to be able to talk to Him through my High Priest and Mediator, Jesus Christ.

Monday, February 26, 2024

God of Nature

Carter Buckner

Today's Scripture: Psalm 34:8

As I explored the vast wilderness alone today, I came across a creek. It was as if I could feel a powerful force of inspiration and peacefulness radiating from it as I stood beside it. The wind calmly blew through the trees, and it felt wonderful because it was so soft and steady. At the same time, the sun slowly trickled through the trees, giving me a greatly renewed sense of energy and warmth. During this time, I thought to myself: if people would just take a break to acknowledge God's great creations, they just might be able to begin to understand how much He gives them every day.

1 Thessalonians 5:18a says, "In everything give thanks." It is often easy to become desensitized to so many of God's blessings. Sometimes we don't stop long enough to appreciate His work, even though it is all around us. My favorite song in the hymn book is "Joyful, Joyful, We Adore Thee" because it reminds me of all the things God does: how He unfolds the flowers, makes and moves clouds, and has designed many different kinds of aerodynamic things.

I think about how God uses light. 1 John 1:5 says that "God is light." This makes me think about how many kinds of light there are. We cannot see ultraviolet light. It amazes me how light from the evening sun can be so peaceful and calming or how a sunrise can be so exciting when seen from a mountain top: it suddenly breaks the darkness, and light pours in over the clouds. There are different kinds of light in the night sky. The effect it has on water is amazing. Sometimes water acts as a mirror, sometimes it looks like it's made of gold, and sometimes it just soaks it up, allowing us to see deep underwater. These are all special, but the sun and lightning are the most powerful lights God created. One is strong enough to instantly destroy a large tree, while the other creates happiness.

Application for the Day: Today I will thank God for the wonders of His creation.

Tuesday, February 27, 2024

Solomon's Wisdom

Carter Buckner

Today's Scripture: Proverbs 2:20

"Wisdom begins when you decide to get wisdom. Love wisdom, and wisdom will make you great. Make wisdom most important, and wisdom will bring you honor" (Prov. 4:7-8). "Give careful thought to the paths for your feet and be steadfast in all your ways" (Prov. 4:26). "The sins of an evil person will trap him" (Prov. 5:22). "Respect for the Lord is the first step toward getting wisdom. Getting knowledge of the Lord is the first step toward getting understanding. If you are wise, then your life will be longer. If you become wise, then you have become wise for your own good" (Prov. 9:10-12). "If any of you lacks wisdom, let him ask God, who gives generously to all without reproach, and it will be given to him" (James 1:5). "A person who talks too much gets himself into trouble. A wise person learns to be quiet" (Prov. 10:19). "People that are proud and boast will become unimportant. But the people who are humble will also become wise" (Prov. 11:2). "The Lord protects good people. But the Lord destroys people that do wrong" (Prov. 10:29). "Whoever is generous to the poor lends to the Lord and he will repay him for his deed" (Prov. 19:17). King Solomon said, "Whoever loves money never has enough; whoever loves wealth is never satisfied with their income" (Eccl. 5:10). "Wine is a mocker and beer a brawler; Whoever is led astray by them is not wise" (Prov. 20:1). "For as he thinks in his heart, so is he" (Prov. 23:7). "A kind word from a friend is more welcome than life-saving advice" (Prov. 27:9). "The righteous person lives a life of integrity; happy are his children who follow him" (Prov. 20:7). "If you trust in the Lord, you will be safe" (Prov. 29:25).

This easy-to-read translation for the deaf was helpful in better understanding the writings of Solomon. When studying these passages, it is good to compare different versions. However, the point is to put them into practice.

Application for the Day: Today I will find ways to put Solomon's words into practice.

Wednesday, February 28, 2024

Truth Is Always Relevant

Carter Buckner

Today's Scriptures: Proverbs 4:26; 2:20

Deliverance is the reward for righteousness (Noah). The sower didn't worry about sowing in the right places. His concern was sowing in enough places (Matt. 13:3-9). God can move mountains, but prayer can move God (Nehemiah). God gave Israel a great victory because of David's faith (1 Sam. 17). Wisdom is seeing things from God's perspective. Joseph is a study on how to become spiritually rich. Moses was highly educated and wholly devoted. God gives time NOT to be wasted (Eph. 5:16-21; Rev. 3:15-16). The king's business requires haste (1 Sam. 21:8). Good friends lead to good places (1 Cor. 15:33). The Lord clearly sees everything we do. He watches where we go (Prov. 5:21). The Bible yields sweet fruits to those who read it. Its depths are unfathomable, and its riches are unlimited (Rom. 11:33). Sin will never make things better for us (Matt. 27:3-4; Rom. 6:23). The Bible is the living word (Heb. 4:12). The best place to pray for potatoes is at the end of a hoe handle (James 2:26). True spiritual enthusiasm is the result of a living, active relationship and involvement with Christ and His work. True freedom is found in Christ (Rom. 8:1-2). Even the tiniest of actions can change the future. Jesus took walks. If we want to be good Christians, then we need to make our spiritual influence outweigh the physical. A negative mind will never give us a positive life. Hate and happiness cannot live in the same heart. Life does not have to be perfect for it to be wonderful. In time, most of life's burdens can become a gift (Psa. 119:71). A place where God fits is a place where a lot of growth takes place. Actions move the Lord to act on our behalf (Matt. 15:21-28). Worship is not a playground (Rom. 12:1). The church does not exist to entertain the saved; it exists to train disciples, glorify God, and reach the lost.

Application for the Day: Today I will write down, meditate on, and pray about one of these passages.

Thursday, February 29, 2024

Where's the Sunlight?

Carter Buckner

Today's Scripture: Luke 12:24

God can be seen in every sunset! 1 John 1:5 states, "This is the message which we have heard from Him and declare to you, that God is light and in Him is no darkness at all." I once wrote in my personal hiking journal: "As Skyler (my little brother) and I hiked 'The Narrows' (a deep, dark canyon in waist deep water), sunlight was very difficult to find, even in the middle of the day. It was also cold and windy, especially during the early morning hours. We were still having motivational issues, even though I had been preaching mind over body all the way to the trailhead. Fortunately, we made progress when Skyler led 'There Is Sunshine in My Soul.'"

Great are the works and wisdom of God. When you climb mountains, you discover many things not made by human hands or man's wisdom. Spiders, ticks, thorns, and bees teach us that small things can cause us pain. Bears teach us that big things can be found, even when you don't know they are there. Lions like to hunt during a thunderstorm to avoid detection from their prey (1 Pet. 5:8). In order for a turtle to move, it has to stick its neck out. You should choose adventure over comfort because someday your body won't let you, but your mind will remember. Without darkness, we'd never see the stars. Not all pioneers head west. A bee is the only creature that can both sting and make honey. Dogs are mentioned forty times in the Bible (NKJV). If you want to be big like an elephant, tall like a giraffe, or hard like a crocodile, then read 2 Peter 3:18. Rhinos are humble animals because they don't go around blowing their horns. If you want to get a horse's attention, just yell "hay." Letting a cat out of the bag is a whole lot easier than putting it back in. Turtles think that frogs are homeless.

Application for the Day: Today I will produce sunshine, as the soul of every Christian should.

Friday, March 1, 2024

Rightly Handling the Scriptures
Chad Garrett

Today's Scripture: Luke 24:44

The title of this devotional may have your mind thinking about 2 Timothy 2:15, "Do your best to present yourself to God as one approved, a worker who has no need to be ashamed, rightly handling the word of truth." This passage was originally written to Timothy, a young soldier of the cross whom Paul had taken under his wings and was training in the ministry. Since this passage is part of the inspired word of God (2 Tim. 3:16), we are also instructed to present ourselves to God as workers, and we are commanded to handle God's word rightly. Well, what does that mean, and how do we rightly handle the word?

Jesus sheds some light on rightly handling God's word when, in Luke 24:44, the Scripture states, "Then he said to them, 'These are my words that I spoke to you while I was still with you, that everything written about me in the Law of Moses, and the Prophets, and the Psalms must be fulfilled.'" Jesus tells us that He saw divisions within the scriptures in relation to the Law, the Psalms, and the Prophets. He did not say these were the only divisions to look at in the scriptures. What He did say is that He fulfilled the scriptures about Him that are found in the Law, the Psalms, and the Prophets. In fact, Jesus quotes from Psalms the most, followed by Deuteronomy. From the prophets, Jesus quotes Isaiah the most. We know that He acknowledged that there are at least three divisions. These divisions must be recognized and studied in their proper time frame and context.

Application for the Day: Today I will think about how Jesus fulfilled the ancient sacred writings (the scriptures) with great accuracy and about how much we can trust Him! I will trust Jesus, who shows me how to handle the scriptures rightly, and I will look for Jesus in the scriptures, trusting Him with my life.

45

Monday, March 4, 2024

Soar Like the Eagles

Chad Garrett

Today's Scripture: Psalms 103:1-5

What comes to your mind when you think about eagles? Perhaps you think about strength, courage, or freedom. Perhaps you think about how big they are or how well they can see and how they soar through the air. That's it! Eagles soar!

David reaches out to God and encourages us to "bless" or "praise" God with our souls. In verse two, our soul is all of our being. Our soul includes our feelings, will, and desires. Notice how this psalm moves through a descending order. The first priority in life is for us to praise God and specifically His holy name; that name is LORD (YAHWEH). That is where our worship begins.

As we worship God, let us not forget all the benefits that God gives us. He forgives, heals, redeems, crowns, and satisfies us. None of these words are written in past tense, but in the present tense, because God continues to extend these benefits to us each and every day! The most important of these benefits is God's forgiveness of our sins! While these other things are less important, they are still important to us. He heals our diseases and redeems us from the pit. The meaning of "pit" could escalate from troubled situations in life to depression, anxiety, and even death itself. God wants to buy us back from those situations so that He can crown us and satisfy us.

Perhaps you are walking through troubled times. Perhaps you are struggling with depression or anxiety. God has the ability to save you from those things and will at some point. Dear brother or sister, what do we do in the meantime? We praise God! We praise God from the depths of our souls (with all of our being). It is only through praising God that He will restore us and renew us like the youthfulness of an eagle—youth, representing energy and resilience.

Application for the Day: Today I will praise God and His awesome name, bless Him, and thank Him with all of my being. I will soar like an eagle!

Tuesday, March 5, 2024

Trustworthy like Tychicus
Chad Garrett

Today's Scripture: Colossians 4:7-9

Have you ever had someone that you truly treasured in your life? Someone whom you could call upon for help? Perhaps they were with you during big events like graduation or when you were in the hospital. Having a treasured friend is a basic need we seem to have. This person may be a spouse, a family member, or a dear friend. First and foremost, this treasured person is trustworthy.

Reading through the letter written by Paul to Colossae, he tells us of a man named Tychicus. He refers to him as a "beloved brother and faithful minister and fellow servant" (Col. 4:7). His purpose for the visit was to provide the brethren with an update on the work being done through Paul and company and to encourage their hearts. Do you know anyone who encourages your heart? How does that make you feel?

Perhaps the timeline worked out that Paul sent the letter to Philemon, Colossae, and even Ephesus with Tychicus. It is very likely that Tychicus stopped at Colossae first and brought Onesimus with him. I don't know at what point Tychicus presented Philemon the letter, but it would make sense to me that Tychicus would have presented the letter to Philemon first, then brought Onesimus before him. Perhaps Tychichus bridged the disconnected relationship between Philemon and Onesimus. This was a moment of high tension. Think about the stress. Perhaps there could have even been a church split due to differences of opinion. Tychichus knew how important it was to be a beloved brother, a faithful minister, and a fellow servant. I believe the relationship was rebuilt through Christ, and the church prospered following the way of Christ.

Application for the Day: Today I will think about two things: 1) First, I will think about someone who has mediated between relationships for me. I will take note of my feelings towards my dear friend. 2) Second, I will seek out someone to encourage and be a faithful and beloved friend too.

Wednesday, March 6, 2024

Grace - 1

Chip Haslam*

Today's Scripture: 1 Peter 5:10

"Amazing grace—how sweet the sound That saved a wretch like me! I once was lost, but now am found—Was blind, but now I see." Of all the hymns written over the last 250 years, without a doubt, the all-time favorite is "Amazing Grace," written in 1779 by a former slave trader, John Newton. The lyrics of this song tell us about God's Amazing Grace.

But what is grace? What does the Bible teach about grace? How is the word "grace" used in the Bible? If we were to go downtown and interview folks on the street, what would they say about grace? As professing Christians, do we really know what the Bible says about grace?

For our devo today, we begin with the basics: some fundamentals, some background information on biblical grace. Over the years, "grace" has been a somewhat elusive word for theologians to define. Because of this difficulty, many believers end up with a "textbook" definition that sounds like this: Grace—a manifestation of favor comparable to mercy. Someone has proposed an acronym: GRACE is God's Riches At Christ's Expense. That's not a bad way to characterize grace, but I do not believe that it is a sufficient definition based on how the Bible uses the word "grace." One of the best-known definitions of grace is only three words: God's unmerited favor, or in five words: the unmerited favor of God. Theologian A. W. Tozer defined grace as "the good pleasure of God that inclines Him to bestow benefits on the undeserving." There was a fellow named Dr. Lindsay, and in teaching a young men's class one day, he said it this way: "Grace is what you need, not what you deserve." Ephesians 2 tells us that we are saved by grace. God gave His son to give us hope and life with Him.

Application for the Day: Today I will grab hold of grace in my life, knowing that my life will be fuller because of it.

*Formatted by Robby Harmon from a lesson series given by Chip Haslam.

Thursday, March 7, 2024

Outrageous Grace - 2

Chip Haslam*

Today's Scripture: Matthew 19-20

Did you know that the Bible never records Jesus saying the word "grace"? Yet we can see the grace of God in virtually everything Jesus did and spoke. Jesus taught and lived grace. When the word "grace" is mentioned, what comes to your mind?

Some may answer like a famous English portrait painter who was asked by a haughty British aristocrat to do her portrait. Then she added, "And see that the painting does me justice." The painter, after taking one look at the hard features of this brash woman's face, observed: "Madame, what you need is not justice, but mercy and grace!" Just a reminder, grace is a gift that costs everything for the giver and nothing for the one who receives the gift. Or another way to put it, grace is love that gives and love that loves the unlovely and the unlovable.

Did you realize that the grace of God is outrageous? Why? Grace is not what we expect. Sometimes grace is not normally what we might think or do! Grace can even seem scandalous! Grace shocks us in what it offers. It is truly not of this world. Sometimes it frightens us with what it does for sinners. Grace teaches us that God does for others what we might never do for them. We are comfortable saying that the good and the not-so-bad should be saved, but God is willing to start with repentant prostitutes and then works downward from there. Grace is a gift that costs everything to the giver and nothing to the receiver. It is given to those who don't deserve it, barely recognize it, and hardly appreciate it. That's why God alone gets the glory in our salvation.

The Christian life is really a series of new beginnings. That is what grace is all about. No one is first, and no one is last. Grace is the land of beginning again.

Application for the Day: Today I will realize that we are all covered by the grace of God.

*Formatted by Robby Harmon from lesson series given by Chip Haslam.

Grace in the Old Testament - 3

Chip Haslam*

Today's Scripture: Jeremiah 31:3

There was a man by the last name of Marcion (85-160 A.D.), who felt that grace and mercy were the only attributes of God. Early historians tell us that Marcion was the son of the bishop in Sinope, an area we know today as Turkey. He was like some folks today when they read the Old Testament: all they can see is a God of wrath and vengeance. When they read the Old Testament, they envision a God with a stern face, eyes of wrath, a quick temper, and a shortage of mercy. When they read the New Testament, the face of God in their mental image softens, the eyes of God are full of compassion, and His arms are outstretched in mercy.

In Marcion's mind, this God of the Old Testament was not the God of the Christian movement he read about in the gospel of Luke and the writings of the apostle Paul. Marcion was not the first to find themes of judgment in the Old Testament that seemed at odds with the message of grace in the New Testament. But this concept cannot be further from the truth.

God's grace in the Old Testament is described as He spoke to Moses at Mt. Sinai. God told Moses, "The Lord, the Lord God, merciful and gracious, longsuffering, and abundant in goodness and truth" (Ex. 34:6). Here is an example of that graciousness: God waited years for humankind to repent and return to Him in the days leading up to the flood. What did they deserve? Death. What did they need? They needed time to repent, so God extended grace by waiting patiently. He also gave grace to the unworthy by warning them of the judgment to come. How? God had Noah preach repentance for 120 years. All told, over 1600 years of grace were given to sinful people to repent.

Application for the Day: Today I will thank God that He does not treat us as our sins deserve (Psa. 103:10).

*Formatted by Robby Harmon from a lesson series given by Chip Haslam.

Monday, March 11, 2024

The Standard of God's Grace - 4

Chip Haslam*

Today's Scripture: Matthew 18:21

I believe that the standard of God's amazing grace is God's seemingly endless ability to forgive. As we begin, let's take a moment to ensure that we all think of the word "forgiveness" similarly. Forgiveness means to dismiss, release, or cancel a debt, to leave or abandon, or to restore someone to their original condition.

Here is an example of forgiveness in action: we hear of a judge that has "dismissed" the charges against a defendant, and, therefore, that person is then forgiven or cleared of any wrongdoing in the case. In a spiritual sense, forgiveness is to restore someone to their original condition. The person who has been forgiven of sin or debt is then restored to the condition of not having sinned, is no longer in debt, and is made clean in God's eyes.

What does the standard of grace mean? I believe the answer lies in the forgiving nature of God and the various definitions of standards. Standard: any figure or object used as an emblem for a leader or people. Something established for use as a rule or basis—a set of criteria for usage and practices. When I say that the standard of grace is forgiveness or a forgiving spirit, forgiveness is the symbol or sign of grace. A forgiving spirit is our measure of grace. The gracious heart is always forgiving. Grace given is the criteria for being a graceful person. A forgiving heart is a forgiving spirit and the minimum standard (or level of attainment) of grace for the Christian. Why must we be forgiving? Why is forgiveness so important? God has forgiven us. It is his standard. It is the bedrock of who he is.

Application for the Day: Today I will remember that our worst days are never so bad that we are beyond the reach of God's grace, and our best days are never so good that we are beyond the need of God's grace.

*Formatted by Robby Harmon from a lesson series given by Chip Haslam.

Tuesday, March 12, 2024

The Scope of God's Grace - 5

*Chip Haslam**

Today's Scripture: Romans 8:35

Some folks would say that life's most important question is, "Do you believe in God?" Maybe a more important question would be, "In what kind of God do you believe?" What is your God like? I believe there is something worse than not believing in God at all, and that is believing in a god but having an erroneous concept. There are many religions in the world today that present differing pictures of God. The saying goes that even a stopped clock is correct twice a day, but a broken clock is worse than no clock because it gives you misleading information. A person can believe in God, but if you have a belief in God that is not based on the truth of the Bible, you are no better off than the non-believer.

What is God like? Is God the god of the Muslim terrorist, is God named Allah, and does he reward murdering terrorists who kill innocent people? Is God the impersonal god of the Deists, who teach that God created the world like a watchmaker and then wound it up and started it? Consequently, God sits by uncaring or unable to get involved in what is happening in the lives of individuals. Is that what God is really like? The Hindu would say that there are many gods. Perhaps New-Age teaching shows that God is the life force in everything, so its followers worship trees, crystals, and even themselves.

When I use the phrase "the scope of God's grace," to what exactly am I referring? The scope has to do with the extent or range of His grace. How long? How wide? Do you have to renew it? We have those answers. The Bible says that our God is everlasting. Our God is long-suffering, patient, kind, slow to anger, forgiving, faithful, gentle, caring, watchful, loving, and full of grace for the undeserving.

Application for the Day: Today I will read Romans 8 and understand the scope of God's love and grace.

*Formatted by Robby Harmon from a lesson series given by Chip Haslam.

Wednesday, March 13, 2024

The Sensitivity of God's Grace - 6

Chip Haslam*

Today's Scripture: John 8

F. B Meyer once said, "When we see a brother or sister in sin, there are some things we do not know: first, we do not know how hard he or she tried not to sin. Second, we do not know the power of the evil forces that attacked them. We also do not know what we would have done in the same circumstances."

We are given insight into how this might happen in John 8. As the accusing Pharisees left the temple area, Jesus was left with an adulterous woman amid the crowd listening to His teaching. Under the Mosaic law, only an eyewitness could accuse a person of adultery, and under the law of Moses, there had to be at least two eyewitnesses. Jesus, even though He knew the heart and sins of this woman, understood that no one could accuse her and follow the Old Testament law.

Jesus said to the woman, "'Woman, where are they? Has no one condemned you?' She said, 'No one, Lord.' And Jesus said, 'Neither do I condemn you; go, and from now on, sin no more.'"

Jesus addressed her as "woman." I want to give you some insight into that term. It is a term of endearment. This is the same word that Jesus used two other times in the book of John, both times in addressing his mother (John 2:4, 19:26). The term was equivalent to calling the woman "lady" and was used to give a woman honor. In this setting, that was certainly not what she was. But Jesus did not simply see a sin-filled woman. He could also see the "lady" she could become. Jesus knew the guilt she must have felt. The One who could condemn and pass judgment did not. There was no lecture or sermon on the sanctity of marriage—just gentle encouragement.

Application for the Day: Today I will not go to others with stones in my hands but with grace in my heart.

*Formatted by Robby Harmon from a lesson series given by Chip Haslam.

Thursday, March 14, 2024

The Sufficiency of God's Grace - 7

Chip Haslam*

Today's Scripture: 2 Corinthians 12:7

There are a few fallacies of thinking with a weak faith. They are as follows: because you are a Christian, all your problems are solved. All the issues you will ever have have been specifically answered in the Bible. If you are having problems, you are somehow unspiritual. Being exposed to sound Bible teaching automatically solves all your problems.

These ideas listed above are fallacies because they are not valid. The apostle Paul was saved by God's grace and empowered to serve and teach by the grace of God. God's grace overcame Paul's past and empowered him for the future. Paul says, and I paraphrase, I have changed my outlook on thorns. I have changed my thinking regarding power and weakness in this life. I choose the power of God for my life. I choose God's sufficient, sustaining grace to handle the hurts and pains of this life for, when I am weak, God is strong in and through me.

Read these scriptures today to see why Paul would proclaim the statement above in 2 Corinthians 12:

And after you have suffered a little while, the God of all grace, who has called you to his eternal glory in Christ, will himself restore, confirm, strengthen, and establish you (1 Pet. 5:10).

Let us then with confidence draw near to the throne of grace, that we may receive mercy and find grace to help in time of need (Heb. 4:16).

For sin will have no dominion over you, since you are not under the law but under grace (Rom. 6:14).

And God is able to make all grace abound to you, so that having all sufficiency in all things at all times, you may abound in every good work (2 Cor. 9:8).

Application for the Day: Today I will be mindful that God's amazing, sufficient grace saves us, changes us, strengthens us, and sustains us through our troubles in this world.

*Formatted by Robby Harmon from a lesson series given by Chip Haslam.

Friday, March 15, 2024

What God's Grace Teaches Us - 8

*Chip Haslam**

Today's Scripture: Titus 2:11-14

If we could live out the first ten verses of Titus 2, our lives would be richer, and we would bless others with the fruit that comes from obeying God's commands. In this chapter, Paul gives instructions on personal behavior for older and younger men and women and enslaved people. Perhaps the reader or listener of Titus' day would read these first ten verses and ask the following questions: Why should we act this way, Paul? Why should we act this way when we are living in such terrible times, are enslaved people, and are treated harshly by the Romans? The beautiful answer is given in the following four verses:

"For the grace of God hath appeared, bringing salvation to all men, instructing [or teaching] us, to the intent that, denying ungodliness and worldly lusts, we should live soberly and righteously and godly in this present world; looking for the blessed hope and appearing of the glory of the great God and our Savior Jesus Christ; who gave himself for us, that he might redeem us from all iniquity, and purify unto himself a people for his own possession, zealous of good works."

Paul is saying to Titus and the readers of this letter that the grace of God teaches or instructs us. In these four short verses, I believe we can see a microcosm of the message of the Bible. By grace, God loves us. By grace, Jesus saved us. By grace, Christians are to lead holy lives of service, and at the second coming of Christ, faithful Christians will have a home in heaven with God. A virtual summary of the Bible message in only four verses teaches us that God's grace requires that we change our lives. This change is how we should live when God's amazing grace has touched us.

Application for the Day: Today I will consider whether my life, actions, speech, and interactions with fellow humans show how much God's grace has changed me.

*Formatted by Robby Harmon from a lesson series given by Chip Haslam.

Monday, March 18, 2024

Questions God Will Not Have to Ask . . . and I Will Not Have to Answer!

Chip Haslam

Today's Scripture: Mark 16:15-16

In Revelation 20, John describes the judgment scene all will face. One day, God and Christ will judge the world. I am not sure if God will ask me any questions, but just in case He does, I want to ensure there are some questions God won't have to ask me and some questions I won't have to answer.

I don't want to answer the question, "Why didn't you read my book?" I don't want to have to explain why I didn't make the time to study and learn what God wanted me to know and do. How could I answer, "I just didn't have time," or "I was too busy with homework, TV, or friends"? Not very good answers for God, are they?

I don't want to answer the question, "Why didn't you attend worship services of My church?" Was sleeping in or recreation more important than regular worship with the church?

God won't have to ask me, "Why didn't you trust my Son and be baptized for the remission of your sins?" Such a simple thing, being immersed in water. Was the water too cold? Did I think baptism was unimportant?

But, there are some questions I will have to answer: "Did you speak the truth in love?" "Did you strive to live at peace with all men?" "Did you visit the fatherless and the widows?" "Were you kind and forgiving?" "Did you love the lost enough to seek and teach them?" "Were you a person of mercy and grace?" and "Did you love the local church?"

When God asks the questions, I believe the best answer is, "I know your Son. I believed the things that He taught, and I tried to live as He commanded. I stand before You clothed not in my own righteousness but in the righteousness of Your Son."

Application for Today: Today I will pray that God will help me live a life to His glory so that one day God won't have to ask, and I won't have to answer.

Tuesday, March 19, 2024

Religious or Biblical Questions?

Chip Haslam

Today's Scripture: 2 Timothy 3:16-17

I remember it as if it were yesterday. Patsy and I walked into the church auditorium with our first baby: Jessica Lynn. We were met by Henry Ragan, who looked at the precious little girl and said, "There are a million questions locked in that sweet little head, and she will ask you all of them." Boy, was he right!

Life is filled with questions. Thankfully, the Bible is filled with answers to life's questions.

    1. Some are good: "Would you rather have ice cream or pie?"

    2. Some give us a feeling of uncertainty: "How much monthly payment can you afford?"

    3. Some leave us with a bad feeling: "How did my favorite dish get broken?"

    4. Some questions are important: "Where will I attend college?" "Should I go to trade school?" "What job will I have?" "Where will I live?"

    5. Then other questions are critical: "Should I marry?" "Who will I marry?" "What church will I attend?"

Has anyone ever asked you a religious question, such as, "Why does your church partake of the Lord's Supper every Sunday?" This is a "religious question," not a Bible one. It is important to understand the difference. The best answer to that question is to turn it into a Bible question: "How often does the Bible teach us to partake of the Lord's Supper?" See the difference? A religious question asks for an opinion, whereas a Bible question establishes a standard by which a question can be answered. The Bible is our standard because the Bible is right; it is God's Word and revelation to mankind.

2 Timothy 3:16-17 – "All Scripture is breathed out by God and profitable for teaching, for reproof, for correction, and for training in righteousness, that the man of God may be complete, equipped for every good work." Will we trust the Word of God? This trust leads us to faith and obedience.

Application for Today: Today I will be thankful for the written Word of God, seek to follow the commands of God, and treasure the hope found in the promises of God.

Wednesday, March 20, 2024

Near the Oil Press

Chris Hedge

Today's Scripture: Hebrews 5:7-9 – "In the days of his flesh, Jesus offered up prayers and supplications, with loud cries and tears, to him who was able to save him from death, and he was heard because of his reverence. Although he was a son, he learned obedience through what he suffered. And being made perfect, he became the source of eternal salvation to all who obey him."

An old hymn by Samuel E. Reed says, "Long in anguish deep was He, Weeping there for you and me, For our sin to Him was known; We should love Him evermore For the anguish that He bore In Gethsemane, alone."

A garden called Gethsemane was nestled on the side of the Mount of Olives less than a mile from Jerusalem. Though not a long walk, its distance from the city provided some tranquility. It must have been a good place to pray.

Its name means "oil press" because of the press located there. Reapers would place olives from the mountain's trees into a large basin, and a heavy stone was tied to ropes maneuvered within the basin. Olives were pressed, and useful oil was harvested. Oil was used in cooking and medicine; it was also used in anointing.

Moses consecrated the tabernacle, its contents, and Aaron the priest with oil. Samuel anointed the future King David. Jesus, the Christ, was the Anointed One. And in the garden named for an oil press, He prayed deeply and intensely: "My Father, if it be possible, let this cup pass from me; nevertheless, not as I will, but as you will" (Matt. 26:39).1

Jesus knew the physical and spiritual agony that was imminent. He was troubled, even sweating drops of blood. Yet there, the Anointed One resolved to fulfill the plan of salvation by going to the cross for our sins. He could not save both Himself and us. He chose us.

Application for the Day: Today I will resolve to live my life as a tribute to the loving sacrifice of my Savior for me.

Thursday, March 21, 2024

Some Mocked, Some Delayed, And Some Believed

Chris Hedge

Today's Scripture: Acts 17:32-34

"Now when they heard of the resurrection of the dead, some mocked. But others said, "We will hear you again about this." So Paul went out from their midst. But some men joined him and believed, among whom also were Dionysius the Areopagite and a woman named Damaris and others with them."

> "What will you do with Jesus, my friend?"
> "Why keep Jesus waiting, Waiting at the door?"
> "Would you be free from the burden of sin?"

"Invitation songs" traditionally follow sermons, and we often sing these questions to each other. It is emotionally stirring when someone, in vulnerability, responds for baptism or for prayers.

The Apostle Paul visited Athens, and he was moved to share the gospel. His brief sermon was powerful! He spoke of the one true God who created the world and everyone in it. Paul said that humanity should seek God, feeling and finding their way to Him. He stated that man is God's offspring and called the crowd to repentance.

Some mocked the news that we will, one day, be resurrected. Others seemed interested, but they postponed their answer to another day. Thankfully, others believed the gospel message.

What is our response to the gospel message? Do we mock Jesus's crucifixion and resurrection by allowing sin to reign in our hearts? Are we convinced of our need to become spiritually focused rather than worldly focused, yet we postpone that life change? Or do we believe, embrace, and embody the gospel message? Do we let it change and direct our lives?

Let us answer the "invitation song" questions with other cherished hymns:

> "I am resolved no longer to linger."
> "Now to be Thine, yea, Thine alone. O Lamb of God, I come! I come!"
> "My heart, my life, my all I bring To Thee, my Savior and my King."

Application for the Day: Today I will resolve no longer to turn my back on Jesus' sacrifice and continue putting off needed spiritual changes in my life; instead, I will answer the gospel call by the way I live my life—every single day.

Friday, March 22, 2024

Why Cabins Without Air Conditioning Are Filled Every Summer

Chris Hedge

Today's Scripture: Acts 2:46-47 "And day by day, attending the temple together and breaking bread in their homes, they received their food with glad and generous hearts, praising God and having favor with all the people. And the Lord added to their number day by day those who were being saved."

We gather in a wooded amphitheater to begin our day in a devotional. Together we sing, pray, and consider scripture. Breakfast is next on the schedule, and we enjoy it as we do the other two meals of the day—in one another's presence. We are dismissed to retrieve our Bibles and proceed to class, where we assemble with those our own age. This is a time for questions to be posed, minds to be challenged, and souls to be guided by seasoned Christians. Then games are enjoyed up until time for congregational singing. The rest of the day follows a similar format as we will spend more time in smaller groups, enjoy meals and activities together, and worship to God.

Perhaps the most spiritually moving part of the day occurs last. Around a campfire, Christians circle late at night for one last devotional of the day. Perhaps it's the darkness that emboldens everyone to sing more fervently than they normally do, but it is a beautiful time.

I have long held the belief that Bible camp is one of the most effective kingdom tools we have. The schedule always reminds me of what the early church experienced. We read in Acts that the first Christians were gladly present in each other's homes and in the temple "day by day." They broke bread, they shared, and they devoted time to God together. My thought is that Bible camp is such a powerfully spiritual week because it looks so much like the early church.

Each year at camp, walls around Christian hearts are lowered, and hearts come together. Tears, love, and mutual support freely flow.

Application for the Day: Today I will strive to pattern my spiritual journey after the early church—together day by day.

Monday, March 25, 2024

Have You Been with Jesus?

Chris McCurley

Today's Scripture: Acts 4:8-13 "Then Peter, filled with the Holy Spirit, said to them, 'Rulers of the people and elders, if we are being examined today concerning a good deed done to a crippled man, by what means this man has been healed, let it be known to all of you and to all the people of Israel that by the name of Jesus Christ of Nazareth, whom you crucified, whom God raised from the dead —by him this man is standing before you well'. . . Now when they saw the boldness of Peter and John, and perceived that they were uneducated, common men, they were astonished. And they recognized that they had been with Jesus."

Some places, after eating there, make you carry the smell for the rest of the day. Barbecue joints are like that. You eat there, and then you smell like smoked mesquite until you change your clothes. The aroma gives you away.

It's been said that couples who stay together for many years start to look like each other. The idea is that the more time you spend with someone, the more you begin to resemble that person.

When I was growing up, I would ask my parents if I could do something with my friends. There were two questions that they would always ask: 1) "Where are you going?" 2) "Who are you going with?" There were places they would forbid me to go and certain people they did not want me hanging out with. In reality, I did sometimes hang out with a few people my parents didn't approve of, thinking that what they didn't know wouldn't hurt them, but my attitude and actions would give me away. My mom would say, "I can always tell when you've been spending time with so and so."

We become like those we behold. In Acts Chapter 4, the Jewish leaders could tell that there was something different about Peter and John. What was it? The resurrected Messiah had rubbed off on them.

Application for the Day: Today I will show that I have been with Jesus because I will give off the aroma of Christ.

Tuesday, March 26, 2024

Living Letters

Chris McCurley

Today's Scripture: 2 Corinthians 3:1-3: "Are we beginning to commend ourselves again? Or do we need, as some do, letters of recommendation to you, or from you? You yourselves are our letter of recommendation, written on our hearts, to be known and read by all. And you show that you are a letter from Christ delivered by us, written not with ink but with the Spirit of the living God, not on tablets of stone but on tablets of human hearts."

People are reading your life to see if your epistle lives up to the intent of the author. There are few things in this world more powerful than a committed Christian. The eye of the world takes in more than the ear. The Christian's life may be the only religious book the world ever reads. There are countless people all around us who will never open the Bible, but they are reading us. Are they able to read Christ clearly and legibly? Do they see a reflection of the author?

There is no denying that people react to our lives. When people read a book, there is usually a reaction—either good or bad. When people read us, there will typically be a reaction—either good or bad. We cannot always control the reaction of the readers, but we can control what they read. When we present the character of Christ, the readers may not like what they read, but at least we have accurately represented the author. Those who reject us are really rejecting the author, but those who accept us are really accepting Christ. Our challenge is to be a living letter that is hard to ignore.

Application for the Day: Today I will be readable because I know that a life lived for Christ is the sermon that one can always preach!

Wednesday, March 27, 2024

Make It Count
Chris McCurley

Today's Scripture: 2 Chronicles 21:20

Does your life matter? In 2 Chronicles 21 we read about the death of Jehoram. Verse 6 tells us that Jehoram "did what was evil in the sight of the Lord." He was a wicked king who was known for abusing his power. As soon as he ascended the throne, he killed all his brothers and some of the princes of Israel. But all you really need to know about this man can be found in verses 10 & 11, which read, "So Edom revolted from the rule of Judah to this day. At that time Libnah also revolted from his rule, because he had forsaken the Lord, the God of his fathers. Moreover, he made high places in the hill country of Judah and led the inhabitants of Jerusalem into whoredom and made Judah go astray."

God eventually became fed up with Jehoram's attitude and antics. As a result, he struck the king with an incurable disease that he suffered with for two years. Verse 19 tells us that he "died in great agony." Then notice verse 20: "He was thirty-two years old when he began to reign, and he reigned eight years in Jerusalem. And he departed with no one's regret. "

"He departed with no one's regret." No one was sad when Jehoram died. His funeral may have been a celebration, but it was not a celebration of the life he lived. It was a celebration of the fact that he was no longer living. Nobody missed Jehoram when he was gone.

I read this and I ask myself, "Will anyone miss me when I'm gone?" I feel confident, that my wife and kids would. Hopefully, some others would miss me. It's a valid question to ponder: would my leaving leave a hole?

Application for the Day: I will begin building my legacy today and strive to live a life that will outlive me.

Thursday, March 28, 2024

Bitterness or Betterness?

Christy Chester

Today's Scripture: Psalm 30:11-12

We see ourselves and view life based upon our perspective. The great thing is that we get to choose our vantage point. We should seek to have God's perspective—the place with the unobstructed view of what is true and important.

Feeling low today? Unworthy? Wounded? Stressed? Is there bitterness in your heart? Is your vantage point affecting your life-view in a negative way?

You can dance in a hurricane, but only if you're standing in the eye.

Joseph had several opportunities where he could have chosen a low vantage point. Joseph's father had elevated him above his brothers, which caused them to hate him (even to the point of wanting to kill him). He was ridiculed by his brothers and rebuked by his father when he shared his God-sent dreams. His brothers sold him into slavery, and Joseph was taken away from his family and homeland. Because of a lie told about him, Joseph was unfairly thrown into an Egyptian prison, and for two years following a fellow prisoner's release, Joseph was forgotten in that prison. These bitter life events could have easily enticed Joseph to choose a low vantage point in his life. He could have chosen to be bitter, but did bitter feelings dictate Joseph's focus?

No matter the situation, Scripture shows that Joseph kept the right perspective by choosing to be better, rather than bitter. Joseph's trust in God allowed him to change his environment with betterness, rather allowing his environment to change him with bitterness. His eyes were focused on the Lord, and his heart set on doing right.

Like Joseph, we can dance in the hurricane, but only if we're standing in the I-AM!

God gives us the betterness perspective! HIS plans are to prosper us, not to harm us (Jer. 29:11). A life directed by God has true love, joy, and peace that passes all understanding—no matter the circumstances.

Application for the Day: Today I will seek to have God's view of myself and my life and will choose to be better, rather than bitter.

Presents or Presence?

Christy Chester

Today's Scripture: Psalm 73:28

When I was a child, I always looked forward to holidays. Birthdays meant a party with cake, ice cream, and gifts! Valentine's Day meant a school party with valentines and candy! Easter came with sweet treats found from an egg hunt! July 4th meant a parade, picnic, and fireworks! Halloween ... candy, Thanksgiving ... great food, Christmas ... presents! My childish mind was focused on what I would receive–I was focused on presents.

As a mother and grandmother, I now realize that the valuable gifts during my childhood were NOT the presents, but the presence. Birthday presents have long been forgotten, but childhood friends will always be remembered. Valentines and candy are long gone, but love from loved ones is still cherished. Easter dresses are outgrown, and eggs are lost, but time spent with family is priceless! I was so blessed by their loving presence.

As a younger Christian, I selfishly thought of heaven as a place where I would receive presents: a golden crown, a mansion, and a perfect city. Oh, how my view has changed! My focus is no longer on God's presents.

Give me God the Father, Son, and Holy Spirit! I desire His Presence!

Holidays spent with my children and grandchildren are all about their presence. I want to be near them, to hug them, to talk with them, to enjoy the time with them. I think that is what God desires from us too. He has done everything for us to be in His Presence. His love is not because of the presents we offer Him. He simply longs for our presence. "One thing I have asked of the LORD, that will I seek after: that I may dwell in the house of the LORD all the days of my life, to gaze upon the beauty of the LORD and to inquire in His temple" (Psalm 27:4).

Application for the Day: Today I will draw near to God by prayer, by praising His name, and by reading His Word to enjoy His Presence.

Monday, April 1, 2024

Losing Your Song

Clarence DeLoach (WSCOC Preaching Minister 1990-2001)

Today's Scripture: Psalm 137:4

Psalm 137 is a lament of the Jewish captives in the land of Babylon. They had lost their freedom, city, land, and joy. They were being challenged to sing a song of Zion by their captors, but they could not! They had lost their song! Christians too can lose their song! What could possibly steal the joy from our hearts? Consider these joy stealers:

1. Satan's influence. He is alive and well! He is desperate to take as many to hell as he can. He is our "adversary" (1 Pet. 5:8). He seeks to "take advantage" (2 Cor. 2:11). We must be alert and aware.

2. A lack of confidence. While the Bible does not teach unconditional eternal security, it does teach that we can have confidence in God's promise. His forgiveness is complete and His pardon abundant (Isa. 55:7). If we confess our sins, He is faithful to forgive (1 John 1:9). We need a growing confidence to maintain a vibrant joy (Phil. 1:6).

3. Prayerlessness. Prayer will intensify our hope. No wonder Paul wrote, "In everything, by prayer and supplication, with thanksgiving, let your requests be made known to God" (Phil. 4:6).

4. Focusing on circumstances. True joy is independent of circumstances. Paul was radiantly joyful, though he was bound "in chains" (Phil. 1:7), because his chains were "in Christ" (Phil. 4:11-12).

5. Ingratitude. Gratitude is the oil that lubricates the cogs of life and makes them run more smoothly. Paul exhorted the Thessalonians, "In everything give thanks; for this is the will of God in Christ Jesus for you" (1 Thess. 5:18).

6. Forgetfulness. David reminds us, "Bless the Lord, O my soul, and forget not all His benefits" (Psalm 103:2). A failure to focus and reflect can cause us to leave our first love (Rev. 2:4-5).

Our worship together should be an anticipation of joy, and our working together must be a partnership of joy. Let us keep that fellowship vibrant, and we will not lose our joy.

Application for the Day: Today I will sing joyfully of the salvation that is mine in Jesus.

Tuesday, April 2, 2024

Spiritual Maturity

Clarence DeLoach (WSCOC Preaching Minister 1990-2001)

Today's Scripture: 1 Corinthians 16:13

Christian maturity is addressed many times in the New Testament. Corinth needed milk because of her immaturity (1 Cor. 3:1-3). The Hebrews could not discern solid food because they had not grown spiritually (Heb. 5:12-14). They were urged to examine and honestly evaluate the progress (or lack of it) they had made.

Frequently, we need to measure our progress in faith. How can we do that? What criteria should we use? Scripture furnishes a gauge by which we can measure maturity. Consider 5 "Ds."

Diet – We are what we eat and digest spiritually! The mature Christian advances from milk to meat. He does not stay on baby food (1 Pet. 2:1-2). He learns to digest more solid food. Facts are acquired, issues are analyzed, and truth is applied to circumstances in life. He grows in appetite as he delights in the Word that is like honey to his taste.

Discernment – We are to learn how to distinguish between right and wrong. Values are learned and priorities recognized. Maturity brings understanding and deeper insight. The Christian begins to appreciate his spiritual blessings more. Making choices about life becomes easier. Wisdom is developed.

Duty – A sense of responsibility comes with experience. The time comes when a person can see the work that needs to be done. He accepts it as his responsibility and performs it to the best of his ability. From such action flows a sense of duty, and, in time, duties become desires. When such occurs, we are really growing!

Discipline – Self-discipline is our greatest challenge. It happens when the maturing Christian integrates the Word of God into his daily experiences. He is not tossed about but has solid footing—knowing Whose he is and what he is.

Devotion – Maturity is evident when one is devoted to the Word, will, worship, and work of God.

Such maturity is not a sudden spurt. It is a lifelong process! But it can be accelerated by quickly taking advantage of God's provisions (Eph. 4:31).

Application for the Day: Today I will take the necessary steps to grow.

Wednesday, April 3, 2024

Are You Up to the Task?
Crystal Loden

Today's Scripture: Hebrews 12:1 "Therefore, we also, since we are surrounded by so great a cloud of witnesses, let us lay aside every weight, and the sin which so easily ensnares us, and let us run with endurance the race that is set before us."

Have you ever wondered "Where am I supposed to be at this point in time?" Or "What am I supposed to be doing with my life?" Have you ever felt lost and wanted guidance? Maybe you have thought, "God, I need to see you doing something in my life."

Apparently, Moses felt that way many times as well. He had the life everyone wanted one day, then found himself running for his life the next. He went from Pharaoh, Jr. in Egypt, to a lowly shepherd in the middle of nowhere. But when it seemed that his life would never amount to anything, God gave him direction. God never tells us to do something that He has not prepared us to do. Moses spent his second forty years being a combination of a Ruler and Shepherd. The Kingly training in Egypt prepared him for leading, and the shepherding trained him to deal with people. That training did not happen overnight. Many a person would have given up and lost out on the blessings and reward of that task. Moses' name is known all over the world because he was willing (reluctantly at first) to be lead and trained for the task set before him. His greatest reward is having his name known by God Himself! Revelation 2:19 says, "I know your deeds, your love and faith, your service and perseverance, and that you are now doing more than you did at first." Wait on the Lord. Keep your eyes open for His direction. And then be ready for what He will set before you!

Application for Today: Today I will pray, "Lord, direct my heart into God's love and Christ's perseverance (2 Thessalonians 3:5). Give me the faith and willingness to wait for you and follow your direction."

Thursday, April 4, 2024

One and Two Hand Rocks

Crystal Loden

Today's Scripture: Proverbs 3:27 "Do not withhold good from those to whom it is due, when it is in the power of your hand to do so."

I collected some river rocks on one of my camping trips. While unloading these rocks I noticed that some could be picked up and tossed with one hand, while others took both hands. My thoughts went to Stephen and others who were stoned. What a horrible, painful way to die! My thoughts then went to those who were throwing the stones. What kind of person could pick up one or two-hand rocks to throw at another person with the intent to harm?

Yet isn't that the very thing done with words and actions? We would never physically pick up a rock and throw it at someone, but we hurl words so easily. What kind of person hurts another easily? There could be several reasons. One would be arrogance. Thinking ourselves privileged enough to put someone "in their place." It might be to take revenge and "make it right." Perhaps, we have been hurt so much that hurting others is all we know. Whatever the reason, throwing "rocks" is condemned in Holy Scripture. There is not one example of this behavior being used as a good thing. If we use Jesus as our example for behavior, we see the opposite. If we find ourselves "throwing rocks" often, it would be wise to look inward and ask ourselves, "Why do I have a heart of stone?" In fact, this is the very thing that Paul tells us to do in 2 Corinthians 11. We are to take the Lord's supper after evaluating our hearts first. If we do this weekly, we will be able to keep a check on ourselves and adjust to any hurtful thinking.

Application for Today: Today I will pray, "Lord, give me a new heart and put a new spirit in me. Remove from me my heart of stone, and replace it with a heart that will be kind and look to you for guidance" (Ezekiel 36:26).

Friday, April 5, 2024

The Faith of a Turtle

Crystal Loden

Today's Scripture: Hebrews 11:3 – "By faith we understand that the universe was formed at God's command, so that what is seen was not made out of what was visible."

We have all found box turtles around our houses. As children, they fascinated us with their slow movements and disappearing appendages. If you picked up a turtle and held it face to face, would that turtle understand what was right in front of it? Would it understand that there is a neighborhood, a city, a state, a country, or a universe around it? Of course not!

That turtle understands only grass, dirt, hunger, fear, and when to procreate. If it is a female, she knows where to lay eggs and how to care for them. These are the things the turtle understands—not because it is stupid, but because that is what it was created to understand. The turtle's lack of understanding does not do away with you or the world and even beyond. It

does mean that God gave it what it needs to survive and even flourish in its world.

It is the same with us. We live in our small circles of familiarity. Yet, there is so much we do not, cannot understand. And that is ok! God has equipped us with what we need to survive and flourish in our world. We need not worry about the things that we do not understand. Paul said, "Do not be anxious about anything, but in every situation, by prayer and petition, with thanksgiving, present your requests to God. And the peace of God, which transcends all understanding, will guard your hearts and your minds in Christ Jesus" (Philippians 4:6-7).

Application for the Day: Today I will be at peace, even though I do not understand all of God's ways. I will pray for patience, while waiting for His clarity, when I WILL understand.

Monday, April 8, 2024

Rescue
Dale Ragan

Today's Scripture: Matthew 25:31-34

Rescue—and attempts to rescue people in life-and-death situations—is frequently covered by news broadcasts around the world. History also records stories of many rescues that have saved the lives of countless people. We all want there to be a plan for rescue and someone to carry it out when we find ourselves facing a circumstance that endangers our lives.

There are numerous stories in the Bible of God implementing the rescue of His people by using men who were willing to follow the rescue plan God had laid out. The *greatest* rescue plan ever devised is already available to every human being, introduced by God at the beginning of time. That plan includes the One necessary to make our rescue possible when time comes to an end for the earth. The One who was designated to carry out God's rescue plan for mankind is Jesus Christ. He came to earth to allow Himself to be crucified as the only sacrifice God will accept. His dying on the cross and His resurrection began the rescue plan. The rescue of mankind will finally be carried out for those who have made the proper preparation when He leaves heaven to return and take to heaven those who have made preparation while living on earth.

The final destination of all humans for eternity will be one of two places. Heaven will be for those who believe Jesus is the Son of God and have followed the rescue plan in the New Testament. Hell will be for those who don't believe and have not followed His plan. The rescue plan is in effect. The choice is up to us and depends on what we decide to do about it (Matt. 25:31-34). When Jesus returns, the choice will have been made, judgment day will be upon us, and eternity will have begun. The time to become part of God's plan of rescue is before that day arrives.

Application for the Day: Today I will follow God's plan, taking great comfort in knowing that my rescue for eternal life is secure.

Tuesday, April 9, 2024

A "Guest" in Heaven

Dan Erranton

Today's Scripture: Acts 2:42-47

For many years I thought that being a missionary meant going to a foreign country or going someplace far away from home. I remember several missionaries visiting WSCOC while I was a young child. They came from Germany, Italy, New Guinea, and other places far away. However, when you look at how the first century church grew, they worked right at home, or as we say in the South, "in their own backyard."

One of the greatest examples of working for the Lord at home that I have ever known was an African-American gentleman in Charleston, SC. His name was Arthur Guest. Bro. Guest attended the Jacksonville Road church of Christ and was employed at the Charleston Naval Shipyard. There were 300 employees in the department in which he worked, and the other 299 knew exactly who Arthur Guest was and knew of his belief in Jesus. He talked to every individual in his department about their soul's salvation, studied with many of them in depth, and converted many of them to Christ. After their baptism, he would take them to the congregation where he attended or to other congregations in the Charleston area. Several of the men became elders, deacons, and faithful members of the Lord's church. He always emphasized that it didn't matter where you attended worship services—just where you would be comfortable doing your best, working for the Lord.

How many people in your workplace know where you attend worship on Sunday? How many of these people have you talked to about the salvation of their souls? I am afraid many of us, including myself, fail to accomplish this very important task. Maybe we could all learn from the example of Bro. Guest.

Bro. Arthur Guest passed from this life to his eternal home on February 22, 2017. I have often made the statement: "If I ever knew someone who would be in Heaven, it would be Arthur Guest." Truly, there is a "Guest" in Heaven.

Application for the Day: Today I will make it my goal to also be a guest in Heaven.

Wednesday, April 10, 2024

Be Like Onesiphorus

Dan Erranton

Today's Scripture: 2 Timothy 1:16-18; 2 Timothy 4:19

The Apostle Paul was an unusual man of many talents. He went on missionary journeys and was shipwrecked, thrown into prison more than once, and beaten on several occasions, all to preach the gospel of Jesus Christ. He made many friends in the brotherhood on those journeys, and he named them as he wrote letters to the churches he had helped establish. We are familiar with names like John Mark, Silas, Barnabas, Timothy, Lydia, and many others.

One of the names that is lesser known to us is Onesiphorus, a name that has intrigued me because of the way in which it is spelled and also the way it is pronounced "On-e-sif-er-ous." The name means "bringing profit" or "being useful." Paul mentions this man only twice in scripture: 2 Timothy 1:16-18 and 2 Timothy 4:19.

Onesiphorus was a Christian who lived in Ephesus but sought Paul out when he was in a Roman prison and stayed with him through thick and thin. Paul praised him for his hospitality, kindness, and courage. Many of Paul's friends had deserted him when he was thrown into prison for preaching the gospel. Rome was not a safe place for a Christian to live in those days because of the persecution of the Roman government, led by Nero. Paul said in 2 Tim. 1:16b that Onesiphorus "often refreshed me and was not ashamed of my chains."

Though at times it may seem otherwise, Paul was not Superman. He was human just like you and me. He had been deserted by his friends, was in jail, and was cold, lonesome, and discouraged. He needed his friends to encourage him, just like we do today. That is why Paul was so fond of Onesiphorus. He was there for him!

Have you ever needed someone to revive you spiritually and emotionally or to help you face the winds of adversity that you couldn't control?

Application for the Day: Today I will strive to be more like Onesiphorus in serving my brothers and sisters in Christ.

Thursday, April 11, 2024

Go Ye into All the World

Dan Erranton

Today's Scripture: Mark 16:15-16

Jesus left this world with these words to His apostles. This passage is referred to by many as the Great Commission. A similar passage is found in Matthew 28:18-20.

All of the apostles died a cruel death for the sake of Christ with the exception of John, who died a natural death while in exile on the Island of Patmos. According to reputable sources, Paul was beheaded, Peter was crucified upside down, Matthew was stabbed to death, James was stoned, and Matthias was burned to death, just to name a few.

The apostles fulfilled their commitment to Christ by traveling to other countries, spreading the good news of Jesus. They had only three primary sources of travel: walking, sailing, or riding on the back of an animal. The world at that time was small as compared to the world in which we live today, but they accomplished their mission. Paul probably traveled more and further distances than most of the other men. I have often wondered what he would have accomplished with a telephone, automobile, airplane, or the Internet.

Sadly, in our brotherhood today, many think of the "world" as a foreign country. Nothing could be further from the truth—Tennessee, Dickson County, and our own community are just as much a part of the world as India, South America, or the Philippines. These people right here in our state and county need to hear the good news of Jesus also. Not everyone can travel to faraway places to spread the gospel, but we can certainly start here at home every day. There are approximately 50,000 people in Dickson County, and the majority of them are not in any "House of Worship" on Sunday.

"Go into all the world" means you and me. The fields of harvest are white right here in our own community. Our friends' eternal salvation may depend on our sharing the gospel of Jesus Christ with them.

Application for the Day: Today I will take the Great Commission seriously and try to influence someone for Christ.

Friday, April 12, 2024

Here Am I! Send Me!

Dan Erranton

Today's Scripture: Isaiah 6:8

I grew up here in Dickson County, where congregations of the churches of Christ were numerous. There was an old saying in Dickson and surrounding counties that there was a "church of Christ on every creek bank." After leaving home for college, I never had a problem finding a congregation in either Clarksville or Memphis.

After graduating from college, I went to work as a pharmaceutical sales representative and moved to Hickory, NC, a beautiful, friendly town of about 30,000 people. That is when I got the shock of my young life. It took me three weeks to find a congregation of the Lord's church in Hickory. Only then did I realize that there was not a congregation of the church of Christ "on every creek bank" in most of the counties in our country. I saw many congregations, even those in the larger cities, struggle just to keep the door open. There was a greater sense of urgency to spread the gospel in these areas. I heard songs that were new to me; for example, "Lead Me to Some Soul Today" was sung at the close of every worship service at the church in Hickory.

The passage of scripture in Isaiah 6:8 came to be an important verse to me. I felt as if the Lord wanted me to see similar small, struggling churches in other places. Having lived in two places in North Carolina, in Upper East Tennessee, and in South Carolina made me aware of the urgency to spread the good news of Jesus. The words of Isaiah 6:8 have been set to music. This song was often led by the late Carl Frazier at several different congregations in Wisconsin.

The call for evangelism, in our country and all over the world, rings loud and clear. Just ask Russell Epperson in Lewistown, Montana; Riley Hendrix in Coral Springs, Florida; Dale Byrum in the Philippines; or our own Chad Garrett, who have all answered the Lord, "Here am I! Send me."

Application for the Day: Today my prayer will be, "Lead me to some soul today."

Monday, April 15, 2024

I Ain't Good Enuf

Dan Erranton

Today's Scripture: I Corinthians 6:9-11

I apologize for using grammar that is not acceptable to many, but I am merely repeating a phrase that I have heard many times while talking to someone about becoming a child of God. Jesus Christ came into this world to seek and save those who were lost. He died that horrible death on the cross and shed His precious blood for EVERYONE.

In the Apostle Paul's letter to the church at Corinth, he told of the unrighteous people who would not inherit the kingdom of God. He named fornicators, idolaters, thieves, drunkards, and many more who would not go to Heaven, but in verse 11, he claimed "and such were some of you. But you were washed, you were sanctified, you were justified in the name of the Lord Jesus."

Several years ago, I was privileged to baptize a gentleman into Christ, who, during his life, was guilty of more than one of those things listed in verses 9 & 10. He would often say, "Dan, I ain't good enough to be a Christian." I would continually refer him to this passage of scripture and explain to him that he was just as good as those people in Corinth. Because of the blood of Jesus, all of his past sins were washed away, and he was pure and holy in the sight of God. He faithfully served God the remainder of his life, during which time he contacted many of his old friends and influenced a number of them to begin attending church services.

The phrase "I ain't good enuf" just ISN'T correct. Paul tells us in Romans 3:23 that we have all sinned and fallen short of God's glory. John also tells us in 1 John 1:7 that "if we walk in the light, as he is in the light, we have fellowship with one another, and the blood of Jesus his Son cleanses us from all sin."

Application for the Day: Today I will strive to walk in the light, knowing that the blood of Jesus continually washes away my sins.

Tuesday, April 16, 2024

I Rang the Bell – Part 1
Dan Erranton

Today's Scripture: Psalm 143:5

In today's scripture, the Psalmist said, "I remember the days of old." The ringing of bells has always played an interesting role in my long life. The first bell that I remember hearing was the "Dinner Bell" at my grandparents' house. My grandmother rang the bell on days when my grandfather was in the field plowing. When she rang the bell, it meant that it was time for him to ride the mules to the barn for food and water, and by the time he finished, dinner would be on the table ready to eat. Hence, the name "Dinner Bell." That same bell was moved to my parents' backyard on Bel Arbre Drive and remains there until this day. George and Virginia Wright lived next door and used that bell many times to call their children to their house.

I have the desk-sized school bell in our bookcase at home that my dad rang to start classes in many of the one-room schools in Dickson County. None of those schools, such as Fairview, Tennessee City, Colesburg, and Eno, exist today. In more recent years, I remember school bells ringing at Oakmont School and Dickson High School to mark the beginning and ending of classes.

One of the most memorable bells that I heard ring was on Sunday morning before church services at the Walnut Street church of Christ. This was especially noticeable during the summer months. There was little or no home air conditioning in those days, so my dad and I would sit on the front step of our house on Church Street and polish our "Sunday shoes." When our current auditorium was built, the original bell was saved from the old building and is in the bell tower today, along with another bell given by Elmer and Pearl Dunn. What a sweet sound it was to hear that bell ring before worshiping the Lord!

Application for the Day: Today I will thank God for precious memories of the past!

Wednesday, April 17, 2024

I Rang the Bell – Part 2

Dan Erranton

Today's Scripture: Philippians 1:21

After writing in yesterday's devotional about the memories of bells during my childhood, I want to tell you about a very different kind of bell today. It was not located on a farm or in a schoolhouse. It is located in the Sarah Cannon Cancer Treatment Center in Dickson, Tennessee. It is the bell patients ring when they have finished their prescribed chemotherapy regimen. Similar bells are located in cancer treatment centers across America. In the six months that I received chemotherapy, I heard that bell ring only one other time on the days that I was there. Some were forced to stop because of side effects of the drug(s), and others passed from this life into eternity.

As I think back to my treatments and the time I was privileged to ring that bell, I am reminded of that old common statement: "Why Me, Lord?" I honestly don't know the answer to that question. Some of my dear friends have told me that God has a reason for me to live a while longer on this earth. I am reminded of the words of the Apostle Paul when he wrote to the church in Philippi that to live is Christ and to die is gain (Phil. 1:21). This I do know: I am indeed a very blessed man, surrounded by a very loving family in my house and in the Lord's house, not only at WSCOC but also in many other congregations of the Lord's family that I have been in contact with for many years of my life.

As a simple reminder, Tennessee Oncology gave me a small replica of the bell that was rung when I finished my chemotherapy. That bell is placed beside my TV cable box in my office. I never turn on my TV without seeing that bell and thinking, "Dan, you are truly a blessed man." Thanks be to God!

Application for the Day: Today I will thank God for my successful treatment for cancer and pray for others who are struggling with that disease.

Thursday, April 18, 2024

No More Pain

Dan Erranton

Today's Scripture: Revelation 22: 1-4

I have spent 68 of the 84 years of my life enjoying the profession of pharmacy, working in a drugstore, being a drug salesman for a large pharmaceutical company, or, for most of those years, working in two different large hospitals.

During these years, the sales or dispensing of medications that were used to reduce pain have been a great part of my work. The past 41 years I have worked at St. Thomas West Hospital, where I spent many hours working under a sterile IV hood, mixing and compounding medications that were administered in the vein. A large number of these IV medications were used to reduce pain. It was not uncommon to mix 15-20 different IV narcotic drips in one 10-hour shift.

It is not a pleasant experience to walk down the hallway of a hospital on the oncology wing, the orthopedic wing, or in the critical care area and hear the moaning, groaning, and screaming of patients who are dealing with excruciating pain. That is one reason that I have so much respect for the people who are taking care of these patients.

For me, in the environment in which I have worked for so many years, it is difficult to imagine a place with no pain and no suffering. Yet, that is exactly what the Apostle John saw when he was given a glimpse of Heaven as recorded in Revelation 21:4. No more death, no more crying, no more sorrow, and no more pain, "for the former things have passed away." As a mortal human being, it is hard to visualize such a place. But we shall be changed, in the twinkling of an eye, this mortal will put on immortality, and we shall live with God forever.

It is my prayer that everyone will obey God, live for Him, serve Him daily, and be faithful to Him so we can all enjoy this wonderful place called Heaven, where there will be NO MORE PAIN.

Application for the Day: Today I will be thankful for a pain-free place that God has prepared for His children.

Friday, April 19, 2024

A Masterpiece

Darlein Sullivan Morse

Today's Scripture: Psalm 139:14 – "I am fearfully and wonderfully made."

I was created to be a masterpiece! We all were. Beautiful, admired, on display as a great work of art. We are God's handiwork (Eph. 2:10), created slightly lower than the angels and crowned "with glory and honor" (Psa. 8:5).

However, as far as a masterpiece is concerned, I feel much more like a Picasso than a Michelangelo. Garish colors, disjointed, all the parts out of place. You have to tilt your head sideways to look at it, and then you're still not exactly sure what you're seeing. My physical being is all right, I suppose. I have arms and legs in the right places, and I don't have an eye on my chin or two ears on one side of my head or anything, but my spiritual being is the problem. It's all over the place! I feel like Paul when he said, (and I paraphrase) 'I just can't seem to get it right" (Rom. 7:18-19, 24).

I've always been that little black sheep that keeps jumping the fence and running off in search of greener pasture only to realize that it's scary and cold outside of the fold. And yet—(Here's the best part)— my Good Shepherd KEEPS coming after me, wooing me back home. "Suppose one of you has a hundred sheep and loses one of them. Doesn't he leave the ninety-nine in the open country and go after the lost sheep until he finds it?" (Luke 15:4). He loves me in spite of me! How awesome is that? He comes and finds me, lifts me out of the pit, brushes me off, and hugs me all the way home! He whispers in my ear and sings over me the whole way and explains to me, yet again, that I am His beautiful creation, created in His image!

I may not be beautiful as the world sees beauty, but to God I am a priceless masterpiece. You are too!

Application for the Day: Today I will meditate on this verse: "Thanks be to God, who delivers me through Jesus Christ our Lord! (Rom. 7:25a).

Monday, April 22, 2024

Lord, Come Quickly

Submitted by Darlein Sullivan Morse in memory of Her mother,
Marion Overton Sawyer, who wrote this poem on 02-24-22.

Today's Scripture: Revelation 22:20 - He who testifies to these things says, "Surely I am coming quickly." Amen. Even so, come, Lord Jesus!

"Oh, Jesus! Lord, come quickly!" I heard my mother say.
I couldn't understand her words. I said, "Jesus, take your time, I pray!"
For I have many things to do. I need to grow and learn.
I could not comprehend her thoughts or the place for which she yearned.

My feeble mind was stuck on earth so far away from God.
I forgot where I had come from with my feet planted on this sod.
But then, one day, Jesus called my name! I heard it, soft and low.
He said, "My child, you are my treasured one. Be careful where you go!

"For your place is here with me, not on earthly soil.
You're only there a little while to bear life's trials and toil.
So keep your eyes on heaven. Don't forget where you came from!
The days are drawing nearer. Don't forget me, as is the way of some.

"For I'm coming back to get you and bring you home to me.
We will dance in joyful union and sing a song of glee!
Remember your dear mother's words and how she longs for me.
The day will come when you'll watch her leave, and then you'll surely see.

"I'll take her hand and lead her home, and we will wait for you.
So tend your life as she does hers, and to me be ever true."
I echo now, my mother's words, "Come quickly, Lord, I pray!"
And I hear my mother's precious voice say, "Lord Jesus, I'm home to stay!"

Application for the Day: Today I will strive to live for Jesus so my prayer may also be, "Lord, come Quickly."

Tuesday, April 23, 2024

It's Time to Let Go!

David Rader (2018 Summer Intern)

Today's Scripture: Genesis 3

I have a problem. Few things excite me like receiving packages in perfect condition. If the box is unique, I have to keep it! In fact, my problem is so severe that my garage has been taken over by a multitude of boxes that, in all likelihood, will never be used. But on the off chance that they could be used, I simply can't let go.

Far too regularly, inability to let go serves as a hindrance in our service to the Lord. A thorough reading of Genesis 3 illustrates the imperative nature of learning to let go. By holding onto pride, God is questioned (Gen. 3:1). By permitting negligence, boundaries are toyed with and negotiations with Satan occur (Gen. 3:2-4). By holding onto doubt, judgment is flawed and sin is committed (Gen. 3:4-6). By internalizing guilt, attempts to cover up and hide are made, rather than pursuing forgiveness (Gen. 3:7-8). By gripping excuses instead of taking accountability, repentance is inhibited, rather than exhibited (Gen. 3:9-13). See how dangerous it is to refuse to let go?

If you've read ahead in Genesis 3, you know that Adam and Eve are banished from the garden for disobeying. However, if that's the only takeaway we glean from this account, we miss the entire message of Scripture: God continually pursues mankind! Before removing Adam and Eve from the garden, God clothes them (Gen. 3:21). His provision alleviates their shame and comforts them in the depths of guilt.

How often do we find ourselves holding onto pride, doubt, guilt, and excuses? An honest assessment likely reflects an answer we don't like. Praise be to God that we aren't left to our own devices to address our shame and guilt! Rather, may we rejoice that our sins and lawless deeds He remembers no more (Heb. 10:17) as He keeps on pursuing and providing for a fallen people! It's time to let go!

Application for the Day: Today I will remember that, despite our struggles to let go of stumbling blocks, God refuses to let go of us!

Wednesday, April 24, 2024

You're Not Dismissed!

David Rader (2018 Summer Intern)

Today's Scripture: Titus 3:4-5

When I was a child, it was always painfully obvious to me when I was in trouble. When my mom changed her tone and utilized my middle name, I clearly understood that I did not meet her expectations. My dad, on the other hand, had the ability to purse his lips together and create a high-pitched whistle that, though no more than a couple of milliseconds in length, could stop me in my tracks. If either of these things happened, I knew I had failed. But do you know what I never once questioned? My parents' unconditional love for me!

Humble introspection, caused by the words of Scripture, likewise provides a clear indication of when we've failed to meet God's expectations. All too often, when we find ourselves guilty of sin or struggling to do the good He commands of us, we ignore the promise of Titus 3:4-5. Despite our lack of merit and our deficiencies of righteousness, His goodness and lovingkindness are manifested in the gift of salvation, provided exclusively by the appearance of Jesus. He has loved us unconditionally!

Yet all too often we question His love. We doubt it. We assume that God must be dismissive of us because of our struggles. Let's be comforted by this reality: that assumption is routinely debunked on the pages of the New Testament. When Mary Magdalene was possessed by seven demons, Jesus didn't deem her incapable of change or categorize her as too far gone because of Satan's influence on her. Instead, he gave her freedom (Luke 8:2). When Peter struggled with doubt and impulsivity, Jesus didn't label him as too inconsistent or too unreliable. He forgave and empowered him (John 21:15-19).

Don't doubt God's unconditional love for you. The New Testament pattern promises God's unwavering faithfulness to you. Regardless of your baggage, God is never dismissive of you!

Application for the Day: Today I will serve the same God who freed Mary and empowered Peter and who stands ready to pour out His goodness and lovingkindness on me.

Thursday, April 25, 2024

Waiting

Debbie Albright

Today's Scripture: Luke 1:37 – "For nothing will be impossible with God."

In the Old Testament books of Genesis and 1 Samuel, stories are told of two women who were waiting for the untimely birth of a son, with contrasting viewpoints for handling their situations. When Sarah, wife of Abraham (Genesis 18), was told by God that she would conceive a son at the age of 89, and her husband 99, she laughed in unbelief, which she later denied. In Genesis 18:13, God spoke to Abraham: "Why did Sarah laugh and say, 'Shall I indeed bear a child, now that I am old?' Is anything too hard for the Lord?" God kept his promise to Abraham and Sarah, and she bore a son, whom they called Isaac.

In 1 Samuel 1, we read the story of Elkanah, who had two wives, Hannah and Peninnah. Every year Elkanah took his family to worship and sacrifice at Shiloh where Eli's two sons served as priests. Whenever the day came for sacrifice, Elkanah would give portions of the meat to his wife Peninnah and her children. To Hannah, however, he would give a double portion because he loved her more and the Lord has closed her womb. Every year, Peninnah would provoke Hannah because she was barren! Hannah would become so upset that she would weep and not eat. Elkanah would ask her why she was downhearted and say, "Am I not more to you than ten sons?" (1 Sam. 1:8b). In bitterness of soul, Hannah wept and prayed to the Lord.

Unlike Sarah, who laughed, Hannah made a vow that if God would give her a son, she would dedicate his life to His service. God heard and answered her prayer, and she kept her vow to give Samuel to the Lord for his whole life. While Samuel was a young boy, her entire focus was on helping God's plan come to fruition.

Application for the Day: Today I will pray that God will help me to dedicate my life to working with Him in the fulfillment of His plan.

Friday, April 26, 2024

Let Go and Let God

Deborah Willis Fuller

Today's Scripture: Philippians 4:6-7

I am ashamed to say that I am a worrier. I worry about my family. I worry about what is going on in the world today. I even worry that I have forgotten something and worry about whether I should worry about that! Why is it that we sometimes let worries consume us? At any time, did worrying help the situation? In Luke 12:25, Jesus said, "And which of you by being anxious can add a single hour to his span of life?"

God does not want us to worry. When we worry, we take our focus off of God and all that He can do for us. God is good. He listens to us when we go to Him in prayer. He cares about us and gives us what we need when we need it. He loves us and blesses us daily.

So why do we worry so much? We let fear take over, and that fear is usually irrational. It is an overwhelming feeling that doesn't help what is going on at the moment, and it takes away our peace. Worrying is basically an inaction. Nothing is accomplished by worrying. In Philippians 4:6-7, the Bible says, "Do not be anxious about anything, but in everything by prayer and supplication with thanksgiving let your requests be made known to God. And the peace of God, which surpasses all understanding, will guard your hearts and your minds in Christ Jesus."

Wow! Do you hear that? God is telling us to let go of our worries. He will protect us and give us peace. He is going to take care of us. We are not alone. Trust that He will be with you in times of trial and in times of triumph, in times of sorrow and in times of great joy. God has got this!

Application for the Day: Today I will go to God in prayer and tell Him about the struggles that weigh heavily on my heart; I will trust in Him that He will give me peace.

Monday, April 29, 2024

No Greater Love

Deborah Willis Fuller

Today's Scripture: John 15:13

Have you ever heard someone say, "I love you," and you wondered if they really meant it? You may have felt that it was a scripted response and that there were no true feelings behind that statement. This takes away the special meaning in those words. I believe that love is an action. It is shown through selfless acts of kindness. Jesus tells us to love one another as He has loved us (John 15:12). Do we actively show love to others? This can simply be by sending a card to let someone know you are thinking of them, bringing a meal to someone who is sick or grieving, or even cutting the grass or helping a parent take care of small children when needed. More importantly, you can just be there and listen when someone needs to talk. After all, the gift of your time is a most precious gift.

Now take that a step further. Would you be willing to die for someone? I am sure that I, like many of you, could say without hesitation that I would die for my family, but what about others? Jesus said, "Greater love has no one than this, that someone lay down his life for his friends" (John 15:13). We have seen several instances in the past few years of people doing just that: teachers and school staff putting themselves in harm's way to protect innocent children; police officers, fire fighters, and those in the military sacrificing themselves to save others; ordinary people from all walks of life risking their lives for someone else. This, my friends, is love in action.

Jesus was the greatest example of this love in action. He bled and died to save all of us from all our sins. How much love He had for us to die upon that cross!

Application for the Day: Today I will pray that God will grant me opportunities to show His love to others through my actions that glorify Him.

Come Share the Lord

Debra Mitchell

Today's Scripture: John 6.54 - "Whosoever eats my flesh and drinks my blood remains in me, and I in them."

I grew up Catholic, attending regularly and receiving all of the required sacraments, including matrimony. A few years into my marriage, my husband pursued a different lifestyle, one that I was not a part of. We divorced, and I was no longer welcome to partake in the Lord's Supper. As a Catholic, I sinned against a sacrament, and until I could get that right, I was not cleansed enough to share in the body of Christ. I would sit in the pew, while the righteous would file by me and receive the body and blood of Christ. This became painful. I felt alone and unwelcomed. I spent years pretending it didn't matter while distancing myself from church and Jesus.

Fast forward, and I am now living in Tennessee. I found myself searching for something, a different way, perhaps a different church. Catholicism was not working for me. Darrell and I visited a church of Christ because it looked like a church I attended in Buffalo. We started attending weekly, we listened, and we prayed. We attended Bible studies and were drawn into fellowship. In 2019, I was baptized, and, by the grace of God, I was forgiven! I could partake of the Lord's Supper again: "Come take the bread, come drink the wine, come share the Lord" (Bryan Jeffrey Leech, 1984). What a beautiful way to come together in fellowship! I have come to acknowledge that I am enough.

In a recent sermon Chris McCurley said, "Choose renewed over removal. Choose to draw closer, not further away." YES!

The Lord's Supper is a vital start to our week. The meditation time has the power to settle our souls. It is a time for fellowship and acceptance. "No one is a stranger here, everyone belongs, finding our forgiveness here, we in turn forgive all wrong" (Bryan Jeffrey Leech, 1984).

Application for the Day: Today I will look forward to sharing in the body and blood of Christ with each Christian in the assembly.

Wednesday, May 1, 2024

Forgiveness

Debra Mitchell

Today's Scripture: Matthew 18:21-22

Our "forgiving muscle" needs to be exercised—not just seven, but many times.

I was raised Catholic, and, in my youth, I was close to God. However, life choices and poor judgment moved me further from God. At the age of 55, I was baptized into Christ. Jesus did the heavy lifting that day, forgiving me of sin. My workout was just beginning while I learned to utilize the muscle of forgiveness myself.

My husband was diagnosed with cancer. In that instant, hardships melted away. Forgiveness was the only option, and I gave it freely. No more counting wrongs, no more nasty tones, no more blame! Our love began to resurface, smiles returned, laughter replaced loud language, and respect replaced reproach. I wonder what kind of life we would have had if forgiveness were part of our lives all along. Darrell, I forgive you!

Forgiving my father was a new muscle I gained. I struggled my entire adult life NOT to be like my father. I moved away from home. I saw him as a bitter man instead of someone with his own hurdles and pain. I prayed for the strength to let go of anger and the wisdom to understand him. I woke up from a dream about my dad, and the peace of forgiveness was upon me. Only love remained. It is incredible not to carry that burden any longer. Dad, I forgive you!

Forgiving myself is a work in process. Jesus is my spotter, holding back my inner critic. For endurance, I pump gratitude into my daily routine. I draw strength from God's word. I journey using Scripture to turn mistakes into life lessons. Like any good routine, some days are harder than others. I have faith I will get there because I am already forgiven by the One who matters most.

So look for opportunities to forgive: the driver who cuts you off, the boss who doesn't appreciate you, the friend who disappoints you, or the child who disobeys you.

Application for the Day: Today I will allow Jesus to motivate my steps toward forgiveness by losing the heavy weight of stress and hostility.

Thursday, May 2, 2024

Think Whatever

Debra Mitchell

Today's Scripture: Philippians 4:8

Are you ready to face the day, to walk out the door and interact with others? To be right with God? To be pure and know what is true? To appreciate the lovely just around the corner? What does it take for you to be ready to face the day?

I've built a morning practice designed to start each day by tapping into my mind, body, and spirit. First, the body. In fifteen minutes, I complete a series of yoga stretches, gently moving through the aches that age brings my way. Next, I shake off the cobwebs of sleep by engaging in a thought-provoking activity, such as reading or writing. And, finally, the highlight of my morning is spending time in God's word. I read and listen to a daily Scripture that guides me throughout the day. I pray and talk with God, aloud, silently, and by writing, inviting Him into my day at first light and asking Him to walk with me throughout. I am not perfect in this practice, but it is a roadmap to guide me every day to wake up, walk out, and meet the world!

Your day may start by hitting the snooze button for the third time or with a child whining for immediate attention or with a to-do list the length of the Dead Sea scrolls. You think, "I couldn't possibly add this to my already busy schedule." But you can! I invite you to add the most important practice: pray and talk with Jesus; invite Him into your day at first light with Scripture. Start your day in a positive light. Prepare yourself to think whatever is true, noble, right, pure, lovely, admirable, excellent, or praiseworthy.

And, finally, brothers and sisters, keep a grateful journal. Get a daily planner or use a simple notepad. Keep it nearby—on your night-stand or kitchen table or office desk. Commit to writing a thank you note to God daily for whatever is praiseworthy.

Application for the Day: Today I will thank God and feel the joy lift my spirit, knowing I am ready to face the day.

Friday, May 3, 2024

Angry Words – Part 1

Del Vineyard

Today's Scripture: James 3:8-10

"But no man can tame the tongue. It is an unruly evil, full of deadly poison. With it we bless our God and Father, and with it we curse men, who have been made in the similitude of God. Out of the same mouth proceed blessing and cursing. My brethren, these things ought not to be so."

Remember the song's words "Angry words! *O* let them never From the tongue unbridled slip; May the heart's best impulse ever Check them ere they soil the lip" (Horatius Palmer, 1867). Why can't I express my anger with words? We used to teach kids, "Sticks and stones may break my bones, but names will never hurt me." NO! That's really not true! Words can hurt! Our words are others' views into our thoughts and feelings.

Angry words are like truth serum: they reveal exactly what is being felt at that moment. We're telling the other person, "This is my unfiltered opinion of you." Regardless of motive or provocation, once the words leave our mouths, they are gone like a bullet fired and cannot be brought back. Words, like a knife, can pierce and hurt. Removing the knife leaves a wound, and words can also leave wounds. Some wounds heal quickly, while others get infected and become a serious condition or could be so serious that they cause death.

So it is with our words. Once spoken, the damage is done. We may be immediately sorry we said what we did, but "Oh, I didn't mean that" probably won't remove the wound. Words can destroy a friendship, kill an influence, ruin a reputation, and end a marriage. Regret, no matter how contrite, probably won't totally erase the harm caused by angry words. How quickly, or even whether, the person hurt by our angry words ever regains respect or regard for us is determined by his ability to forgive.

Application for the Day: Today I will choose words that bless others.

Monday, May 6, 2024

Angry Words – Part 2

Del Vineyard

Today's Scripture: James 3:8-10 – "But no man can tame the tongue. It is an unruly evil, full of deadly poison. With it we bless our God and Father, and with it we curse men, who have been made in the similitude of God. Out of the same mouth proceed blessing and cursing. My brethren, these things ought not to be so."

If we are the person hurt by someone's words, we should remember what Jesus taught: that we must forgive if we want to be forgiven by God (Matt. 6:12-15). No one said that would be easy. If we are the one who hurt others with our angry words, we need to ask sincerely for their forgiveness and ask for God's forgiveness (Matt. 5:23-24).

If we are people who tend to let our anger explode out of our mouths, we need to remember the following verses:

- Ephesians 4:26 – "'Be angry, and do not sin': do not let the sun go down on your wrath."

- James 1:19b – "Be quick to hear, slow to speak, slow to wrath."

- Proverbs 16:32 – "He who is slow to anger is better than the mighty, And he who rules his spirit than he who takes a city."

- James 3:5-6 – "Even so the tongue is a little member and boasts great things. See how great a forest a little fire kindles! And the tongue is a fire, a world of iniquity. The tongue is so set among our members that it defiles the whole body, and sets on fire the course of nature; and it is set on fire by hell."

- Ephesians 4:31-32 – "Let all bitterness, wrath, anger, clamor, and evil speaking be put away from you, with all malice. And be kind to one another, tenderhearted, forgiving one another, even as God in Christ forgave you."

- Proverbs 15:18 – "A wrathful man stirs up strife, But he who is slow to anger allays contention."

Application for the Day: Today I will think about my words before I say them and work to control my urge to retaliate verbally if I am offended or angered by someone.

Tuesday, May 7, 2024

Responsibility

Del Vineyard

Today's Scripture: 1 Corinthians 12

1 Corinthians 12: 18-19 – "But now God has set the members, each one of them, in the body just as He pleased. And if they were all one member, where *would* the body *be?*"

Several years ago, Charles Osgood wrote a poem about responsibility. It captured the various facets of responsibility and implied accountability so well that someone condensed it into what we now call a meme. Memes are phrases, videos, images, etc., often humorous, which are copied and distributed over the Internet. There have been many variations but here is one of my favorites (by an anonymous author):

> This is a story about four people named Everybody, Somebody, Anybody, and Nobody. There was an important job to be done, and Everybody was sure that Somebody would do it. Anybody could have done it, but Nobody did it. Somebody got angry about that because it was Everybody's job. Everybody thought that Anybody could do it, but Nobody realized that Everybody wouldn't do it. It ended up that Everybody blamed Somebody when Nobody did what Anybody could have done.

I have seen several variations of this meme used in various management, sales, and leadership training settings. It has widespread application to many facets of our lives beyond work responsibilities. Unfortunately, the "it's-not-my-job" attitude or the "someone-else-is-better-suited-for-that-job" attitude also affects the church. It's not so humorous when human nature starts to prevent things that the church needs to be doing from being done. There is a job for everyone to do in the church. For starters, it is everyone's job to find his or her job. 1 Corinthians 12 tells of the diversity of parts (members) of the body (church) and how each is valuable and necessary for the wellbeing of the whole body. It strongly implies that each part must do his or her part, however small it might seem to be, for the body to thrive.

Application for Today: Today I will resolve to do what I can to see that jobs that I can do get done.

Wednesday, May 8, 2024

Jesus Is the Anchor of My Soul

Elsie Kees

Today's Scripture: Hebrews 6:19

As an anchor holds the ship when the storms are raging, hope in Christ holds the soul steadfast. Jesus offers hope to all, not only to those who are religious. Christians are looking for that blessed hope of eternal life as they wait for the great God and Savior Jesus Christ.

Abraham trusted completely in God. He packed up and left his family for a place he had never been with only God to guide him. This is what Christian hope is all about, trusting in God completely (Rom. 4:17-18).

In reading stories of hope in the Bible, there is joy in just knowing that all has been done for us. Jesus paid it all. Moses's farewell sermon reminds us how much God loves us and is always nearby. This love brings us joy and hope. We probably will never be able to understand how deep this love is, but we can see His love in action by reading stories of His love and what He has done for others. As people of hope, we know that God will make a way where there is no other way.

Something that really bothers me is to hear someone say that no one loves him. That is the feeling of a heavy heart—to hear those words and realize that this person must not know God. To be without the hope of God's love is hard to comprehend.

To know what God has done for me, even when I did not know He was doing it, was hard to understand. I have come to learn and understand that, when I give my all to God, His love will take care of me! Not having the hope of God's love and care would be very drastic for me.

- Hope of the Christian – Titus 2:11-14
- Holding on to hope – Romans 8:24-25

Application for the Day: Today I will pray that, with God's help, I can take confidence in the two readings above as a Christian.

Be Different

Erin Webb

Today's Scriptures: John 15:19; John 17:14-16

The Commodores clearly didn't have children--there's not much "easy" about Sunday mornings. And once we make it to the pew, there's a series of tricks, snacks, and activities to keep our crew occupied so that we can participate in worship. Even still, we sometimes need to remind our kids that, when they try to talk to us or wallow around in the aisle, they're actually distracting us from giving our full attention to our Creator, the one who deserves our attention.

But what about outside of the building? Can our lives be a distraction that might keep others from seeing our Lord? The way we treat others, the conversations we have, even the looks that we give—what do they communicate to the "world" about followers of Christ? WE WERE MEANT TO BE DIFFERENT. In John 17, Jesus prays to His Father, not to take us out of the world, but to keep us from the evil one.

My challenge to you is to find ways in which you are tempted to be "in the world" and choose to BE DIFFERENT from the world. Instead of joining in the gossip, choose not only to walk away but also to be bold enough to challenge and change the conversation. BE DIFFERENT. When a person offering you a service messes up, extend grace and patience, not anger and poor reviews. BE DIFFERENT. Don't take to social media to air out opinions about others. Instead, approach the subject with love and prayer, allowing God to open doors for you.

BE DIFFERENT. If we look like the world, we aren't doing it right. One of my favorite sayings is, "God has called us to BE DIFFERENT." We use this reminder with each other at home when we find ourselves being tempted to be worldly. It takes thick skin, but it's a change worth making if it keeps us from distracting from the One who deserves our attention.

Application for the Day: Today I will show Christ to others by the ways in which I am different from what the world expects.

Friday, May 10, 2024

Where Does Your Wealth Come From?

Erin Webb

Today's Scriptures: Romans 5:8; Psalm 139:14

One thing I know is that my first thirty years of life would have been more enjoyable if I had learned earlier where my worth comes from and who is responsible for my happiness! Don't get me wrong —I lived a charmed life: great parents, husband, family, home, schools, teammates, and friends. Still, I felt incomplete. My life was spent chasing something to make me feel whole. If I'm a great student… If I'm a good athlete… If I'm a good friend… If I'm a good daughter… If I'm a good wife… If I'm a good mama… What an endless cycle of feeling "less than" and unloved!

Only one person made me feel this way—not parents, not friends, not husband or kids. I felt this way because I was chasing something that was never going to fulfill me. If I'm in pursuit of being the best student and that is how I measure my worth, what will happen to me after graduation? If my desire is to be the best athlete and my worth is tied to that, what happens when I play my last game? If my desire is for others to like me and someone doesn't, what happens to my self-worth? If I disappoint my parents, how does that affect my self-worth? If my husband and I go through a rough patch, my self-worth tanks.

Remember that you were created! The Lord knew you while you were still in the womb, and Christ died for you despite your shortcomings. Those two truths can and should be the foundation of our self-worth. We can't make everyone like us, but Christ loved us enough to die for us. When we cause someone to feel disappointment, let's apologize and remember that His mercies are new every morning. Every earthly thing we love and enjoy will one day pass away. One thing can't be taken from us, and it is in that one thing that we should find our worth.

Application for the Day: Today I will push myself and others to remember that worth comes from God.

Monday, May 13, 2024

Our Planning

Gary Brunett

Today's Scripture: James 4:13-16

Do we leave God out of our daily planning? James 4:13-16 states, "Come now, you who say, "Today or tomorrow we will go to such and such city, spend a year there, buy and sell, and make a profit; whereas you do not know that will happen tomorrow. For what is your life? It is even a vapor that appears for a little time and then vanishes away. For we ought to say, if the Lord wills, we shall live, and do this or that. But now you boast in your arrogance. All such boasting is arrogance."

James is speaking in this passage about leaving God out of our planning. We need to consider at least four things when we make plans for the future. We should consider the uncertainty of life. Many things can happen to alter our plans, so we certainly need to include God in our planning.

We need to consider the brevity of life. All of us realize, that life can be cut short for a variety of reasons, and we do not need to take life for granted. Even if we live to a ripe old age, life is so short. James seems to be stressing that we cannot even count on getting old.

We can be foolish because we do not take into account THE WILL OF GOD. We need to understand that planning ahead is not discouraged here, as long as one understands that all plans are subject to the will of God.

We can also be foolish because we are proud of ourselves and our abilities. Instead of trusting in God and submitting to His will, we can be proud of what we have done in the past and boast about what we plan to do in the future. It is permissible to be proud of some things, but it is a sin to be proud of one's own accomplishments, failing to give God the glory.

Application for the Day: Today, I will remember to include God in all my future plans.

Tuesday, May 14, 2024

Practical Christianity

Gary Brunett

Today's Scripture: James 5: 7-12

The emphasis in James 5: 7-12 is on patience. This is an extremely important subject. Patience is not our greatest virtue. One old saying is "Lord, give me patience and give it to me right now." The dictionary says that patience is "the quality or habit of enduring without complaint." In the KJV patience is equated with the term "long-suffering or long tempered."

In this devotional, we will focus on three areas where we need to have patience. The first is to be patient in your work. James 5: 7 states "Be patient therefore, brethren, unto the coming of the Lord". James stresses that his readers should not be wasting their time being overly concerned about whether their persecutors would be punished or not. That is God's business, not theirs. In Romans 12: 19 Paul said, "Beloved, do not avenge yourselves, but rather give place to wrath; for it is written, "Vengeance is Mine, I will repay," says the Lord. One of the important lessons we can learn from verses 7-8 is the need to be patient in our work for the Lord.

The second area is to be patient with each other. Have you ever noticed when we get frustrated or angry or we are hurt by others, that we tend to take it out on those nearest and dearest to us. Although this is illogical, it is very common. Christians need each other and how foolish it is to murmur and complain about each other. Let us learn to pray for those whom we criticize. It is hard to murmur and pray at the same time.

The third area is to be patient in the midst of trials. One of the most important lessons we can learn is that we can endure, we can remain faithful to the Lord no matter what comes. We will have peace that comes from doing what we know to be right.

Application for the Day: Today, I will pray asking God to help me develop patience to bring glory and honor to Him.

Wednesday, May 15, 2024

Worldliness

Gary Brunett

Today's Scripture: James 4:6-10

How can we be faithful or if we have been unfaithful, how can we return? First, we need to accept the grace of God. If we had only our own strength on which to rely, the situation would be hopeless. But we have the grace of God to help us meet the challenge. Philippians 4:13 states, "I can do all things through God who strengthens me." The need for God's grace did not cease once we were Christians. In Proverbs 3:34 it states "God giveth grace to the humble." There are so many ways that God helps us: He has given us His word. We can pray to Him. He has given us meaningful work to do. He has given us His divine protection.

Verse 7 tells us to be obedient. God is our spiritual Commander-in-Chief, let us submit to Him, obey Him without question. We are told to resist the devil and he will flee from us. Our enemy is formidable but not irresistible. We need to continue to strive to be more like God. James tells us to draw near to God and He will draw near to us. The bottom line is we need to strive to become more like God.

Verses 9, 10 tells us to humble ourselves before God. So closely tied with cleansing the hands and purifying the heart is the matter of penitence. It is with this that James closes his discussion of how to cure worldliness; "Be afflicted, and morn, and weep: let your laughter be turned to mourning, let your joy to heaviness, Humble yourselves in the sight of the Lord, and He will lift you up. Is James against one being happy? Absolutely, not! James 5:13 answers that question. Sin is no laughing matter. When sin runs rampant in our country, our hearts should be grieved. When sin is tolerated in the church, our heart should be enraged. When sin is in our lives, our hearts should be broken.

Application of the Day: Today, I will strive to move closer to God and do His will in all things.

A Cup of Cold Water

Gaylan Brown

Today's Scripture: Matthew 10:42

My mama sang, "I come to the garden alone, and that I will remember from the spring of my life, until the last day of December. For the small things done at the Master's invitation, are seed-producing fruit, exceeding all expectation!" The sound of my mother's voice singing that song is one of my earliest memories. The small things stick with you. She sang it as she rocked me in the old rocking chair.

I remember my first Bible schoolteacher at Water Street church of Christ in Charlotte whose name was Alize Southerland. I remember the flannel graph pictures, the stories, and her sweetness. I've told many people that all the important principles in life were taught in Mrs. Alize's Bible Class.

And I can't say enough about my dearest Melissa, always being there for our children, picking them up after school, supplying them with snacks, love, and encouragement. They always described her as the best "cooker" in the whole world.

Let us not take for granted the "cups of cold water" given to others by godly servants. "Now there was in Joppa a disciple named Tabitha, which, translated, means Dorcas. She was full of good works and acts of charity. In those days she became ill and died, and when they had washed her, they laid her in an upper room. Since Lydda was near Joppa, the disciples, hearing that Peter was there, sent two men to him, urging him, 'Please come to us without delay.' So Peter rose and went with them. And when he arrived, they took him to the upper room. All the widows stood beside him weeping and showing tunics and other garments that Dorcas made while she was with them" (Acts 9:36-39). Peter raised her from the dead.

Our lives have been blessed with Dorcases. Our church family is full of godly women, going about God's business, often unnoticed and undervalued. God notices and values them highly. So should we!

Application for the Day: Today I will be intentional in recognizing and thanking godly servants!

Friday, May 17, 2024

Milk Fever

Gaylan Brown

Today's Scripture: John 6:48-51

I was blessed to grow up on a dairy farm. In my father's eyes the breed of cows best suited for dairying was Jersey. A Jersey is a smaller breed than some, but is attractive and intelligent (for a cow) and is known for the high butterfat content of their milk, bringing a higher price per pound of milk. One downside to Jersey cows is a predisposition for milk fever, known as hypocalcemia, a condition caused by insufficient blood levels of calcium which would commonly occur soon after calving. This mineral deficiency would result in muscle paralysis, requiring IV administration of glucose, minerals, and electrolytes.

God's Word provides essential "nutrients" for *our* spiritual well-being. We need regular infusions of spiritual minerals and electrolytes to prevent "paralysis" which hinders our effective service in God's kingdom. The Psalmist describes the fruitfulness of the tree planted by streams of water, delighting in the law of the Lord (Psalm 1:3). We too can be healthy and vigorous for God if we drink daily from the sweet stream of God's Word.

The prophet Ezekiel is instructed to eat the word of God. Ezekiel 3:1-3 - And he said to me, "Son of man, eat whatever you find here. Eat this scroll, and go, speak to the house of Israel." So I opened my mouth, and he gave me this scroll to eat. And he said to me, "Son of man, feed your belly with this scroll that I give you and fill your stomach with it." Then I ate it, and it was in my mouth as sweet as honey." When we ingest, absorb, and digest, the Word, it becomes part of our existence.

Jesus speaks of Himself as the bread of life in John 6:48-51 where he said" I am the bread of life…. I am the living bread that came down from heaven…the bread that I will give for the life of the world is my flesh."

Application for the day: Today I will absorb God's Word and allow it to bring fruit in my life.

Monday, May 20, 2024

Sing Louder

Gaylan Brown

Today's Scripture: Matthew 28:18-20

In his book *How Do You Kill 11 Million People?*, author Andy Andrews tells the story of how Hitler and his regime were able to murder over 11,000,000 people during World War II. One of the key elements in this horrific undertaking was the use of deception and lies. Jews and other "undesirable" groups and classifications of people were herded into barricaded areas under the pretense of protection. This took place in many cities throughout Europe. Later, the people were told that they were going to be relocated to a better place. They were warned that the transfer would not be pleasant but that they would be much better off and that the families would remain together.

The process was controlled to prevent hysteria while people filled railroad cars designed to transport cattle. The cars were big enough for eight-ten cows, but were now crammed full with 100 people, and the doors were locked behind them. They were doomed. The trains delivered their loads to a large group of concentration camps. Some were immediately murdered and cremated, while others were used for forced labor under impossible conditions, resulting in more lingering deaths.

One of the amazing things that took place was the attitude of complacency and denial of what was going on exhibited by the people not in captivity. One such person told about hearing the train whistles while sitting in church buildings. The people heard the crying and wailing coming from the railroad cars, and in their hearts, they knew what was happening. Their solution to shield their consciences was to sing louder to drown out the cries of the prisoners headed for destruction.

It is our God-given task to share the message of salvation to a lost and dying world headed for destruction. John 3:16 states, "For God so loved the world, that he gave his only Son, that whoever believes in him should not perish but have eternal life."

Application for the Day: Today I will open my ears and heart to those who are perishing.

Tuesday, May 21, 2024

A Heart for God

George Caudill
Formatted by Isaiah Leninger from a Class Manuscript

Today's Scripture: John 1:15-34

Perhaps at no time in history have we needed a voice like John the Baptist more. This world is full of evil. Mass shootings are common. Millions of babies have been aborted. The rates of divorce, homosexuality, single-parent homes, and suicide are all at all-time highs. Christianity is removed from popular culture. We need someone to stand up and speak the truth boldly and tell the world about Jesus. We cannot sit silently or support those living in sin (Rom. 1:32). We need to be an influence on the world.

John (the Baptist) teaches us three very important things about how to be an influence on the world:

1. Do not conform to the world to convince the world. John did not care about fitting in with the world around him. Mark 1:4-6 tells us that John lived in the wilderness, wearing camel's hair and eating locusts. But more importantly than what he wore or what he ate, he was never content to sit back and let God's Word go unspoken. John lived in a way that made everyone take notice. He lived in a way that was not conformed to the world, but transformed (Rom. 12:1-2).

2. It is not necessary to understand everything to preach about Jesus. When John saw Jesus, he said, "I myself did not know him" (John 1:31), yet John was still the voice crying in the wilderness to make straight the way of the Lord (John 1:23). The power of the gospel is not in the messenger. It is in the message that Jesus saves (Rom. 1:16).

3. One doesn't have to do it all to do a lot. Even when John was in prison for speaking the truth, he was still sending his disciples to Jesus. He knew that his influence was limited at that moment, but, even then, he was still leading people to Christ.

Application for the Day: Today I will pray for boldness to be different from the world and to be an influence in all I say and do to lead people to Christ.

Wednesday, May 22, 2024

If I Were Starting My Family Again – Part 1
George Caudill
Originally Published in Opening Doors, WSCOC 2011 Devotional Book

Today's Scripture: Ephesians 5:25

Through inspiration of the Holy Spirit, the apostle Paul wrote, "Husbands, love your wives, just as Christ also loved the church and gave Himself for her. If I were starting my family again, I would show love for the mother of my children more. I would try to love Sara even more the second time through than I did the first time. People who know us well may find that strange because I've always loved her so much and for so many reasons, but there are a lot of ways to experience love and a lot of ways to express love.

I would be freer to let my children know that I love their mother. We are told that the most powerful expression of love between spouses are those non-verbal expressions of love. Children learn more when we place the chair at the table for our wives, when we open the car door, when we bring a special gift, or send flowers on a special occasion, than they do by verbal expressions of love. There are ways to demonstrate love that, when practiced, become second nature to us.

Men, the greatest thing we can do for our children is to love their mother. Women, the greatest thing a mother can do for her children is to love her husband. When children know their parents love each other, there is security and a stability that is gained in no other way.

The best thing parents can give their children is their love for one another. Nothing makes them feel quite so secure as knowing mom and dad love each other.

Application for Today: Today, I will be intentional in expressing my love for my spouse both verbally and non-verbally. I will strive to love her like Christ loved the church!

Thursday, May 23, 2024

If I Were Starting My Family Again – Part 2
George Caudill
Originally Published in <u>Opening Doors</u>, WSCOC 2011 Devotional Book

Today's Scripture: Ephesians 6:4

Through inspiration of the Holy Spirit, the apostle Paul wrote, "And you, fathers, do not provoke your children to wrath, but bring them up in the training and admonition of the Lord." If I were starting my family again, I would try to laugh more. *Proverbs 15* and *Proverbs 17* dwell at some length on what a happy spirit does for a person. Norman Cousins, editor of "The Saturday Review" (1942-1972) traveled widely and sometimes he'd come home with jetlag. He'd crossed two or three time zones and it takes a day or two to get over that; however, this time he just didn't get over it, and he decided he needed to see a physician. He did and was put through a series of tests and was finally told that he was terminally ill and there was really nothing medical science knew to do for one in his condition.

Cousins later wrote a story in his book *The Anatomy of An Illness* where he said he decided if medical people could not do anything for him, he had to do something for himself. One of the ways he decided to treat his illness was through humor. He'd go to the public library and check out old Laurel and Hardy films. He would do anything that would give him a belly laugh and bring humor into his life. He would get with friends who liked to have a good time. For whatever it's worth, he lived a good ten years more. In another book he wrote called *The Healing Heart,* he emphasized the power of humor in one's life to overcome illnesses and obstacles of various sorts.

Oscar Wilde once said the best way to make children good is to make them happy. Charles Buxton said the first duty to children is to make them happy. We should never fear spoiling children by making them happy because happiness is the atmosphere in which all good affections grow.

Application for Today: Today, I will seek humor in life and spend more time in laughter.

Friday, May 24, 2024

If I Were Starting My Family Again – Part 3

George Caudill
Originally Published in Opening Doors, WSCOC 2011 Devotional Book

Today's Scripture: Ephesians 6:4

If I were starting my family again, I would try to be a better listener. Researchers say men have no greater problem than a lack of communication. If my children were small again, I'd stop reading the newspaper when they wanted to talk with me, and I would try to refrain from words of impatience at the interruption, because such times can be the best opportunities to show love, kindness, and confidence.

A survey was conducted of 500 professionals (doctors, teachers, nurses, psychiatrists, ministers) listing the top fifteen characteristics of a healthy family that they had known. When the fifteen characteristics of a healthy family were ranked, number one was communicating and listening. Learning to listen to each other, just laying the newspaper down. It's difficult for many men to lay the newspaper down when he talks to his family.

When we hear our child calling and do not answer, it's as if we are thinking, "It's only the kid calling." If that is continued, it will not be long before fathers will call their children and they will say, "It's only the old man calling."

The parent who listens to their children in the early years will find that they will have children who care what their parents say later in life. There is a vital relationship between listening to children's concerns when they are young and the extent to which children will share their concerns with parents when they are teenagers. Parents who take their time to understand what their children say and feel early in life will be able to understand their children later in life.

Parents who listen to children in their early years will be listened to by their children in their later years. When parents spend time, take real interest and listen to their children when they are very young, they will have children who listen to their parents when they become older.

Application for Today: Today, I will spend more time listening than talking.

If I Were Starting My Family Again – Part 4

George Caudill
Originally Published in <u>Opening Doors</u>, WSCOC 2011 Devotional Book

Today's Scripture: Ephesians 6:4

If I were starting my family again, I would let my children know that they are valuable and they don't have to get good grades to be valuable. Somehow, we have to be able to translate that and say to them, "I won't love you anymore if you make A's, and I won't love you any less if you make F's. You are loved. You don't have to earn my love. My love is a gift to you, and it's because you are valuable and you are made in God's image, and you have intrinsic value and worth that you don't have to earn my love."

Now, the more we develop our gifts, the better we like ourselves. We need to say that to them when they are young and won't understand it; but if we keep saying it to them and say it enough times they will begin, hopefully, to hang on to that as the years go by, and it will make such a difference. We must communicate to our children that we won't love them more, and they won't be more valuable because they already have value, but the more they develop those gifts, the better they will like themselves.

I would, also, let my children know that the past doesn't equal the future. Just because children fail doesn't mean they have to fail in the future. If they couldn't change, we would have to cut repentance out of the Bible. I would let them know that they don't have to go back and clear up all the deadwood in the past, but they can start from today. That's the good news that Jesus gives. That's the good news of repentance, of change. The past doesn't have to equal the future and the past can simply be the

I would do a better job of teaching my children that they become good people first and everything else comes later. We must convince our children that they must work on self more than anything.

Application for Today: Today, I will thank God for the value He places on me.

Tuesday, May 28, 2024

If I Were Starting My Family Again – Part 5

George Caudill
Originally Published in Opening Doors, WSCOC 2011 Devotional Book

Today's Scripture: Ephesians 6:4

If I were starting my family again, I would teach my children that there are no little decisions, and every decision is for or against greatness. I would teach them that good work is often wasted for a lack of a little more. I would try to impress upon them that when they work to accomplish something, they will get tired, and if they give up and quit, they will never know how close they were to success. Success doesn't come in stages; it comes all at once. And I would encourage them to just give one more push, one more try. Studies prove that the difference between the good and the elite is not ability, it's effort.

I love the comic strip *Peanuts*. There is so much wisdom in *Peanuts*. Lucy said to Linus one day, "Linus, if you use your imagination, you can look in the clouds and you can see all kinds of things. What do you see?" Linus said, "Well, that group of clouds over there looks like a map of the British Honduras in the Caribbean, and that group of clouds over there looks like a profile of the face of Thomas Eaken, the great sculptor and painter, and those clouds over there look like the stoning of Stephen." Lucy said, "That's great, Linus. Charlie Brown, what do you see?" He said, "I was going to say a horsey and duckey, but I changed my mind." Our children may see a horsey and duckey a lot, and we must help them understand that effort will almost always overcome ability.

I would work harder to help them believe in themselves. I would help them to understand that to believe that they can and never quit believing is so important. I would try to teach them that what they say to themselves when they fail is what ultimately makes a difference, and the key as to whether they try again is what they say to themselves when they fail.

Application for Today: Today, I go the second mile and give my best effort.

Wednesday, May 29, 2024

If I Were Starting My Family Again – Part 6
George Caudill
Originally Published in <u>Opening Doors</u>, WSCOC 2011 Devotional Book

Today's Scripture: Ephesians 6:4

If I were starting my family again, I would try to let my children understand as early in life as possible that there is a connection, a link, between behavior and consequences. They must experience that, and the earlier the better. We can't bail them out of everything in their lives and never allow them to experience consequences. If we do, when they get in late adolescence, they can't accept it. We must teach them to accept responsibility and not blame others. We must help them see that they are responsible for their education as well as their success.

Study after study has shown that the more parents are involved in their children's education, the better they learn. Across the board that is true. The more the children see us read and the more we read to them, the better they will read. The more we are involved in school, their world, and their education, the more responsible they will become. We must teach them that they are responsible since they are the ones who are going to pay, and they must not blame others. The reason blame is so serious is that there is no progress when it happens. The day we take complete responsibility for ourselves, that's the day we stop making excuses and things start turning around in all aspects of our lives, at home, at school, and with friends. There are two kinds of pains: the pain of discipline or the pain of regret. The parents must begin letting the children experience that and as early as possible.

Yes, the link between behavior and consequences is caught much easier than it's taught. That's where it starts. What our children need is to see that and to experience that, and there's got to be a life of that. It's got to start in their own world, and we must hand it over to them. It just means taking control of their lives.

Application for Today: Today, I will encourage my children to take responsibility, even when they fail.

Thursday, May 30, 2024

If I Were Starting My Family Again – Part 7

George Caudill
Originally Published in <u>Opening Doors</u>, WSCOC 2011 Devotional Book

Today's Scripture: Ephesians 6:4

If I were starting my family again, I would do more encouraging the next time through. I would seek to be freer to express words of appreciation and praise. I reprimanded my children for making mistakes and would scold them at the slightest infraction, but my children seldom heard words of commendation and encouragement when they did a job well. I learned a little late, but eventually I did learn that just saying, "I love you," and just saying "I'm proud of you," can be very important no matter what age they reach.

I would provide more hope to my children. All children want to win. When they begin to play baseball, they must have some success and believe they can hit it. When I pitched to our sons, I tried to strike them out; however, when I pitched to our four grandsons, I tried to hit the bat. Is there a message here for all of us?

My mother was always an encourager. Regardless of what I did, she was for me and would encourage me. I can remember teachers of mine from the first grade through college who were encouragers and those who were not.

Today, I would seek to remember the good things my children do and express more freely my feelings of joy, gratitude, and praise of them. I would remember that each day holds many opportunities for encouragement even in the smallest things and fault finding, not followed by encouragement, hurts rather than helps. All of us desire deeply to be appreciated. The ability to encourage the hidden resources of children must be cultivated so that we see not only where the child is now but what they can be and encourage them to become. I know now that when we express appreciation in the many small things of life, love and appreciation grow for one another. If I were to start my family again, I would persist in daily praise.

Application for Today: Today, I will be intentional in encouraging others.

If I Were Starting My Family Again – Part 8

George Caudill

Originally Published in <u>Opening Doors</u>, WSCOC 2011 Devotional Book

Today's Scripture: Ephesians 6:4

If I were starting my family again, I would stress that the family is for ministry and service. If a child learns to serve and instead of take, more than likely it will be learned at home. A study by Harvard University in 1980 shows—that in families who read the Bible together, study together, pray together, come to church and worship together, serve together, and minister together—the divorce rate is 1:1286. God makes a difference in the family. He is the glue who holds it together.

If I were starting a family again, I would share God more intimately with my boys. I would seek, like Christ himself, to choose the ordinary things of life to illustrate the God we serve. This deep desire must somehow pervade and permeate all other desires.

I don't know if one ever reaches his real desire along that line. We don't have to *talk* about God all the time, but we must *teach* about God all the time. I'm not discouraging verbalizing our faith. But the most serious lessons children learn about God are probably the ones when we are teaching about God but not talking about God. It may be that the intimacy between parent and child has something to do with the intimacy between the child and God later. A child has an innocent world in which it is easy to believe. If parents can perpetuate that, they will accomplish the greatest thing in life.

If I could do it over, I would help my child think of God in terms of love, helpfulness, kindness, compassion, and the Giver of all good things. This is the God of Scripture. I would seek to use the creation to call attention to God's care, love and provision. An understanding of nature can help in understanding the Book of Life later. I would read the Book of Life to my boys, but I would relate it more to where my boys were. I would read other books showing God's care and compassion. I would seek to show them what God is like in my life and the lives of others. Dads, don't just love your children every now and then. It's a love without end.

Application for Today: Today, I will model ministry and service to others.

The Freedom to Pursue Christ

George Caudill
Formatted by Steve Baggett from a Bible Class Manuscript

Today's Scripture: Hebrews 11:6

God wants to forgive us! Thus, the restoration movement, out of which the churches of Christ grew, has at its core the simple conviction that the gospel is an easily understandable and transmittable message (1 Corinthians 15:1-4).

Pursuing the truth of the gospel (developing our own faith) is a process, one which involves four stages:

1. The Infancy of Faith – This stage is where we experience the faith of others. An infant hears someone singing "Jesus Loves Me," and praying "Now I lay me down to sleep." The child doesn't really have a faith of his own, he just experiences what he sees and hears.

2. The Childhood of Faith – This is when we believe what we believe because folks with whom we are affiliated with, also believe it. It's not necessarily our own...we haven't thought through it, but we believe it.

3. The Adolescence of Faith – This is the time when we start challenging what people have told us is true. A child raises questions at the breakfast table or in Bible classes at church. He is honing or developing his own faith.

4. The Adulthood of Faith – The final stage is when you own your own faith. You are not necessarily right about everything, you don't necessarily have an answer for everything, you have a long way to go and a lot to learn, but it is your faith.

It is that adulthood of faith, an owned faith, which we strive to acquire. So, let's love God, study His truth for ourselves, pursue His truth at whatever cost, believe in the Lordship of Jesus Christ, confess that before others, repent of our sins, and be buried in baptism for the remission of our sins. Then, let's find a church family that is more nearly like the one mentioned in the New Testament. Let's strive for an owned faith, not someone else's faith!

Application for Today: Today, I will assess my faith and do whatever is necessary to make it mine, not someone else's.

Tuesday, June 4, 2024

Prioritizing Your Life

Greg Camarata

Today's Scripture: Mark 12:28-31

Most people have issues with prioritizing in many areas of their life. Many will put everything off until the last minute or until a decision must be made. Many times, this is human nature and even applies to our Christian walk. Let me take a moment and allow Jesus to address priorities. If you find prioritizing difficult, Jesus does it for you in Mark 12:28-31.

A scribe had an issue with prioritizing in life and asked Jesus what is the most important command? Read Mark 12:28-31.

In this passage, Jesus offers two priorities for life:
> Priority 1: "Love the Lord your God with all your heart and with all your soul and with all your mind and with all your strength."

> Priority 2: "Love your neighbor as yourself. There is no other command greater than these."

So how are these priorities to play out in our day-to-day lives?
- When you graduate from high school or college, love the Lord your God with all your heart, soul, mind, and strength.
- When you fall in love and get married, love the Lord your God with all your heart, soul, mind, and strength.
- When you get laid off or lose a job, love the Lord your God with all your heart, soul, mind, and strength.
- When your children are born healthy, love the Lord your God with all your heart, soul, mind, and strength.
- When your child is born with a handicap, love the Lord your God with all your heart, soul, mind, and strength.
- When a loved one passes away, love the Lord your God with all your heart, soul, mind, and strength.
- When your final days of life are upon you, love the Lord your God with all your heart, soul, mind, and strength.

We all go through good times and rough times in life. Jesus said that no matter what happens in this life, love the Lord your God with all your heart, soul, mind, and strength.

Application for the Day: Today I will renew my decision to love God no matter how the day goes.

Wednesday, June 5, 2024

Coming to the Table with Jesus – Part 1

Holly Spencer

Today's Scripture: Luke 19:1-10

I love to cook. I love great food–it is a huge part of my life. While Chris McCurley speaks in sports analogies, I speak in food analogies. I tell food stories! Whenever Jeremy and I travel somewhere new, I can't wait to dive into a new culture and cuisine, try the local specialty, or maybe even learn to cook it! I love to see how cultures linger over long meals for fellowship—not just for the food, but also with a sense of place and belonging. Sitting around the table is not just the meal; it's the evening's activity.

The Table is a timeless concept. It hasn't changed. We can identify with it and understand it. It combines the basic human need for food and sustenance with another need that we might not realize is almost as important: community and belonging.

Jesus spent time teaching in formal settings—in the synagogue or with "teachers of the law"—but often He was also "coming to the table" in community with others. One of my favorite accounts is the story of Zacchaeus. Zacchaeus was not just any little guy. He was the *chief tax collector*. It was a position of power, known to be dishonest and defrauding—and even worse—in cahoots with the Roman government. Jesus said to him, "I'm inviting myself over for dinner!" No time to prepare, no time to put the skeletons in the closet, no time to sweep anything under the rug. This really was a "come as you are" moment, and it was transformative!

I know we aren't told the whole story. We don't know exactly what Jesus said, but the Bible account does teach us this: when Jesus comes to dinner, He's coming to change your life. He's not just a good person or wise teacher. He's God incarnate, and He wants to turn our lives and our hearts on end.

Application for Today: Today I will accept Jesus' dinner invitation so that I can be in a relationship with Him and let Him change my life.

Thursday, June 6, 2024

Coming to the Table with Jesus – Part 2
Holly Spencer

Today's Scripture: John 21:4-17

When we think about coming to the table with Jesus, probably the most obvious moment was just before His death when He instituted the Lord's Supper. This is a part of the gospels you might have studied more often than most. But when I think about "moments at the table," the one that resonates most with me is found in John 21.

This is the final glimpse that John gives us of Jesus while on earth with His disciples. Peter, John, and several other disciples had been out fishing all night. One of the last things Jesus did before returning to heaven was to make breakfast for His friends. This is a setting that I think we can all imagine very clearly: a campfire on a little beach with the people we are closest to in the whole world.

What follows is a conversation Jesus had with Peter.
15 When they had finished breakfast, Jesus said to Simon Peter, "Simon, son of John, do you love me more than these?" He said to him, "Yes, Lord; you know that I love you." He said to him, "Feed my lambs." 16 He said to him a second time, "Simon, son of John, do you love me?" He said to him, "Yes, Lord; you know that I love you." He said to him, "Tend my sheep." 17 He said to him the third time, "Simon, son of John, do you love me?" Peter was grieved because he said to him the third time, "Do you love me?" and he said to him, "Lord, you know everything; you know that I love you." Jesus said to him, "Feed my sheep."

Gathered around the breakfast table, Jesus commissioned Peter to lead the world to HIM. To lead the world to the greatest community that has ever been—to a community and relationship that are eternal.

Application for Today: Today I will accept Jesus's invitation into His community, love Him more than anything or anyone, and share the Good News with everyone I can.

114

Friday, June 7, 2024

Coming to the Table with Jesus – Part 3
Holly Spencer

Today's Scripture: Galatians 6:2

We spend a lot of time thinking of "church" as the formal corporate times of worship, but it is obvious that Jesus put a lot of emphasis on the in-between times: the natural times that occur, where conversation is easy and informal. There was no distinction between church life and personal life, in contrast to the way many of us try to live today. Today's verse from Galatians speaks of carrying one another's burdens. God's plan for us is to walk through life in connection with other believers, not to try to do it on our own.

One of the things I have always loved about owning a coffeehouse is looking out and seeing people connecting. And it is often more than just a casual interaction. If someone asks you, "Can we get coffee?" there is probably more meaning to that question than meets the eye, but don't let it make you nervous! It might mean:

- I want to catch up with what's going on in your life.

- I need to have a real conversation with you that may take more than the five minutes we have in passing.

- I want to build a deeper connection with you.

- Let's set aside some time in our busy schedules to talk.

- I'm dealing with some hard things that I really need you to pray about.

Now each of those things might be a little harder to say, but "Can we get coffee?" is easy to say! Face-to-face, intimate conversation while going beyond normal polite greetings is needed, so don't be afraid of it! And don't be afraid to initiate it. I think it is safe to say that ALL of us crave deeper connections! God created us to be in communion and in connection with Him and with each other.

Application for Today: Today I will deliberately make time to connect with someone. Who knows how God might work through something as simple as a meal together or a cup of coffee?

Monday, June 10, 2024

Overcoming Failure

Hunter Webb

Today's Scriptures: Romans 7:24; 1 John 1:7

As a teenager, one of the things that I am learning is that life is often a series of failures. It seems that, no matter how hard I try, sometimes I fail. One of my favorite sports is baseball, and baseball is a game of failure. If you can get a hit in three out of ten bats, you could probably play college baseball and maybe even beyond. A batting average of .300 sounds pretty good, but, in reality, that means you failed 70% of the time.

I find that life seems to be a lot like baseball. In 1 John 1:7, the Bible says, "If we walk in the light, as he is in the light, we have fellowship with one another, and the blood of Jesus his Son cleanses us from all sin." This verse means that the person who walks in the light lives every day trying to please God. By contrast, people who walk in the darkness try only to please themselves. The person who walks in the darkness sins, and the person who walks in the light also sins. So what is the difference between the two? The difference is that, even though the person walking in the light fails, he continues to pick himself back up and tries to please God. Even though he sins, he is like David, about whom the Lord said, "I have found in David the son of Jesse a man after my heart, who will do all my will" (Acts 13:22). Listen to the words of the apostle Paul, who knew a little about failure himself. In Romans 7:24-25a, he wrote, "Wretched man that I am! Who will deliver me from this body of death? Thanks be to God through Jesus Christ our Lord."

Application for the Day: Today I will strive to remember that failure does not have to be final, and I will begin again when I fail.

Tuesday, June 11, 2024

Unconditional Love

Hunter Webb

Today's Scripture: Luke 15:11-32

One thing you might not know about me is that I am a big fan of baseball. One day I was outside in the yard hitting baseballs. I hit for a long time, and when I was done, I started to pick all of my baseballs up. I found a lot, but I was missing a few. I looked and looked, but I could never find them. I really love my baseballs, but I then it hit me: it's JUST A BASEBALL.

Think about losing a person, A SOUL! Think about how God feels when He loses a soul. This makes me think about a scripture in Luke. Luke 15 tells the story of the prodigal son. When the son realized that he had made a mess of his life and returned home to ask his father if he could just be a hired servant to him, the father was overjoyed. When he saw his son returning, he ran to meet him, embraced him, gave him fresh clean clothes, put a ring on his finger, and threw a great "Welcome Home" party for him, even after everything he had done. What was the father's reasoning? Here was his answer: "For this my son was dead, and is alive again; he was lost, and is found" (Luke 15:24a). I like to think that this is how God, our Heavenly Father, feels when we turn towards Him and away from the world.

 At the end of the day, a baseball is just a baseball. But a soul was created in God's image and, in the Father's mind, was worth the death of His son. The apostle Paul said, "But God shows his love for us in that while we were still sinners, Christ died for us" (Rom. 5:8).

Application for the Day: Today I will give my life to Him, return to Him, or start living an abundant life with Him like the prodigal son who returned home.

Wednesday, June 12, 2024

Love One Another

Isaiah Leininger (2023 Summer Intern)

Today's Scripture: John 13:34-35

There was once a small country congregation of the Lord's church. They were few in number, but they were all faithful. They worshiped together for many years, growing closer together and to the Lord. Not only were they a spiritual family because of their love for God, but almost all of them were also related physically. All was well until the father of the family passed away. His children and grandchildren began to argue and bicker over what to do with his belongings. Who would get the house? Who would get the car? They fought so much that the congregation ended up dividing, and some members left to worship elsewhere.

This kind of event gives unbelievers a chance to drag the church through the mud. They will say things such as, "You Christians talk about God's love so much, but you can't even love each other! Why would I want to become a Christian if that's how you treat each other?"

Our job as the church is to spread the saving message of Jesus. How can we do this if we do not first love one another?

Jesus spoke to His apostles in John 13:34-35, where He said, "A new commandment I give to you, that you love one another: just as I have loved you, you also are to love one another. By this all people will know that you are my disciples, if you have love for one another."

If we want the world to know about the love and mercy God has offered to all mankind, it starts with us loving one another. This is not just some happy feeling towards our brothers and sisters. This is the kind of love that Jesus had for us; it is completely dedicated and sacrificial. That's the kind of love that we need to have for other Christians.

Application for the Day: Today I will pray to God to help me see my brothers and sisters as Jesus sees them and to love them as He loves them.

Thursday, June 13, 2024

More Than Meets the Eye

Isaiah Leininger (2023 Summer Intern)

Today's Scripture: Romans 3:23-25

Sometimes in life, things are exactly what they seem. We can examine them and quickly understand what we are seeing. But often there is more than meets the eye. We judge something or someone from one brief encounter, though we may miss several crucial details.

Are we guilty of doing this with Scripture also? Do we sometimes get lazy and take a verse at eye level instead of digging into it and its context? The answer may sometimes be yes. There are many verses that Christians use as stand-alone phrases, which remove them from the deeper meaning in their contexts.

One such passage is Romans 3:23a, which simply says, "For all have sinned and fall short of the glory of God." This verse, though absolutely true by itself, is a part of a much richer story. Paul, at this point in the book of Romans, has established that there is no difference between Jews and Gentiles. Neither is better than the other because no man is perfect—all have sinned. But reading only verse 23 takes away the message of hope Paul gives afterward in verses 24-25: "For all have sinned and fall short of the glory of God, and are justified by his grace as a gift, through the redemption that is in Christ Jesus, whom God put forward as a propitiation by his blood, to be received by faith. This was to show God's righteousness, because in his divine forbearance he had passed over the former sins" (ESV).

Yes, all have sinned. That statement is completely true. But the gospel message is not one of condemnation; it is one of salvation! There is hope for everyone to escape the consequences of their sins, but only for those who are saints (Rom. 1:7). This requires washing our sins away in the waters that represent the blood Christ shed on the cross.

Application for the Day: Today I will thank God for the message of hope found in the gospel, which lets me know that Jesus died for my sins.

Friday, June 14, 2024

Rest for Your Souls

Isaiah Leininger (2023 Summer Intern)

Today's Scripture: Matthew 11:28-30

Have you ever been so exhausted that you couldn't move? You might have been fatigued because you exercised, had a long day at work, didn't sleep, or for some other reason.

We can experience physical exhaustion for many reasons, but the cure is the same. We need rest. But what about spiritual exhaustion? What do we do when the cares of the world are weighing us down and we are longing for home? Again, we need rest! So where can we go to find rest? We turn to Jesus because He has promised us rest. Matthew 11:28-30 says, "Come to Me, all who are weary and heavy-laden, and I will give you rest. Take My yoke upon you and learn from Me, for I am gentle and humble in heart, and you will find rest for your souls. For My yoke is easy and My burden is light."

This life is not easy, especially for those who are Christians. At times, we feel like we are fish trying to swim upstream. Paul challenged the Romans, "Do not be conformed to this world, but be transformed by the renewing of your mind" (Rom. 12:2). We are living in a way that is opposite from the world around us, and, as a result, we will face opposition and difficulties. Paul said to Timothy, "Indeed, all who desire to live godly in Christ Jesus will be persecuted" (2 Tim. 3:12).

It can be tiring for us physically, emotionally, and spiritually to continue. Sometimes it feels like it would be easier to just give up and go along with the sinful flow of the world, but remember when you are tired and weary that Jesus is there. He will give you the rest you need to keep going. "When you are discouraged, just remember what to do; reach out to Jesus; He's reaching out to you" (Ralph Carmichael).

Application for the Day: Today I will pray that, when I am weary, I will turn to Jesus for the rest that I need to keep following Him.

Monday, June 17, 2024

The Day of My Distress

Isaiah Leininger (2023 Summer Intern)

Today's Scripture: Genesis 35:3

"Distress: (the feeling of) extreme anxiety, sorrow, or pain." (*Oxford Languages*)

Have you ever experienced any of these emotions? If you have, then you know that they are not pleasant. When someone is in distress, he is suffering. Oftentimes, the suffering is made worse because of loneliness. When others are around, they can help provide comfort, strength, and encouragement for the one who is hurting. But when a person is alone, feelings of hopelessness can be overwhelming. That anxiety, sorrow, or pain can be difficult to try to carry by oneself. As an old hymn says, "But I don't know a thing in this whole wide world that's worse than being alone" ("Where No One Stands Alone," Mosie Lister, 1955).

Thankfully, we are never truly alone. Even when no one is standing next to us, the Lord is always there. In Genesis 35:3 Jacob says, "Then let us arise and go up to Bethel, so that I may make there an altar to the God who answers me in the day of my distress and has been with me wherever I have gone." Jacob's life was full of ups and downs. He was forced to run from his brother, Esau, who wanted to kill him. He had been tricked by Laban into marrying Leah instead of Rachel. Laban also tried to cheat Jacob out of the percentage of the flock he had been promised. However, through it all, Jacob knew that God had been with him. God blessed Jacob and continued to provide for him at every turn. Jacob was never alone because the Lord was always with him, helping him when he was in distress.

We too have a source of comfort when we are in our day of distress. No matter what we are going through, Jesus understands (Hebrews 4:15). Jesus is always there, providing comfort and strength in every step.

Application for the Day: Today I will thank God for always answering me in my distress, and I will ask God to help me trust in Him when times are tough.

Tuesday, June 18, 2024

What Does the Lord Require of You?

Isaiah Leininger (Summer Intern 2023)

Today's Scripture: Micah 6:8

In any relationship, the expectations need to be known for both sides to function properly within the relationship. In a romantic relationship, each partner needs to know what the other expects and needs. The same goes for the relationships between parents and children, between boss and employees, and even between friends. We need people to communicate what is expected of us in order to have a happy and successful relationship.

For Christians, the most important relationship we will ever have is the relationship we have with our Heavenly Father. For that relationship to function the way God designed it, we need to know what God expects from us. Thankfully, God has communicated that to us.

The prophet Micah was sent by God to the nations of Israel and Judah to warn them about the destruction that would soon come if they didn't repent. Toward the end of his book, Micah wrote, "He has told you, O man, what is good; and what does the Lord require of you but to do justice, and to love kindness, and to walk humbly with your God?"

The expectations that God has for us are simple. First, we are to do justice. We are to do what is right. In Micah's time, the rulers and false prophets took advantage of the poor and took away what rightfully belonged to them. God loves justice and hates robbery (Isa. 61:8).

Second, we are to love kindness. We are to value mercy, unlike those stealing from the poor in Micah's day.

Finally, we are to walk humbly with our God. We need to recognize that God is superior and that His word is law. He will be the one to judge us for how we live in this life, whether we are just and kind to those around us.

Application for Today: Today I will pray to God to help me do what is right, to show kindness to all, and to humble myself before God.

Wednesday, June 19, 2024

Who Can Be Against Us?
Isaiah Leininger (Summer Intern 2023)

Today's Scripture: Romans 8:31-32

This world is full of conflict. Some people even make their entire livelihood from it. Professional athletes compete against one another to win the game. Lawyers and politicians compete in court or to win an election. Sometimes, though, it is not people against people. It is rather two ideas against one another. Christians understand this concept because Christians are to be countercultural. We are to be against the wickedness of the world.

Because of that, we face opposition. We are constantly against people who oppose God and reject the truth that we stand for. And because Christians are against the world, we are a minority. It is easy to get worn down and discouraged because we face so much opposition. In such times, we must remember what Paul tells us in Romans 8:31-32: "What then shall we say to these things? If God is for us, who can be against us? He who did not spare His own Son but gave Him up for us all, how will He not also with Him graciously give us all things?"

Paul reminds Christians that we are on the winning side. No one will be able to stand against us because no one can stand against God! Paul would finish the chapter by saying that no one can condemn us if we are right with God. Best of all, there is nothing that can separate us from the love of God! No matter what people say or what people do, God's love will forever reign supreme. No matter what we endure, it will be worth it if we remain faithful till the end. Paul makes this point earlier in the chapter in verse 18, where he says, "For I consider that the sufferings of this present time are not worth comparing with the glory that is to be revealed to us."

Application for the Day: Today I will pray to God, thanking Him for His steadfast love, and I will pray for strength to endure the hardships of life.

Thursday, June 20, 2024

An Amazing Godly Woman

Jane Petty

Today's Scripture: 1 Samuel 1-2

Hannah was one of the wives of Elkanah. She was the preferred wife but was childless, a source of great distress to her. Her sister/wife Peninnah had children and greatly provoked Hannah in order to irritate her.

On one of Hannah's visits to the Lord's house in Shiloh, she wept bitterly and prayed to the Lord. In the first recorded mention of a woman praying in the Bible, she prayed for a son and promised to give him to the Lord and to raise him as a Nazarite (Num. 6:1-21).

Eli, the high priest, saw Hannah's mouth moving but heard no words and thought she was drunk. He rebuked her, but she explained that she was in great distress and wasn't drunk. He answered, "Go in peace, and may the God of Israel grant you what you have asked of him" (1:17).

In the fullness of time, Hannah had a baby boy, weaned him at probably two or three years of age, and brought him back to the house of the Lord at Shiloh to leave him with Eli.

Elkanah could have nullified the vow made by his wife (Num. 30:11-13) by registering an objection when he heard of it. In Leviticus, provisions were made to redeem a vow by giving money to support the priests and sanctuary. However, Hannah was careful to keep her vow, even though it was at great personal cost. In an extraordinary sacrifice, she gave Samuel back to God as she promised.

Then Hannah prayed again in a song of praise to God and confidence in His sovereignty:

"My heart rejoices in the LORD; in the LORD my horn is lifted high. My mouth boasts over my enemies, for I delight in your deliverance. There is no one holy like the LORD; there is no one besides you; there is no Rock like our God" (1 Sam. 2: 1-2).

The continuation of her song praises God for his knowledge (vs.3), power (vs.4-8), and judgment (vs. 9-10).

Application for the Day: Today I will remember Hannah and her amazing faith.

Friday, June 21, 2024

Butterflies

Jane Petty

Today's Scripture: 2 Corinthians 5:17

Recently I took a trip to Niagara Falls, Canada, and visited the Niagara Parks Butterfly Conservatory, the largest facility of its kind in North America. This facility has 2,000 free flying tropical butterflies in a glass enclosed conservatory, and visitors may walk through and observe the butterflies. They were enchanting and beautiful.

Butterflies and moths go through a process called metamorphosis. There are four stages in the life cycles of these insects (egg, larva, pupa, and adult). A butterfly egg has a shell to protect it and a yolk for food for the embryo. When they hatch, they are caterpillars, or larva, and they are eating machines. They grow and grow, shedding skin as they go and sometimes ending up 100 times larger than when they began. In the next life phase, the pupa, or chrysalis, encloses itself in a shield to protect it while the amazing metamorphosis occurs. In this phase, the caterpillar completely dissolves into a liquid soup with all its DNA intact and transforms at the cellular level into the body parts of a butterfly or moth.

Think about that for a moment. Can anyone deny the existence of a divine creator when confronted with these facts? Can anyone believe that this just happens by chance? Genesis provides the creation story, and nature proves that it is true.

We can also go through a personal metamorphosis. "Transformation" is a synonym for "metamorphosis." 2 Corinthians 5:17 tells us that if we are in Christ, we are a new creation; old things have passed away, and new things have come. 2 Corinthians 3:18 talks about our being transformed into the image of the glory of the Lord.

So how do we transform? By believing in Jesus and His sacrifice for us, being baptized and becoming a Christian, and then continuing the Christian walk. Easier said than done? Perhaps, but we will surely find it the most rewarding thing we ever do in this life and the next.

Application for the Day: Today I will think about my transformed life and seek to help others in their transformations.

Monday, June 24, 2024

Earthquakes

Jane Petty

Today's Scripture: Psalm 46:2,3

Reelfoot Lake in northwest Tennessee was created by a series of magnitude 7.5 or greater earthquakes in 1811-1812. The series of earthquakes between November 1811 and February 1812 caused the Mississippi River to run backward for a time and created the lake. There was total darkness at times and the pervasive smell of sulfur. Entire settlements were destroyed or flooded. Desperate people and spooked animals frantically looked for a safe place. It must have been terrifying.

Scientists and engineers have now begun to build earthquake-proof houses in known areas of earthquake activity. Building codes have been strengthened, and while earthquakes still occur, damage and loss of life have been minimized in some areas.

In life we also experience spiritual earthquakes. Perhaps the death or serious injury or illness of a loved one has shaken your faith. Maybe the loss of a job or a home has stunned you. There are numerous circumstances that can cause a questioning of faith. Are there things we can do to make our faith "earthquake proof"?

We can confidently say yes. Think about Mary, the mother of Jesus. She was visited by an angel and told she would have a son, even though she was a virgin. This news must have disrupted her life and her plans. Surely, she knew that some people would think ill of her. Yet, she trusted God.

Or what about the apostle Paul? He had striven his whole life to be a good Jew. He was zealous tracking down Christians and persecuting and executing them. The Bible says that he breathed threats and murder against Jesus' disciples. But when he met the Lord on the road to Damascus, he was astonished and trembled. He heard the Lord's voice and believed and obeyed his commands. He completely changed his life. For the rest of his life, he was the Lord's disciple.

Both Mary and Paul were "earthquake proof" because of their faith. We today must draw closer to God by studying and praying.

Application for the Day: Today I will strengthen my faith through Bible study and prayer.

Tuesday, June 25, 2024

G-Men and G-Women

Jane Petty

Today's Scripture: Romans 14:8

I recently listened to an audiobook about J. Edgar Hoover, the man who served as Director of the Federal Bureau of Investigation and its predecessor, the Bureau of Investigation, for forty-eight years. Before 1934, government agents were known as "G-Men," slang for "Government Men." There wasn't anything about the Bureau of Investigation's agents to make them noteworthy. On September 26, 1933, Tennessee police officers and Bureau of Investigation agents arrested criminal kidnapper George "Machine Gun" Kelly in Memphis, Tennessee. When Mr. Kelly emerged from the house he was staying in, his hands were up, and he was saying, "Don't shoot! G-Men, don't shoot!" This story made the papers, and in a few months the bureau's agents were the ones known as "G-Men." Mr. Hoover was not pleased with this nickname at first, but after a while he enthusiastically embraced it. Women were not allowed to be agents at the time, but "G-Women" came later.

Although we may not be FBI agents, we are still G-Men and G-Women. We are God's men and God's women. We were all created by God, and we were bought at the terrible price of Jesus' body and blood on that horrible cross.

Psalm 100:3 – Know that the LORD Himself is God; It is He who has made us, and not we ourselves; We are His people and the sheep of His pasture.

1 Corinthians 3:23 – And you belong to Christ, and Christ belongs to God.

1 John 3:1 – See how great love the Father has given us, that we would be called children of God; and in fact we are.

2 Corinthians 10:7 – You are looking at things as they are outwardly. If anyone is confident in himself that he is Christ's, have him consider this again within himself, that just as he is Christ's, so too are we.

May we feel privileged and greatly blessed to be God's men and God's women.

Application for the Day: Today I will seek to be a blessing to others in Jesus' name and act as God's man or God's woman.

Wednesday, June 26, 2024

God of Grace and God of Glory

Jane Petty

Today's Scripture: Hebrews 13:5-6

Do you have a favorite hymn? Perhaps "Amazing Grace," "Just as I Am," or others. Hymns touch our hearts and souls through lyrics, music, and life experiences. One that I have thought about during the Covid-19 global pandemic is "God of Grace and God of Glory." Written in 1930, in the midst of the Great Depression by Henry Emerson Fosdick, the hymn implores God to give us courage during difficult times.

God of grace and God of glory, on thy people pour thy pow'r; crown Thine ancient church's story, bring her bud to glorious flow'r. Grant us wisdom, grant us courage for the facing of this hour, for the facing of this hour.

Lo, the hosts of evil round us, scorn Thy Christ, assail His ways! From the fears that long have bound us, free our hearts to faith and praise. Grant us wisdom, grant us courage, for the living of these days, for the living of these days.

Cure Thy children's warring madness, bend our pride to Thy control; shame our wanton selfish gladness, rich in things and poor in soul. Grant us wisdom, grant us courage lest we miss Thy kingdom's goal, lest we miss Thy kingdom's goal.

Set our feet on lofty places, gird our lives that they may be armored with all Christlike graces in the fight to set men free. Grant us wisdom, grant us courage, that we fail not man nor Thee, that we fail not man nor Thee. Amen.

We know that difficult times are always with us. Just in our lifetime, people have experienced the Great Depression, World War II, Korean War, Vietnam War, Gulf War, War on Terror, riots, mass shootings, 9/11/2001, (President Bush reportedly thought of this song when told of the terrorist attacks.), Covid-19 pandemic, and others of a personal nature. The Bible reminds us that this world is not our home. (Heb. 13:14, John 14:2, 2 Cor. 5:1). We must look past our current circumstances and trust in God.

Application for the Day: Today I will pray for God's strength and courage during my earthly sojourn.

Thursday, June 27, 2024

Mulligans

Jane Petty

Today's Scripture: Matthew 18:21-22

I recently saw a movie entitled *Mulligan*. A mulligan in golf is an extra stroke allowed after a poor shot, not counted in the score. In the movie a high-powered, middle-aged businessman played in a Pro-Am golf tournament, where professional golfers and amateurs are teamed together. After he made a poor putt, he became angry and broke his putter. After the round, someone suggested he talk to the "old pro," who taught him about life and suggested that God gives us mulligans all the time.

The Parable of the Prodigal Son (Luke 15:11-32) illustrates this principle explicitly. When the younger son returned from his life of sin, the father welcomed him with open arms. He gave his son a mulligan.

We all need mulligans. We say or do something we shouldn't, or we fail to say or do something we should. But God will forgive. Isn't that what a mulligan is? Forgiveness and grace.

Peter asked the Lord how many times he had to forgive and was probably astonished at the answer. Yet Peter is the person who really needed forgiveness. Remember his three-time denial of the Lord on the night before the crucifixion? He had vowed that he would never fall away, but Scripture records his behavior that night. Can you imagine how he felt at the crucifixion?

After the resurrection Peter and the other disciples saw Jesus that first day of the week, but there was no specific message to Peter. He saw Jesus a week later when Thomas saw the Lord. Later Peter, Nathanael, James, John and two other disciples went fishing and fished all night. Early in the morning, Jesus called to them from the shore and told them to fish on the other side of the boat. Their catch was so tremendous that the nets started to break. When Peter realized it was Jesus, he jumped into the water and swam to shore. After breakfast Jesus gave Peter a mulligan when, three times, He told Peter to feed his sheep.

Application for the Day: I will thank God for the mulligans given me and offer them to others.

Friday, June 28, 2024

The Beginning, the Back, and In Between

Janice Lampley

Today's Scripture: Psalm 119:97 – "Oh how I love your law! It is my meditation all the day."

The Bible I carry is not a new one. Over the years, I have used the blank pages in the back, the side margins, and the spaces at the top and bottom of its pages to jot down truths that have caught my attention and nourished my soul.

Some of these truths are sermon notes, and some are general comments from Bible class discussions. All are helpful in understanding what God is saying to me.

See what God says FIRST. Genesis 1:3 is only the first of a series of times in the first chapter of the Bible that "God said" is recorded. I have them underlined in my Bible. How many "God said" scriptures do you count in yours?

We are not the light source, but the light's reflection. See what God says FIRST in the following passages:

1 Peter 2:9: "But you are a chosen race, a royal priesthood, a holy nation, a people for His own possession, that you may proclaim the excellencies of Him who called you out of darkness into His marvelous light."

Philippians 2:15: "That you may be blameless and innocent, children of God without blemish in the midst of a crooked and twisted generation, among whom you shine as lights in the world."

Ephesians 5:8: "For at one time you were darkness, but now you are light in the Lord. Walk as children of light."

1 Thessalonians 5:5: "For you are all children of light, children of the day. We are not of the night or of the darkness."

The Lord wants my precious time to learn these truths, not my spare time. Who is motivated to serve God based on seeing my reflection of Jesus, our only true light source?

Application Today: Today I will endeavor to know and do the will of God as I study the word of God from the beginning, the sides, and the back of my Bible!

Monday, July 1, 2024

Benefits of a Giving Lifestyle

Janie Jones

Today's Scripture: John 3:16

There is no questioning the fact that God is the great giver: "For God so loved the world that he gave his only Son, that whoever believes in him should not perish but have eternal life" (John 3:16). He gave us not only life, but all the blessings associated with it; He gave His only Son for us!

There are many benefits of a giving lifestyle:

- According to Malachi 3:10, when we are tested, our faith will be strengthened: "Bring the full tithe into the storehouse, that there may be food in my house. And thereby put me to the test, says the LORD of hosts, if I will not open the windows of heaven for you and pour down for you a blessing until there is no more need."
- Giving will make me happy, and I will be blessed in return. Jesus said, "Give, and it will be given to you. Good measure, pressed down, shaken together, running over, will be put into your lap. For with the measure you use it will be measured back to you" (Luke 6:38).
- Giving keeps our minds on the eternal and brings recognition from God (Matthew 6:33).
- When I give, I am protected from material enslavement (Matthew 6:24).
- By giving, my perspective on material things will be put in its proper place.
- My spiritual commitment will be tested by my giving.
- Giving will keep me from losing my assets. We never lose what we give away.

Most importantly, giving is an expression of obedience. Does God need any material things we give Him? NO, all God needs is for us to show our love for Him. God will bless us abundantly when we give with a cheerful heart. By giving, we can be more like God.

Application for Today Today I will ask myself this question: What other person or being would I want to be like, but God, my Father?

Tuesday, July 2, 2024

Examples in the Bible

Janie Jones

Today's Scripture: Psalm 32:8

In Psalm 32:8 David wrote, "I will instruct you and teach you in the way you should go; I will guide you with My eye." God teaches and instructs in many ways. On Wednesday night ladies' class recently studied several minor New Testament figures. The Bible is a treasure of lessons if we sift and dig through the maze of words. Through these people we learned many valuable lessons.

- Lydia exhibited leadership, caring and generosity. The Lydias of our lives teach us about being prepared.
- Nicodemas and Joseph of Arimathea illustrated that serving the Lord is not always easy.
- Dorcas (Acts 9:36) used her gifts.
- Titus had great zeal for the Lord.
- Tychicus modeled being trustworthy, involved, and encouraging (Col.4:7).
- Demas was not a positive person but teaches us to stay rooted in God.
- Epaphroditus is a great example of discipline.
- John Mark illustrated that God forgives, and we can continue to serve Him.
- Priscilla and Aquila served together and bloomed where they were planted.
- Zacchaeus did not allow his physical stature to keep him from drawing near to Jesus.
- Jude taught us to fight the good fight, because if we stop, the bout will be over for us.

The lessons continued to be apparent as we studied:
- Lois and Eunice and saw the value of sharing spiritual truths with our children.
- Silas who praised God instead of whining. His influence continued as he and Paul encouraged and strengthened "the brothers with many words" (Acts 15:32).

Isaiah 7:9 says, "If you will not believe, surely you shall not be established."
- Phoebe showed her firmness through her integrity and Christian character.
- Philemon was forgiving.
- Chloe showed us that women can have an important influence for Christ.
- In Archippus, we see that we must complete the work we have received from the Lord. (Colossians 4:17). God has given us talents to use, none of which are more important than others.

Application for the Day: By practicing what we learn from examples even in Scripture, the peace of God will be with us.

Wednesday, July 3, 2024

Headed in the Right Direction

Janie Jones

Today's Scripture: Proverbs 3:5-6

My friend Bernadette and I were working in her living room one day last year. I was trying to unscrew a bracket, and I had the ladder I was on facing in a direction that had me turned backward, trying to manage that screw. I was having no luck–that screw would not budge. I decided to turn the ladder around so that I was facing the bracket. Do you know what happened? The screw turned easily. I exclaimed to Bernadette, "You know, if you are in the right direction, things will work out. I think there is a lesson here."

Rick Crandell said, "Our life here is a walk–but are we headed in the right direction?" Spiritually, am I headed in the right direction? Are you? Are your family members? Is your church family? And how do I know the right direction? Proverbs 3:5-6 states, "Trust in the Lord with all your heart, and do not lean on your own understanding. In all your ways acknowledge him, and he will make straight your paths." I am going in the right direction when I rely on God's guidance. The Bible is filled with Scripture about God's desire to direct us if we will listen–if we will read His Word. "Your word is a lamp to my feet and a light to my path" (Psalm 119:105). "I have stored up your word in my heart, that I might not sin against you" (Psalm 119:11). "Enter by the narrow gate. For the gate is wide and the way is easy that leads to destruction, and those who enter by it are many" (Matthew 7:13). I can trust the Lord with all my heart, and He will direct me in the right direction. I must take action to be headed in the right direction. I must be in prayer, follow and obey His commandments, and surround myself with people who will help me.

Application for Today: Today I will be in the right direction by turning from my way and looking to God's way.

Thursday, July 4, 2024

Jesus as Our Friend

Janie Jones

Today's Scripture: John 15:13

Jane McWherter in her book <u>Friendship</u> tells us what friends do for us.

- They give us roots and loving acceptance. The second greatest commandment is to "You shall love your neighbor as yourself." (Matthew 22:39).
- A friend will help us with our burdens and share the load when we cannot bear them alone. "Two are better than one, because they have a good reward for their toil. For if they fall, one will lift up his fellow. But woe to him who is alone when he falls and has not another to lift him up! (Eccl. 4: 9-10).
- Friends help to complete what is lacking in our personalities. *"As iron sharpens iron, so a man sharpens the countenance of his friend" (Proverbs 27:17).*
- In times of happiness, friends heighten our joy by being there for us. "Rejoice with those who rejoice, weep with those who weep" (Romans 12:15).
- Friends help us grow spiritually by helping us when we make mistakes. "Faithful are the wounds of a friend..." (Proverbs 27:6).
- Friends will also provide an opportunity for us to be givers of the benefits of companionship.

Isn't Jesus that friend for us? In John 15:13 Jesus said, "Greater love has no one than this, than to lay down one's life for his friends." He wants the best for us – heaven. Jesus will always be at our side, and He will lift us up. Jesus accepts us no matter who we are. Jesus draws near in our suffering and will love us to the very end. We can know our Father with Jesus as our friend. Jesus is the friend who laid down His life for us.

Application for Today: Jesus will be our friend if we are faithful, loyal, and obedient. Since He has chosen us, how can we not look to Jesus and say, "my friend?"

Friday, July 5, 2024

Waiting

Janie Jones

Today's Scripture: Psalm 62: 1, 5, 8-11

Do you have trouble waiting? You have probably heard the phrase "hurry up and wait." Generally speaking, people tend to want to move on rather than wait. Isaiah said, "But they who wait for the Lord shall renew their strength; they shall mount up with wings like eagles; they shall run and not be weary; they shall walk and not faint" (Isaiah 40:31). In Scripture the word "wait" means to "hope, to anticipate, and to trust." Waiting on the Lord does not mean being idle or indifferent because sometimes waiting is harder than working. For your waiting to be meaningful and spiritually productive, you should do what David did.

Wait silently. This means not telling your trials to everybody who will listen or even telling them repeatedly to the Lord. He probably knows them already. When a child rests in the arms of his/her mother or father, there is no need to make noise. "But the LORD is in his holy temple; let all the earth keep silence before him" (Habakkuk 2:20).

Wait expectantly. God will work as we trust Him and let Him have His way. Our hope is not in human or material resources. Our hope is in the power of God.

Wait continually. It is not easy to wait "at all times," especially when you feel that God is not following your schedule. If your time is in His hands (Psalm 31:15), you will have perfect peace as you wait for Him to work (Isaiah 40:31, Psalm 27:14).

Wait steadfastly. That means to wait resolutely, unwaveringly, and immovably. Paul stated it like this: "Therefore, my beloved brothers, be steadfast, immovable, always abounding in the work of the Lord, knowing that in the Lord your labor is not in vain" (1 Corinthians 15:58).

Application for Today: Today I will wait on the Lord by trusting in Him, by seeking Him, and by praying to Him.

Monday, July 8, 2024

He Leadeth Me

Janine Tuggle

Today's Scripture: Psalm 23:2-3

When I was young, I got tired of the old songs. They were led often because the song leaders did not know some of the newer songs.

Now hearing songs like "He Leadeth Me" by William B. Bradbury brings back so many memories. I visualize my dad standing in front of the congregation, songbook in hand, leading this song, not just because my dad was leading it, but especially because of what the words say.

The song teaches about God, our Father, leading us, and what a blessed thought it is. He will comfort us in any situation if we are anxious in whatever we do or wherever we are. It's God's hand that leads us; where there is a leader, there are followers. Faithful followers we must be.

When my dad would mow the lawn, I loved to follow behind him. As he pushed the mower, making those rows, back and forth or around in circles, I was right behind him. Walking on the mowed path was fun. I guess I was his faithful follower. My dad for the most part was a calm person. When I would visit him in later years, he always reached his hand out to me to say hello. My dad never murmured or complained about what lot he was dealt.

This is a lesson I have learned: to let God lead me and to take His hand. The song says, "By his own hand He leadeth me; His faithful follower I would be, For by His hand He leadeth me." It could be in our darkest moments or when everything is looking up. It could be when waters are still or when seas are troubled, but it is still God's hand that leads us. We won't be able to get out of bad situations unless we follow Him.

Application for the Day: Today I know that when I come to the end of my journey, just as I watched my dad on his dying bed, I can know that by God's grace the victory is won "since God thro' Jordan leadeth me."

Tuesday, July 9, 2024

I Feel Broken

Janine Tuggle

Today's Scripture: Psalm 31:12 – "I have been forgotten like one who is dead; I have become like a broken vessel."

When I go with my husband to the lumber store to pick out lumber for a fence, he sorts through the pieces, choosing those without flaws or splits in the wood. He would like the perfect pieces, not broken ones.

Some things that are torn or broken can be mended and fixed. If you get a hole in your pocket, it can be mended. A broken porcelain dish can be glued back together. A fence that blows down can be nailed back up. When a bone is broken, it mends back either when the bone is set or when screws or rods are put in place to fix the broken bones.

What happens when we have problems in our lives, emotionally, mentally, and spiritually? To whom do we go? Granted, some mental illnesses that are clinical should be seen by a doctor. But there is a great physician who can heal our broken spirits. As David speaks to the Lord God in Psalm 31, he asks for deliverance and rescue. David praises God for being a rock, his rock and fortress, knowing that God will lead and guide him.

David is in a low place, feeling troubled and distressed. Concerned for his soul, he goes to God in prayer, petitioning his needs. He commits his spirit into God's hand, saying he will rejoice and be glad. God has seen his afflictions and has known his distresses. God has redeemed him.

In the same way, God knows when we are down, distressed, afflicted, or broken. This is the time we are to trust in the Lord. We must go to him in prayer and ask as David did, "Be gracious to me, O Lord" (31:9a).

Application for the Day: We sometimes feel so low, or we are carrying such a large burden, that we feel broken. It is then when we need to trust in the Lord, our Lord, and ask to be strengthened.

Wednesday, July 10, 2024

Tuck Me In

Janine Tuggle

Today's Scripture: 1 Samuel 25:29a (CSB) – "Someone is pursuing you and intends to take your life. My lord's life will be tucked safely in the place where the Lord your God protects the living."

Occasionally, as I am going to bed, especially when it is cold, I like to get the covers all tucked in on my sides. That reminds me of when my mom would tuck me into bed and give me a kiss good-night. I remember as a young child, calling for my mom, "Come tuck me in!" if she hadn't done so already.

The version for the scripture of our text in 1 Samuel is about the only version which uses the word "tucked." Other versions use "bound in the bundle of life" (KJV) or "bound in the bundle of the living in the care of the LORD your God" (ESV). ("Bound" here means as you would tie a bundle of twigs or some other item together, tied securely.)

Here we can visualize the concept of security, as one who is tucked into bed by their mother. The child feels secure and safe. There is the feeling and awareness that they are loved and the knowledge that there will be no harm to them.

There's another story of a mother hen found in the rubble of a burned down chicken coop. Underneath her wings and close to her breast were her little chicks safely tucked away—a precious example of being tucked in, safe and secure from harm's way.

"Fear not, for I am with you; be not dismayed, for I am your God; I will strengthen you, I will help you, I will uphold you with my righteous right hand" (Isa. 41:10 ESV).

Application for the Day: Today I will learn that, when I have anxiety and pressures from the world, I can ask God in prayer to "come tuck me in" and know that I will be tucked away in the safety of my Lord.

Thursday, July 11, 2024

Vultures

Janine Tuggle

Today's Scripture: "Wherever the corpse is, there the vultures will gather" (Matt. 24:28).

Vultures are considered some of the most unclean and hated birds. When I travel along the roads, I frequently see an animal that has been killed in one way or another—most usually hit by a vehicle. Soon after, there will be a wake of vultures gathering around this dead animal, cleaning up the carcass. There are times we see vultures flying around in circles in the air, and we can assume there is something dead nearby.

Vultures have the keenest eyesight, equal to eagles, and a sharp sense of smell. They are always in search of food, using their senses to find something that has died. Vultures usually eat on the carcass after death. But there are some species that will attack sick or injured animals.

Just like these birds of prey, there are vultures that hover around ready to swoop down on those who are near spiritual death. If we start to get weak, miss services, slow down in our prayer life, or stop picking up our Bibles, there's something inside telling us it's all right. There could be someone or something that is drawing us away from His word.

We must be careful if we become weak and start dying spiritually, or we will become victims of the birds of prey. There are vultures (friends, evil companions, or our minds) in our lives who will swoop down to eat us. "Therefore we must pay much closer attention to what we have heard, lest we drift away from it" (Heb. 2:1).

We must keep ourselves strong: "Be strong and courageous. Do not be frightened, and do not be dismayed, for the LORD your God is with you wherever you go" (Josh. 1:9b). "He gives power to the faint, and to him who has no might he increases strength" (Isa. 40:29).

Application for the Day: Today I will be strong and stay strong because the vultures do not go after the strong, only the weak and dead.

Friday, July 12, 2024

Who Has the Best Seat?

Janine Tuggle

Today's Scripture: Ephesians 2:6

Everywhere we go, we all try to find the best seat in the house. We want the best seat at a theater. Some like to be up close, some farther back. How about on an airplane? I like a seat by the window. Others might like an aisle seat. What about when booking a seat for a ballgame? You look for a seat that's good but in your price range.

Growing up, we each had our own seat at the kitchen table. My dad sat at the end, the head of the table. Even at church, all of us seem to have their own seats. Don't sit in that seat; it is Brother so-and-so's seat, which has been said many times.

In Scripture, we are told how the scribes and the Pharisees were very hypocritical by doing all their deeds to be seen with long fringes on their clothing, for "they love the best places at feasts, the best seats in the synagogues" (Matt. 23:6). Also, we're told in Luke, "Woe to you Pharisees! For you love the best seats in the synagogues and greetings in the marketplaces" (Luke 11:43).

The seat in which we choose to sit is important! At some functions, such as wedding receptions or retirement parties, there are seats for the guest of honor. Paul states that Christ is seated at the right hand of God. (Col. 3:1). Today we should avoid the practices of the scribes and Pharisees, who boasted about their status and position. But we can be assured that, when we have died to our sins and have been raised from the grave of baptism (Col. 2:12), by the grace of God we will be seated in the heavenly places in Christ Jesus.

Application for the Day: Today I will remember that, as long as I continue to live a faithful life in Christ, I have a seat reserved for me in heaven. "For we must all appear before the judgment seat of Christ" (2 Cor. 5:10a).

Monday, July 15, 2024

Wisdom

Janine Tuggle

Today's Scripture: Proverbs 3:13 - "Blessed is the one who finds wisdom, and the one who gets understanding."

Wisdom: there are so many who try to define wisdom. There are many quotations about it. Some talk about how people acquire it. In an online article from Psychology Today entitled "The Wisest Quotes on Wisdom," many quotations come from famous people, such as William Shakespeare, Socrates, Charles Dickens, and Albert Einstein, yet no quotations from the Bible.

The Bible speaks about many people with wisdom. We are told that God "gave him [Joseph] favor and wisdom before Pharaoh, king of Egypt" (Act 7:10b). "And Moses was instructed in all the wisdom of the Egyptians" (Acts 7:22). Joshua was "full of the Spirit of wisdom" (Deut. 34:9). Excellent wisdom was found in Daniel (Dan. 5:14). Stephen was among "seven men of good repute, full of the Spirit and of wisdom" (Acts 6:3). "Solomon's wisdom surpassed the wisdom of all the people of the east and all the wisdom of Egypt" (1 Kings 4:30).

Proverbs gives us insight into many aspects of wisdom. We are told, "The fear of the LORD is the beginning of knowledge; fools despise wisdom and instruction" (1:7). The writer Solomon gives wise instructions to his son: "Get wisdom; get insight; do not forget, and do not turn away from the words of my mouth" (Prov.4:5).

Someone can be streetwise, book wise, or wise in business but this isn't the wisdom coming from God. "Wisdom from [God] above is pure, then peaceable, gentle, open to reason, full of mercy and good fruits, impartial and sincere" (James 3:17).

"Give instruction to a wise man, and he will be still wiser; teach a righteous man, and he will increase in learning. The fear of the LORD is the beginning of wisdom, and the knowledge of the Holy One is insight" (Prov. 9:9-10).

Application for the Day: Today I will look to the Bible for wisdom and read its words because I know that there is always great wisdom and understanding therein.

Tuesday, July 16, 2024

Find Your People

Jeremy Spencer

Today's Scripture: Proverbs 18:24

In a song by Nashville recording artist Drew Holcomb, he sings:
> You gotta find your people
> The ones that make you feel alright
> You gotta find your people
> The ones that make you feel whole
> That won't leave your side when you lose control
> The ones that don't let you lose your soul
> You gotta find you people
> The ones that get the joke
> Who understand what you're saying before a word is spoke

It's so important to find your people to do life with. We are surrounded by people who love us, but in the core, we have people we know will always be there, who literally come running during life's emergencies, who tell us hard truths, who support us in every step of life, and who sit there in silence and solidarity when there are no words left to say. These are the people we need in life!

Holly and I have wondered, at different times in our lives and the lives of others, "What do you do when you don't have a church community surrounding you?" One of the biggest blessings of the family at Walnut Street is the love that is shared and the countless ways that we support one another. Community is one of the greatest blessings that the church brings to us. But being part of that community takes more than just attending worship and Bible classes. It takes getting to know people and letting them know you, sharing meals together, raising kids together, supporting each other in the unexpected, socializing and enjoying life together, and being there for one another.

Don't miss out on being a part of this great community God created for us, and within that community, find the people that are your core support group—those people you know who will show up for the ups and downs in life. They're the "family," those friends who are as close as family. Find your people and cling to them.

Application for Today: Today I will not only find my people, but I will *be* the person others can count on.

Wednesday, July 17, 2024

Groanings Too Deep for Words

Jeremy Spencer

Today's Scripture: Romans 8:26

Romans 8:26 has always been a favorite verse of mine. The Holy Spirit intercedes for us when we do not know what to pray for—with groanings too deep for words. This has always been comforting to me, and I like the language of "groanings too deep for words." I think we often find ourselves in life not knowing exactly what our prayer needs to be, but God anticipated this, and the Holy Spirit is ready to intercede on our behalf.

Another verse related to prayer is 1 Thessalonians 5:17, which says, "Pray without ceasing." Although I don't think the literal translation of this verse means that we are to be in a constant state of prayer, I have found myself in need of just that at times. I needed to pray over and over, and I wasn't quite sure what the words of my prayer needed to be. I recently spent several months teaching the high school class on Wednesday nights. In that class we read an excerpt about a person in a similar situation who needed constant prayer. He found himself praying a 3- to 4- word phrase over and over. This is what I found myself doing, praying the same couple of phrases over and over—I didn't know what else to pray or what specifically to say, but I knew the Holy Spirit was there and was ready to take my words and intercede with "groanings too deep for words." It was comforting to know that my simplistic prayer was reaching God's ears in the way it needed to be heard.

Too often we may think we have to have it figured out before we go to the throne of God. But God does not require that! He is ready to accept us and redeem us right where we are at that point.

Application Today: Today I will not wait until I am ready or until I think I've got it figured out to talk to God; instead, I will start today, where I am, and let Him take me to where I need to go.

Thursday, July 18, 2024

A Place for You
Joe Corlew

Today's Scripture: John 14:2-3 – "In My Father's house are many mansions; if it were not so, I would have told you. I go to prepare a place for you. And if I go and prepare a place for you, I will come again and receive you to Myself; that where I am, there you may be also."

In June of 2023, my wife and I were blessed to be able to experience a Disney Cruise with two of our grandchildren and our daughter and son-in-law. Not only did we enjoy wonderful entertainment, food, sights, and activities, but being able to experience it with family made it even more enjoyable.

Even though the rooms on a cruise ship are not huge, we had a very comfortable room. Whenever we would leave our room for breakfast or dinner, we would return to find that the bed had been made, and the bathroom and other parts of the cabin had been cleaned as well. Although we would not see the room steward waiting in the hall to watch us leave, somehow, he always seemed to know when we had left. Each night there would be some type of animal or sea creature created from folded towels lying on the bed in addition to chocolate candy on our pillows.

As I was thinking about how nice the daily preparation for our lodging was on the cruise ship, I couldn't help but think about Jesus's promise that He has gone to prepare a place for us, and not only has He prepared a place for us, but He has promised to come and take us to that place. I am looking forward to experiencing an eternity with God in the place that Jesus has prepared for me, and I want my family, friends, and acquaintances to experience it as well.

Application for Today: Today I will be prayerful and actively engaged in trying to help as many folks as possible experience the blessing of discipleship on this earth and an eternity with God, Jesus, and the saints of all ages.

144

Friday, July 19, 2024

Quiet Quitting
Joe Corlew

Today's Scripture: Matthew 9:37-38 – "Then he said to his disciples, 'The harvest is plentiful, but the laborers are few; therefore pray earnestly to the Lord of the harvest to send out laborers into his harvest.'"

As Jesus was going around to the cities and villages near Jerusalem, He had compassion on the multitudes of people and instructed His disciples to pray for laborers to go and reach the multitudes with the gospel. Jesus was not just asking His apostles to be laborers in His vineyard but for all disciples to be involved in spreading the gospel.

In recent years (especially during the last three years with the COVID-19 pandemic), our nation's workforce has been significantly diminished. This is due to a combination of free money (stimulus payments and unemployment benefits) from the government, government-forced shutdowns of some businesses, COVID-19 related school closures, paranoia of being near other people, and sometimes just because folks have become lazy and complacent. For those still employed, a relatively new term called "Quiet Quitting" has been coined to describe the phenomenon of workers who do only the bare minimum of job requirements and are not motivated or enthusiastic about their jobs. Could this term also apply to members of the church? Are we failing to accomplish the mission of spreading the gospel and interested only in being pew sitters and being fed and not engaged in discipleship?

We have been challenged from the pulpit for the past few months to be "All In." One of those sermons reminded us that we are to be Salt and Light. In Matthew 5:13-16, Jesus calls us to be the Salt of the earth and the Light of the world. For Salt to be effective, it needs to leave the shaker and get into the food. For Light to be effective, it must not be hidden but should illuminate the path that one should follow.

Application for Today: Today I will determine to do a better job in sharing the gospel with my family, classmates, co-workers, neighbors, and others with whom I have occasion to interact.

Clearly Seeing the Invisible

Joe Deweese

Today's Scripture: Romans 1:20

In today's scripture Paul said, "For His invisible attributes, namely, His eternal power and divine nature, have been clearly perceived, ever since the creation of the world, in the things that have been made. So, they are without excuse."

It's a peculiar thing for Paul to say that God's invisible attributes can be clearly seen. After all, doesn't "invisible" mean that we can't see them? Follow his logic and you'll find the wisdom in Paul's statement. First, he specified the attributes: "eternal power" and "divine nature". While we do not fully understand the breadth of these statements, we can reasonably see that these are meant to represent attributes we would associate with an omnipotent Creator God. His power is eternal, and His very nature is divine.

Second, he specified the means by which we "see the invisible"—he said these attributes were clearly seen "in the things that have been made." The phrase "things that have been made" is a reference to the world around us and the entire cosmos. As we look out at the stars and examine plants and animals on our planet, we are left with clear evidence of a designing intellect that brought all of this into being.

Third, this has been going on "ever since the creation of the world." God's handiwork is evident in His creation–this was true in the beginning and is still true today. This places humanity all the way back at the beginning since it is humanity that has the ability to perceive God's handiwork.

As you go through the day today, see how many creations you come across and pause as you consider God's eternal power and divine nature reflected in the things that have been made. Where will you see God's attributes today?

Application for Today: Today, I will look for God's attributes in all created things.

Tuesday, July 23, 2024

Live For Him

Joe Deweese

Today's Scripture: 2 Corinthians 5:14-15

"For the love of Christ controls us, because we have concluded this: that one has died for all, therefore all have died; and He died for all, that those who live might no longer live for themselves but for him who for their sake died and was raised" (2 Corinthians 5:14-15).

Why did Jesus die? And what impact should that have on me?

Jesus' death represents a sacrifice for our sins as discussed in Hebrews 9 and 10. Without His blood being shed, we would have no hope of having our sins forgiven (Hebrews 9:24). That seems odd to us, but this is the system God put into place. It underscores the value God places on blood and what it represents. Yet, that's not the end of the story. Yes, Jesus died, and yes, we are redeemed through that sacrifice, but that should be the beginning not the end of the story.

Paul points out in the passage above that the sacrifice of Jesus should motivate us to live selflessly. So, rather than taking the freedom we have in Christ to pursue our own desires, we are to surrender our desires to Him and pursue living a life for Him. Paul said in Romans 12:1-2, "I appeal to you therefore, brothers, by the mercies of God, to present your bodies as a living sacrifice, holy and acceptable to God, which is your spiritual worship. Do not be conformed to this world, but be transformed by the renewal of your mind, that by testing you may discern what is the will of God, what is good and acceptable and perfect." When we do this, we point others to the love that sets us free, and we seek to do what pleases Him and help set others free through the message of His love which is demonstrated in our lives. This idea is brought out also in Philippians 2 with the example of Christ and His willingness to "empty Himself."

Application for Today: I will go through the day today in a way that reflects my desire to live for Him?

147

Wednesday, July 24, 2024

New Creatures

Joe Deweese

Today's Scripture: 2 Corinthians 5:17

Today's scripture states "Therefore if anyone is in Christ, he is a new creature; the old things passed away; behold, new things have come."

Newness is something we tend to value. New clothes or shoes. New house. New car. New toys. New tools. New job. Why do we value newness?

Perhaps, newness comes with a sense of cleanness—no dents or scratches or dings. Perhaps, it comes with a sense of completeness—all parts in working order, all functions operating. There is a sort of excitement that comes with newness—like undiscovered potential waiting for us.

Newness is something we are drawn to. Paul says in Romans 6:4, "We were buried therefore with him by baptism into death, in order that, just as Christ was raised from the dead by the glory of the Father, we too might walk in newness of life." We are raised from the watery grave of baptism to "walk in newness of life." The cleansing of baptism brings with it a sense of newness—new creatures. We are redeemed and in a right relationship with God. We are connected, reconciled to Him—all parts in working order.

But some may say, "That was so long ago, I don't feel new anymore." We often feel the sticky nature of sin clinging to us and making us feel guilt or shame. Let go of that sin and let the blood of Jesus be enough. "Therefore, since we are surrounded by so great a cloud of witnesses, let us also lay aside every weight, and sin which clings so closely, and let us run with endurance the race that is set before us, looking to Jesus, the founder and perfecter of our faith, who for the joy that was set before him endured the cross, despising the shame, and is seated at the right hand of the throne of God. (Hebrews 12:1-2). In Christ, you are a new creature. Now live like it!

Application for Today: I will lay aside every weight and sin, and focus on Jesus.

Thursday, July 25, 2024

Spoken to Us by His Son

Joe Deweese

Today's Scripture: Hebrews 1:1-4

"God, after He spoke long ago to the fathers in the prophets in many portions and in many ways, in these last days has spoken to us in His Son, whom He appointed heir of all things, through whom He also made the world. And He is the radiance of His glory and the exact representation of His nature, and upholds all things by the word of His power. When He had made purification of sins, He sat down at the right hand of the Majesty on high, having become so much better than the angels, to the extent that He has inherited a more excellent name than they."

What would it have been like to be Adam and Eve walking with God in the garden? Or a patriarch like Noah or Abraham? Or Moses and the Israelites standing at the base of the mountain? Or the Jews hearing from the prophets the message of God?

God has used various means to communicate with humanity. He has sent angels and prophets. He has spoken and performed various miraculous wonders. Now He has spoken through His Son, Jesus Christ. Note that Jesus is not just a passive element in this process. He is "heir of all things" and was one "through whom He also made the world." Jesus was an agent in creation (see also John 1 and Colossians 1 for this same theme).

God has chosen in this era to send a message directly through His Son. Jesus came to this earth to deliver God's message. The next few chapters after this statement note how much greater the message is coming from Jesus than from the angels or prophets or even from Moses. If those other messages proved true, how much more the message from Jesus (Heb. 2:1-4)? Heed the warning: pay attention to what we have heard so that we do not drift from it! How have I drifted from God's message? What course corrections do I need to make today?

Application for the Day: Today I will determine what course corrections I need to make.

Friday, July 26, 2024

Visible Made from Invisible

Joe Deweese

Today's Scripture: Hebrews 11:1-3

"Now faith is the assurance of things hoped for, the conviction of things not seen. For by it the people of old received their commendation. By faith we understand that the universe was created by the word of God, so that what is seen was not made out of things that are visible."

Hebrews 11 is filled with a message of faith through examples of those who have gone before. Their example and testimony stand as a witness to the faithfulness of the Lord and the trustworthiness of His promises. But before the writer gets to these other testimonies, he makes this statement about the creation: "The universe was created by the word of God, so that what is seen was not made out of things that are visible" (Heb. 11:3).

What does this mean? Certainly, the reference to the universe being created "by the word of God" sends our minds back to Genesis 1 where God spoke the world into existence. I find the last part of the sentence even more interesting; how did God make what is seen? The scripture tells us that it was not made out of "things that are visible."

While this is not the meaning intended by the writer of Hebrews, it seems worth noting that the atoms and particles that make up matter are individually invisible. In this sense, what is seen is literally made out of molecules that are not visible. It is quite humbling indeed to consider the amazing design of nature and the fact that God's power is seen even in the atoms and molecules of the creation. Yet, here the writer is more likely referring to God speaking creation into existence in such a way that the power of His voice brings the physical into being. God is the greatest physicist and chemist of all!

What can I learn from considering God's power to bring things into existence by His word? What does that say about my own challenges and problems and frustrations?

Application for the Day: Today I will look for God's power of creation.

Monday, July 29, 2024

Who Built This Place?

Joe Deweese

Today's Scripture: Hebrews 3:1-4

"Therefore, holy brethren, partakers of the heavenly calling, consider the Apostle and High Priest of our confession, Christ Jesus, who was faithful to Him who appointed Him, as Moses also was faithful in all His house. For this One has been counted worthy of more glory than Moses, inasmuch as He who built the house has more honor than the house. For every house is built by someone, but He who built all things is God."

We take for granted that structures, houses and buildings, all have a builder. Probably there are also architects, contractors, construction workers, and others involved in modern building projects. In the passage above, the Hebrew writer is pointing out that God built everything and thus is over everything—sovereign (which means He can decide who has charge over His house). Here the writer is trying to make the point that while Moses is important, the Son has even greater importance—Moses was faithful IN the house, but Jesus is faithful OVER the house. In other words, Jesus is greater than Moses; thus, we ought to heed His Words.

Let me take a tangent for a moment. The idea that every house has a builder is the basis of something called the design argument. The basic idea is that design implies a designer. Just as a house has a builder or a painting has a painter, design has a designer. William Paley (1743-1805) coined his famous "watchmaker" argument upon the idea that if we found a watch in the woods, we would assume that there must be a watchmaker since watches (with their intricate detail, clear purpose, and complex mechanisms) don't happen by accident.

The world is full of designs: animals, plants, humans. Where did all of these come from? Do they not demand the same level of explanation? How have I taken for granted God's designs in nature?

Application for the Day: Today I will determine where to look to see God's design.

Tuesday, July 30, 2024

What a Day That Will Be

Joey Holley

Today's Scripture: Luke 23:43

My job as principal of Dickson County High School comes with several "opportunities" daily. Dealing with 1,500 teenagers always makes the day interesting. One thing I tell anyone who asks is that my job is no different than most. While 99% of my job is great, the other 1% has its moments, but it is no different than most other jobs. I often hear, "Boy, kids sure are crazy now," or, "They have lost their minds!" My response is, "Kids are no different today than we were in high school; the only difference is that they come to our school with more 'baggage.'" The problems kids face today are overwhelming.

Often our kids are told, "You better enjoy your high school years because this is the best time of your life." For some students this statement is mind blowing. Some are living in homes that are struggling to make ends meet, and they are working to help Mom pay bills. Others have parents who don't really want them around, or their parents are abusers of drugs or alcohol. And they are being told by well-meaning adults that this is as good as it gets? Wow, what a life! Let's all try to be careful when using that statement with teenagers.

Without question, we are all shooting for heaven. That will be the greatest time ever! We believe that the day we walk through those pearly gates will truly be the best time of our lives! The Bible also tells us that heaven is the dwelling place of God. His throne is there, the angels are there, and the Lord Jesus Christ is there. Philippians 3:20 says very plainly that "our citizenship is in heaven. And we eagerly await a Savior from there, the Lord Jesus Christ." That's why Jesus told the thief on the cross, "Today you will be with me in paradise" (Luke 23:43b). What a great day that will be!

Application for the Day: Today I will carefully encourage youth with the promise of a greater day to come!

Wednesday, July 31, 2024

Sound of the Rooster Crowing

Joey Turbeville

Today's Scripture: Luke 24: 54-62

God created us with many amazing bodily functions, and one is our brains' memory. You can probably recall memory clips as far back as childhood. Many times, these memories are triggered in my brain as a result of something I hear.

While the brain is powerful, it doesn't translate the true meaning of negative words like don't. To illustrate this, I will tell you, "Don't think of a pink elephant!" What are you picturing in your mind?

The same can be true when negative thoughts and feelings are aroused in our memories from our past. When this occurs, the more we tell ourselves not to think of it, the more we do. Psychologists suggest using positive affirmations regarding negative thoughts such that we replace the negative with a positive.

Can you imagine what the sound of a rooster crowing did to Peter for the rest of his life?

In Luke 22:54-62, we are told Peter denied Jesus three times before the rooster crowed:

"But Peter said, 'Man, I do not know what you are talking about.' And immediately, while he was still speaking, the rooster crowed. And the Lord turned and looked at Peter. And Peter remembered the saying of the Lord, how he had said to him, 'Before the rooster crows today, you will deny me three times.' And he went out and wept bitterly" (Luke 22:60-62).

Suddenly, the rooster blared an alarm that perhaps caused guilt and shame every time Peter heard that sound.

But what if, instead of feeling guilty every time he heard a rooster crow, he replaced that thought with a positive affirmation: "I deserve death, but Jesus is my Savior, and I am forgiven!" Peter seemed to do just that, as he dedicated the remainder of his life to Jesus and his teachings.

Application for the Day: Today, as I am reminded of my past failures, I will carry the positive affirmation of God's grace and be thankful that I have been forgiven and that God "remembers my sins no more!"

Thursday, August 1, 2024

Fun and Games or Broken Legs

John Lampley

Today's Scripture: Philippians 4:2 – "Let each of you look not only to his own interests but also to the interest of others."

We heard sirens, and Wendy's dad said, "Y'all just go before the police get here." This was the unexpected end to a typical night hanging out with friends in the youth group. Because we were bored, we decided to go rolling (toilet papering) a friend's house. Since Wendy wasn't with us and lived nearby, her house would be the target. We quickly assembled a small group of amateur rollers, gathered some rolls, and began to stake out the house. When we arrived, we noticed that the family was still milling around, but we decided to dive in anyway.

The excitement escalated quickly when a member of Wendy's family spotted us hiding behind some bushes, and the chase was on. We sprinted up the street towards our car with Wendy's dad in hot pursuit. After he caught up to us (not all of us were track stars), he realized we were friends. At that point, breathing heavily, he told us he was glad he had not taken Laura's legs out with the baseball bat he was carrying. Then we heard sirens, and Wendy's dad said, "Our house was broken into last week. Y'all just go before the police get here. I'll let them know that tonight was a false alarm." We then understood that Wendy's family was dealing with fear and anger from someone breaking into their house. We had made a very poor choice of which house to roll that night.

Even with close friends, we will not always know what's going on in their lives. All the more, we will not know what's going on with our church family, passing associates, and strangers. Many of the people we will meet today have struggles that we likely will never know.

Application for Today: Today, before each interaction with others, I will take a moment to remind myself that each individual is made in the image of God, has eternal value, and is dealing with unseen challenges.

Cloud Watching

John Petty

Today's Scripture: Exodus 40:34-38

Today is an August day in the year 2023, and I am looking at the clouds in the summer sky. Whenever I read Psalm 19, I think first of the clouds: "The heavens declare the glory of God" (v. 1). If I lived out of town, I might also think of the night sky. On some days, the lovely blue sky and the stately white clouds are so exquisitely beautiful as to seem designed entirely to delight us. That may well be the exact purpose intended! For me, a glance at the daytime sky is an assurance that God is there and in control.

Come to think of it, clouds are mentioned in several ways in the Bible. There was, of course, the pillar of cloud that guided the Hebrews through the wilderness by day and also filled the tabernacle (Ex. 24-38).

Then the cloud covered the tent of meeting, and the glory of the Lord filled the tabernacle. And Moses was not able to enter the tent of meeting because the cloud settled on it, and the glory of the Lord filled the tabernacle. Throughout all their journeys, whenever the cloud was taken up from over the tabernacle, the people of Israel would set out (Ex. 40:34-38).

I wonder how big it was. Did it create its own rain? Was it a puffy white cloud or something else? A dark and angry cloud maybe?

The faithful that are alive at Christ's return are promised to be caught up in the clouds (1 Thess. 4:17) to meet the Lord in the air, which I guess means we will be transported up there somehow. To be suddenly snatched up and removed from the cares of the present world would certainly be a change. Sounds pretty neat, doesn't it?

Lastly, Christ ascended into Heaven via a cloud (Acts 1:9) and is coming back in a cloud (Luke 21:27)—this time with power and glory. We don't know when, but it could be anytime now.

Application for the Day: Today I think I'll do some more cloud watching.

Monday, August 5, 2024

Shelter from the Storm

Joshua Grooms (2022 Ministry Intern)

Today's Scripture: Matthew 6:31-34

Matthew 6:31–34 (ESV) – "Therefore do not be anxious, saying, 'What shall we eat?' or 'What shall we drink?' or 'What shall we wear?' For the Gentiles seek after all these things, and your heavenly Father knows that you need them all. But seek first the kingdom of God and his righteousness, and all these things will be added to you. Therefore, do not be anxious about tomorrow, for tomorrow will be anxious for itself. Sufficient for the day is its own trouble."

The imagery of our trials surrounding us as a storm is one that relates closely to all. At some point most of us have felt that the best we can do is to keep our heads above the waves and tread water until the storm subsides enough for us to gather a breath and collect our wits. We see the waves building around us and the misfortunes gathering like clouds, obscuring our sight so that the hopes and goals we use as guiding stars are no longer in view. There, in the darkness, life hits us the hardest. It feels as if the devil himself is sending wave after wave to beat our little boat to pieces.

The waves are building. An unexpected bill arrives. The waves are building. A job is lost. The waves are building. Family relationships are strained. The waves are filling the boat. Hope is lost.

"Peace, be still!" The gentle voice of the Savior pierces the winds, and all is calm.

The Gospels recount the time that Jesus calmed the winds and waves to save the apostles from the storm that surrounded them (Mark 4:35-41, Matt 8:23-27, Luke 8:22-25). Even though we are not on a physical boat with Jesus, we put our faith in the One who commands the winds and the waves. The God who made heaven and earth protects and guides us. Jesus never promises to dispel all the storms, but He does promise to protect us. He is our shelter from the storm.

Application for the Day: Today I will rest in His shelter.

Tuesday, August 6, 2024

A Happy Face
Judy Hinson

Today's Scripture: Proverbs 15:13

Proverbs is an amazing book. The wisdom instilled in it describes a way of life that springs from reverence for God and from loyalty to His revealed Word and will. It has been called the book of "truisms" for its conventional wisdom, and it makes this book absolutely unique.

"A glad heart makes a face happy, but heartache breaks the spirit" (Prov. 15:13, CBJ). A glad heart lights up the face because it cannot be contained just to the inside of a person. It bursts forth for all the world to see.

There are many verses in the New Testament that reveal the way to have and to sustain a happy heart and, therefore, a glad and happy face. The following verses show us that Jesus wants us to know how to achieve happy hearts in our daily lives: Matthew 6:34; Romans 15:13; John 14:27; 2 Timothy 1:7; John 15:11; Philippians 4:4-5.

When one has God and a relationship with Him in his heart, can he be sad, fearful, worried? Yes. When one has God and a relationship with Him in his heart, can he stay in this frame of mind? No.

Although this proverb speaks to the individual, there is another point to this proverb. What is the second one? To show God to others. My granddaughter's homeschool philosophy is "To Know God and To Make Him Known." This is what truly makes for a glad heart. Sometimes I struggle to find happiness in a season of anxiety, and my prayer is from St. Francis of Assisi: Please be with me and guide me toward You as I desire happiness with You. Make me an instrument of Your peace. I want to know what it's like to follow You. When men look at me, I want them to see the Light of the world inside.

Application for Today: Today I will pray for the Holy Spirit to clothe me in a spirit so that I may be a source of joy for others today.

Wednesday, August 7, 2024

A Shield about Me

Judy Hinson

Today's Scripture: Psalm 121:7-8

What a world we live in today! Sin is now the "in thing," and we, as God's children, are bombarded from every side: social media, companies who openly declare hostility toward us (yet continue to accept our money), people of faith being sued for not making a cake or even being jailed for not issuing a marriage license. If we don't jump in and agree 100%, we are labeled as haters, which is so far from the truth.

Jesus wept over the people of Jerusalem. These were His people. They were the very ones who persecuted and killed the righteous, but He loved them. He deeply yearned to gather them all to Him, but they would not. We, too, want to bring all people to our Jesus. We love them as He did, and, like Him, we cannot condone sin.

We are reminded to "fight the good fight" in 1 Timothy 6:12. So into battle we go with love, and we are protected in this struggle by our God, who Is a shield about us.

Genesis 15:1 – "Do not be afraid, Abram. I am your shield."

Deuteronomy 33:29 – "Happy are you, O Israel! Who is like you, a people saved by the LORD, the shield of your help and the sword of your majesty!"

2 Samuel 22:31 – "As for God, His way is perfect; the word of the LORD is proven; He is a shield to all who trust in Him."

Psalm 3:3 – "But You, O LORD, are a shield for me, my glory and the One who lifts up my head."

Ephesians 6:14-16 – "Stand therefore, having girded your waist with truth, having put on the breastplate of righteousness, and having shod your feet with the preparation of the gospel of peace; above all, taking the shield of faith with which you will be able to quench all the fiery darts of the wicked one."

Application for Today: Today I will stand with my brothers and sisters, knowing that we have a Savior who wields a mighty shield and sword.

Thursday, August 8, 2024

Are You Full?

Judy Hinson

Today's Scripture: Galatians 5:22

"Where two or three are gathered"-There Will Be Food! I'm not sure about the rest of the country, but this is The South. These occasions include but are not limited to dinner on the ground, sporting events, birthdays, anniversaries, deaths, family reunions and all the holidays. And of course, one must always be prepared with a cake, pie or cobbler on hand at all times for the drop-in visitors along with coffee and sweet tea. I think we can say, "Yes, we are full," physically that is.

What about Spiritually? Are we full of the fruit of the Spirit? Does our cup run over with love, joy, peace, longsuffering, kindness, goodness, faithfulness, gentleness, and self-control. "If we live in the Spirit, let us also walk in the Spirit," Galatians 5:25. Jesus was full of these qualities in His walk on this earth (Luke 4:1). His physical life was dominated by His devotion to do the will of the Father. Our lives should reflect Him by being zealous to also be full of the fruit of the Spirit.

For us, this is often not that easy. We want to walk with the Spirit, but so often we let the flesh creep in and dictate our walk instead of the Spirit (Romans 8:5). Peter stated, "Beloved, I beg you as sojourners and pilgrims, abstain from fleshly lusts which war against the soul," 1 Peter 2:12.

To walk in the Spirit, we must exercise our faith, practice these virtues, and let go of anyone or anything which threatens to lure us away. We must be prepared to be vigilant (1 Peter 5:8). We must be prepared for battle (Ephesians 6:13). We must be steadfast in prayer (Colossians 4:2). We must keep watch over our hearts (Proverbs 4:23). We must guard our ways (Psalm 39:1). We must always be alert and stand firm (1 Corinthians 16:13).

Application for Today: Today, I will read, sing, pray about, and meditate on that old song, "Earth Holds No Treasures."

Friday, August 9, 2024

Journeys
Judy Hinson

Today's Scripture: Zephaniah 3:17

Often it has been said that life is a journey. However, is it a single trip, or is it smaller steps, which, when put together, make up the entire journey of life? Think back on happy times when you sat on top of the world: marriage, your first car or first home, the birth of your children. Remember the journeys that have brought you to your knees: lost expectations, frustrations, sicknesses, or death of a spouse, mother, father, child, or others we hold most dear.

It is easy to make the journey when it fills our hearts with joy, but how do we face difficult times as we travel through life? Jesus said in Matthew 11:28-29, "Come to me, all who labor and are heavy laden, and I will give you rest. Take my yoke upon you, and learn from me, for I am gentle and lowly in heart, and you will find rest for your souls." The psalmist said that God is our "refuge and strength" (Psa. 46:1). Moses proclaimed that God never leaves us (Deut. 31:8). He is the warrior who gives us victory, and He is our helper who rejoices over us with gladness and loud singing. In times of trouble, think of those old songs, such as "Lean on the Mighty Arm of Jesus" and "Leaning on the Everlasting Arms."

One last thought: we do not travel alone. Along the way, we will observe others who need our help. "There are feet to steady, hands to grasp, minds to encourage, hearts to inspire and souls to save" (Larry Page). Be observant of those around you who may be on their own difficult journeys. Show them through you the light, the love, the peace, and the comfort that is in you, which is the Lord Jesus.

Application: Today I will remember that "the Lord your God in your midst, a mighty one who will save; he will rejoice over you with gladness; he will quiet you by his love; he will exult over you with loud singing" (Zeph. 3:17).

Monday, August 12, 2024

Just a Closer Walk with Thee
Judy Hinson

Today's Scripture: 2 Corinthians 5:7

> I am weak but Thou art strong; Jesus, keep me from all wrong.
> I'll be satisfied as long As I walk, dear Lord, close to Thee.
> Thro' this world of toil and snares, If I falter, Lord, who cares?
> Who with me my burden shares? None but Thee, dear Lord, none but Thee.
> When my feeble life is o'er, Time for me will be no more,
> Guide me gently, safely o'er To Thy kingdom shore, to Thy shore.
> Just a closer walk with Thee, Grant it, Jesus, is my plea.
> Daily walking close to Thee, Let it be, dear Lord, let it be.

The author of this old folk song is unknown, although circumstantial evidence strongly suggests it dates back to Southern African-American churches of the nineteenth century, possibly even prior to the Civil War. It has been performed and recorded by many artists over the years. By the end of the 1970's, it had been recorded by over 100 artists, including Pat Boone, Tennessee Ernie Ford, Louis Armstrong, Willie Nelson, Gladys Knight, and Charlie Daniels. It was even featured on the Veggie Tales from their "I'll Fly Away" album in 2003.

What is it about this 150-year-old song that has made it so moving and touching to so many? Job 33:4 says, "The Spirit of God [Elohim] has made me, and the breath of the Almighty [El Shaddai] gives me life." If His very breath is in us, can we not help but feel the need of Him in our souls?

Read these Scriptures as you look at a few of the lyrics:
"I am weak but Thou art strong." Psa. 6:2, Psa. 28:8, 1 Cor. 4:10, 2 Cor. 12.9
"If I falter, Lord, who cares?" Deut. 33:26, 2 Chron. 16:9, Psa. 124:7-8
"Guide me . . . safely o'er to Thy kingdom shore." Ex. 15:13

Application for the Day: Today I will remember that Jesus will be strong for me and that He cares for me and is more than willing to supply all my needs—physical and spiritual.

Tuesday, August 13, 2024

Reading the Bible like a Book

Judy Hinson

Today's Scripture: 2 Timothy 2:15

Do you love to read? Do you enjoy romance, historical, or biographical? My favorites are mysteries and murder mysteries! It started when I was young. I devoured them. I read every Agatha Christie, Edgar Allan Poe, Sir Arthur Conan Doyle, and Daphne du Maurier I could get my hands on. There's nothing like the joy of curling up on the couch on a dreary, rainy day—forget the laundry, cooking, and cleaning.

What about the most published and most important book of all time? The Bible. How do we read the Bible? Do we pick a few verses a day as part of an organized schedule or as part of a workbook study?

Every book in the Bible has its own unique story. Genesis is the beginning of the Jewish nation. Esther shows how God places us in positions to accomplish His plans. Acts is the history of the early church, and, of course, there are Paul's letters to the churches.

Paul's letters were correspondence written from the depths of his heart. They were friend to friend, preacher to brethren, and some to individuals like Timothy and Philemon. Beyond teaching, these letters reveal relationships, disappointments, and even dreams. Choose one of Paul's letters, and read it from start to finish in one sitting. You'll discover an amazing display of emotion between Paul and his readers. For instance, he closes Romans, 1 Corinthians, Philippians, and Colossians with personal greetings, calling his coworkers and friends by name. Paul grieves eloquently over the Galatians' willingness to stray from the true gospel. He admonishes the Corinthians over their petty divisions. He founded churches all over the known world, but there's no doubt that Paul loved the people in the churches he founded: "We were ready to share with you not only the gospel of God but also our own selves, because you had become very dear to us" (1 Thess. 2:8b).

Application for the Day: Today I will remember that every book in the Bible has a unique story to tell and that I will be richer by reading each one.

Wednesday, August 14, 2024

Standing on the Promises

Judy Hinson

Today's Scripture: Psalm 139:13-14

Why are we so stirred by beautiful hymns? There are a lot of studies and papers out there by scientists and doctors on this very question, and there are as many different theories as the number of people doing the studies. However, they all agree on these points: Singing can change the brain, it is almost exclusively developed in human beings, and we are wired for it—it is built in us. Songs evoke powerful responses, and they arouse deep emotions. They make us happy; they make us cry; they make us sad; they comfort us. Singing has some of the same health benefits as exercise. Whether it's a song of delight or a song of sorrow, it releases endorphins, the brain's "feel good" chemicals.

So why do we, as the children of God, sing? First, God sings and rejoices over us. Zephaniah 3:17 says that God "will rejoice over you with gladness." We sing to Him because it inspires a heart worship to our God. Worship is the recognition of God's incredible worth, and when we sing, we can better see who He is. As is in this song, we acknowledge that we can stand on His promises, and He has promised to:
Send us a Savior (Genesis 3:15)
Fight for us (Exodus 14:14)
Put a wall of protection around us (Job 1:10)
Deliver us from our troubles (Psalm 54:7)
Build a place for us (John 14:1-4)
Give us peace (John 14:27)
Give us what we ask in His name (John 14:13-14)
Give us strength (Philippians 4:13)
Never leave us (Hebrews 13:5)
Forgive us (1 John 1:9)

How do we know that He will keep His promises? "For all the promises of God in Him are Yes, and in Him Amen, to the glory of God through us" (2 Cor. 1:20).

Application for the Day: Sing this old hymn aloud, and let it fill your heart and soul with the majesty, power, and might of our God.

Thursday, August 15, 2024

The Story of the Crocheted Shell

Judy Hinson

Today's Scripture: Isaiah 1:18

Several years ago, I was wearing a crocheted shell, and a friend remarked that it was very pretty. I recalled when I had received it as a gift some fifty years before. It was handmade of raw silk and sported a unique design. It was a very dark ecru with little dark-brown spots. Of course, I didn't have a clue what raw silk was supposed to feel like, but I loved it at first sight. Since I was keeping foster children at the time, beautiful clothing was a luxury we couldn't afford. I couldn't wait to try it on. IT WAS AWFUL! It was the roughest and the itchiest thing I had ever tried to wear. I was so disappointed that I put it away in a drawer.

After a while, I got the shell out again and put it on; nothing had changed. It was still just as rough and itchy as the first time I had worn it. Back in the drawer it went. Then after several years passed, I tried putting a shirt on under it, making sure it was large enough so the shell didn't touch me anywhere. And it worked. I would wear it a few times a year, gently hand wash it and put it back in the drawer. After a while, I noticed that it was much lighter and no longer itchy. Year after year, I continued to do the same thing. It became lighter and softer year after year.

Like this shell, we are all a beautiful and unique creation of God, but because of sin, we are brown and rough. But Abba had a plan conceived even before He created us. Through His work of redemption, we can become like this shell. Because of His mercy and grace, He continually washes us clean. We are still a work in progress as we are continually washed by Jesus' blood, and one day when we will stand before our God, we will be as white as snow.

Application for the Day: Today I will ask God to wash me anew.

Friday, August 16, 2024

This One's for the Girls

Kayla Fuller

Today's Scripture: Mark 15: 40-41

Growing up in the church today can be confusing for women. In this society of equality and feminism, we hear conflicting reports about what it means to be a strong woman. Some churches seem to treat women as less important, ignoring passages Proverbs 31 and 1 Peter 3:1-4. Whereas, in some congregations women are honored because of the teaching of those very same passages.

I grew up being taught to be a Christian lady quietly serving in the background and supporting your husband. Today, however, many women are loud and outspoken, rather than soft and quiet.

When strong women in the Old Testament are discussed, many times Ruth and Esther are among the first who come to mind. Ruth was doing what she could for her and her mother-in-law to survive. Esther actually risked her life for her people. She became queen when the former queen was deposed because she refused to entertain the king who had been drinking and the men were afraid that other women would follow her example. Providentially, she was in the right place at the right time and took advantage of that opportunity.

When it comes to women in the New Testament, besides the Marys, we often study about:
- Phoebe in Romans 16. She is called a servant in some translations, but the Greek word *diakonos* has also been translated deacon elsewhere. Paul even refers to her as a patron.
- Priscilla, in Acts 18, who became a missionary (with her husband).
- Lydia, in Acts 15, who brought her family and friends to faith.
- Euodia and Syntyche who were key leaders in the church at Philippi.

Ladies remember that after Jesus was crucified, many of the men left, and the women stayed until the end and brought the news of Jesus' resurrection. Let us strive to be the Christ-like women of God who are among the first to tell others about Jesus.

Application for the Day: Today I will pray, thanking God for godly women.

Monday, August 19, 2024

A Kind Heart

Keely Webb

Today's Scriptures: Proverbs 16:24; Ephesians 4:32

In middle school, I realized that you could make "friends," and not really have "friends" at the same time. Many of my "friends" acted one way with me and another way with others. I felt defeated and thought something was wrong with me. At times, I would reciprocate the hatred. But when I cried to my parents at night, they told me the same thing repeatedly: kill them with kindness. It seemed silly! If somebody was mean to me, why should I be kind to them? They don't deserve my kindness.

I read about Jesus's crucifixion and noticed the lesson my parents were trying to teach me. Even when Jesus was hanging on the cross, He asked the Lord not to blame us. He died on the cross for us. I feel like sometimes we don't realize how big that is. Did we deserve Jesus's love and kindness? The kindness He still shows us today? We hung Him on a cross to die—yet-He still loves us? Proverbs 16:24 says, "Kind words are like honey—sweet to the soul and healthy for the body."

As I was reading about Jesus and taking in what is meant to "kill them with kindness," it seemed silly to hold a grudge against people who aren't kind to me. If Jesus can be kind to His trespassers, I can be kind to mine. We are called to walk in the way of the Lord and to be different. "Instead, be kind to each other, tenderhearted, forgiving one another, just as God through Christ has forgiven you" (Eph. 4:32). It's hard to be mean to someone who is always kind. If someone says, "I don't like your hair," and you say, "Well, I think your hair looks amazing," what are they going to do?

When Jesus was crucified and resurrected, all our sins could be forgiven! It leaves me speechless to think about that sometimes. Although we don't deserve it, He shows us kindness.

Application for the Day: Today, even though my enemies don't deserve it, I will "kill them with kindness."

Tuesday, August 20, 2024

Give It to God

Keely Webb

Today's Scriptures: Philippians 4:6; Matthew 6:34

"Don't worry about anything; instead, pray about everything. Tell God what you need, and thank him for all he has done" (Phil. 4:6). Sometimes, anxiety overwhelms us, and we lose sight of the Lord. We get so distracted that we forget that God is always with us. When that happens to you, take a moment to talk to the Lord, and see how much easier it is fighting your battle with the Lord on your side.

Truthfully, anxiety will arise within us at some point in our lives. The way we handle it determines the result. Trying to overcome anxiety with substitutes, such as illegal drugs that numb your senses, can lead to a worse result. Taking the time to talk to God and letting Him guide you through your troubles will reduce the storm within you. Without the Lord, it's like trying to put out a fire with gasoline. "So don't worry about tomorrow, for tomorrow will bring its own worries. Today's trouble is enough for today" (Matt. 6:34).

A good example of someone anxious in the Bible is Martha. One day when Jesus visited, Martha was so focused on getting everything prepared for Jesus that she didn't take time to listen to Him. She became angry with her sister, Mary, who was listening to Jesus instead of helping her with the preparations. Martha's worry pulled her attention away from what really mattered: Jesus.

I have struggled with anxiety and worry throughout my life. A good step to overcoming anxiety and worry is putting your trust in God and believing that He will take care of you. Pray about your anxious thoughts, and know that God hears you. He is working in your life, even if you don't see Him there. If you are feeling like you are trapped and the worries of tomorrow are overtaking you, go to God in prayer. Everything in this life happens in God's timing, and He has a plan.

Application for the Day: Today I will give my worries to God and let Him guide me through the storm.

Wednesday, August 21, 2024

Jesus and James

Ken Cargile

Today's Scripture: Matthew 5:1-2 - "Seeing the crowds, he went up on the mountain, and when he sat down, his disciples came to him. And he opened his mouth and taught them. . . ."

The Sermon on the Mount has long been regarded as one of the greatest collections of Jesus's teachings. While studying to teach a Bible class on James recently, I came across several similarities between James and the teachings of Jesus in Matthew. Here are some examples:

Matthew 5:11-12 - "Blessed are you when others revile you and persecute you and utter all kinds of evil against you falsely on my account. Rejoice and be glad, for your reward is great in heaven, for so they persecuted the prophets who were before you."

James 1:2 - "Count it all joy, my brothers, when you meet trials of various kinds, for you know that the testing of your faith produces steadfastness."

Matthew 7:21 - "Not everyone who says to me, 'Lord, Lord,' will enter the kingdom of heaven, but the one who does the will of my Father who is in heaven."

James 1:22 - "But be doers of the word, and not hearers only, deceiving yourselves."

Matthew 7:1 - "Judge not, that you be not judged."

James 4:12 - "There is only one lawgiver and judge, he who is able to save and to destroy. But who are you to judge your neighbor?"

Matthew 6:14-15 - "For if you forgive others their trespasses, your heavenly Father will also forgive you, but if you do not forgive others their trespasses, neither will your Father forgive your trespasses."

James 2:13 - "For judgment is without mercy to one who has shown no mercy. Mercy triumphs over judgment."

Other examples could be given, but these comparisons show that the Scriptures are consistent in their teachings. Both Jesus and James present a unified description of life under the New Covenant.

Application for Today: Today I will thank God for the consistency of Scripture and will try to pattern my life after its teachings.

Thursday, August 22, 2024

Go with God

Kerry Scruggs

Today's Scripture: Revelation 22:18-19

"I warn everyone who hears the words of the prophecy of this book: if anyone adds to them, God will add to him the plagues described in this book, and if anyone takes away from the words of the book of this prophecy, God will take away his share in the tree of life and in the holy city, which are described in this book."

When reading a passage, I ask myself two questions: What does God want us to learn about Him, and what do we learn about ourselves? Here, we learn that God wants us to keep His Word pure and untouched and that there are consequences if we change His Word. For readers, this passage shows that we can, and often do, change the words in the Bible to fit into our lives, to make things fit the way we want.

Revelation teaches us that God wants us to keep His Word the way it is. There are profound consequences if we change his Word. What are these consequences? According to verse 18, if we add to the Bible, as many have done, the plagues from Exodus will be added onto the person who adds to His Word. Verse 19 says that if we take away from His Word, our share and our place in the book of life (and therefore heaven) will be taken away.

Throughout the Bible, we are shown the love and protection that God offers, and we learn that God always keeps His promises. If we keep His Word, our reward is a home with Him forever.

But what are our consequences if we take away or add to His Word? The horrible plagues listed in the Bible, our share in the tree of life, and our share in heaven. But there is always hope! We can always repent, change our ways, and go with God.

Application for the Day: Today I will ask God to help me live a life true to His Word.

Friday, August 23, 2024

God's Love

Kerry Scruggs

Today's Scripture: Genesis 29:31-35

Have you ever felt unloved and completely alone? The story of Jacob, Leah, and Rachel is one crazy love triangle. Leah was forced to marry Jacob when it was Rachel and Jacob who were in love. Leah spent her marriage trying to get her husband to love and honor her. She felt completely and utterly unloved.

We do not know much about Leah from her story in Genesis. The things that we do know can tell us a lot about her. We know that her father worshiped idols, which leads us to believe that she did not initially know God. We follow her story and watch as she had children, yearning for her husband's love. Let's look at the names she gave her sons. Reuben means "behold, a son." Leah said that the Lord had seen her misery and had given her a son. Next is Simeon, which means "to hear." She said that the Lord heard that she was not loved. Third is Levi. His name means "joined." Leah believed that Jacob would join her because she had given him three sons. Her fourth son, she named Judah. This is where we see a change in Leah. When Leah named Judah she said, "This time I will praise the Lord" (Gen. 29:35). Leah's fourth son's name means "to praise God," reflecting her love of God. The names of Leah's first three sons showed how she longed for her husband to love her, but by her fourth son, she knew that God loved her and had blessed her.

When reading about Leah, some may think that she was the most unloved woman in the Bible. She may have been unloved by man, but she was dearly loved by God with pure, whole, and completely undefiled love. Jesus came from the tribe of Judah to save us, and there is no bigger love than that!

Application for the Day: Today, if I feel unloved, I will read my Bible to get to know God better, and I will ask Him to open my heart so that He can fill it with His love.

Monday, August 26, 2024

Home Sweet Home

Kerstin Galloway Shafer

Today's Scripture: Philippians 1:3-5

I had an assignment in high school to deliver a speech introducing myself, and, wanting to stretch my creative muscles, I wrote it as though I were a tour guide of my own life. Tour stops included my house, my favorite restaurant and store, and the church, which I described as my home away from home, because, at that time, I had spent a lot of my life in the church building. Since delivering that speech, that description has taken on a whole new meaning for me. When I went to college, I found myself missing not the building but the people. I missed the people who knew me by name, greeted me with a smile or a hug, and asked me about my life. I missed the surrogate grandfathers who shared peppermints and stories. I missed the surrogate grandmothers who shared recipes and wisdom. I missed the brothers and sisters with whom I shared memories and laughter. I missed the men and women who showed me how to sing and serve and study. I missed the community who celebrated with me and cried with me. I missed the family who showered me with prayers and support in my walk of life and, more importantly, my walk with Christ, and later, in my mission trips and my marriage.

There are many clichés about home. "Home is where the heart is." "There's no place like home." While there may be some truth to these statements, they often refer to home as a place, and I am convinced that home is not a place but a person or a people. The church, not the building, but the people, is our home away from our eternal home. One day, we will gather together around the throne, and we will smile and share stories and sing and celebrate again in our home, sweet home.

Application for the Day: Today, I will thank God for my home away from home and the hope of my forever home.

Tuesday, August 27, 2024

Wisdom and Wisteria

Kerstin Galloway Shafer

Today's Scripture: James 5:16

When my husband, Jacob, and I moved into our home, we inherited a wisteria plant. Wisteria is beautiful when it blooms bright purple in spring. However, it has fast-growing vines, aggressive roots, and requires seasonal pruning. Not knowing its power and the responsibility it requires, I let it grow. Then I started seeing vines growing out along the ground. I tried trimming them myself until I realized that this was not a one-person job. Those vines became woody roots that sent shoots along our house. The runners shot into our shrubs, wrapping around the base and blending in with branches, and the top vines stretched and began strangling the tree nearby. It was time to ask for help. Jacob and I worked together until we realized that this was not a one-day job. To this day we still struggle with this stubborn plant from time to time.

Our sin can be like that plant. It may start as something that looks harmless, beautiful even, but behind the beauty are those harmful habits that take root in our hearts. Unaware of the grip it has on us, we let it grow. Then we start seeing the effects of it creep and crawl into our lives. We try to tackle it on our own, until we realize, due to its nature, it is not a one-person job. Then we see it stretching and becoming stronger, and before we know it, it is not only affecting our own lives but also the lives of those around us and those we love. If this sounds familiar, it is time to ask for help. After doing the work of confessing and praying, we may realize that this is not a one-day job. But we don't have to struggle with that sin alone. We can find comfort in knowing that we have ALL sinned (Romans 3:23), AND we are justified by His grace (Romans 3:24-25).

Application for the Day: Today, I will ask for help in my struggle with sin, remembering my need for grace and giving grace as I have received.

Wednesday, August 28, 2024

Our Father in Heaven – Part 1

Kevin Turbeville

Today's Scripture: Exodus 20:1-6

I am Kevin, your brother, who wrote this devotional for today. There is almost assuredly another Kevin with whom you have a closer relationship. It is extremely likely that I am not the only Kevin you know. There is a very good chance that I am not your only brother. There is also a chance that this will not be the only devotional you read today. If you are keeping count, the only exclusive characteristic of our relationship thus far today is that I wrote these words down for this page in this book. If you believe what has been preserved in Scripture, then you know that the same cannot be said of Yahweh, God, who brought the Israelites out of the land of Egypt, from the house of slaves, before Whom Israel was to have no other.

There is only one Yahweh. This is likely the greatest problem humanity has with our Creator. We do not do well when asked to have only one of anything. Imagine going to the polls and having one candidate from which to choose or going to the grocery store only to find saltines and water. Had God been more open to the idea of sharing His space with at least one other, then more of humanity would be on board with the relationship He has purposed.

A very close second to our problem of one is that no created thing can come before this One. I am married to my God-ordained one. My wife and I are one flesh according to God. However, on the days I place her above Him, I know it, she knows it, and He knows it. While she and I might enjoy being in that number-one spot for a moment, it usually ends up with one or both of us feeling alone because neither of us was created to be there in that spot.

Application for the Day: Today I will ask my Father, who is in heaven, to grant me the willingness to be His creation, not the other way around.

Thursday, August 29, 2024

Hallowed Be Thy Name – Part 2

Kevin Turbeville

Today's Scripture: Exodus 20:7

In junior high school I wanted to do what John Fogerty did. My parents agreed to pay for guitar lessons at the music shop in downtown Dresden. After a couple of months of lessons and zero practice on my own, I decided to go back to wanting to do what Michael Jordan did. The money spent on those lessons, my parents' time in shuttling me back and forth, their encouragement and enthusiasm regarding my ill-fated venture, and the time slot my lessons consumed turned out to be in vain, except to learn that, honestly, I lacked the interest and longsuffering required to become John Fogerty.

I loved listening to Creedence Clearwater Revival. I would imagine being on stage, fans going wild, while I screamed "doo, doo, doo, lookin' out my back door" into the microphone. My buddies and I would ride down the road, pretending the cab of my pickup was a recording studio and we were in the middle of an audition. However, despite all the joy, camaraderie, and ambition CCR's music provided us, my faithfulness to that dream ultimately waned, considering the trial it would be to follow in John Fogerty's footsteps.

I am reminded of that whole season of life almost every time I hear CCR today. It is comical how fast and hot my passion for glory burned only to fizzle at the expectation of learning the three chords required to play every CCR song. Obviously, I was not the Creedence disciple I alleged to be.

This is probably the most harmless example of vain discipleship from my life. Vain discipleship that causes harm means a disciple has repented, turned to go in the opposite direction from the way his teacher is going. Who suffers when discipleship is in vain? The disciple suffers when he stops following a good teacher. The teacher suffers because He loved us enough to lead us in the first place.

Application for the Day: Today I will ask my Father, who is in heaven, to grant me the willingness to hallow His name, not the other way around.

174

Thy Kingdom Come, Thy Will Be Done On Earth As It Is In Heaven – Part 3

Kevin Turbeville

Today's Scripture: Exodus 20:8-11

Mema Jean Turbeville was my Memaw. Memaw and Pepaw's house is 6-T's Farm on Turbeville Road in Latham, Tennessee. During Memaw's lifetime, 6-T's Farm was a dairy and Belgian horse farm. Memaw revered education, especially grammar. She is responsible for everyone in our family pronouncing our last name "Tur-BE-ville," rather than sliding "Tur-buh-ville" lazily out of our mouths. She is why her four children, my sister and I, and a cousin who lived forty-five minutes away have any ability whatsoever to speak publicly.

In the fourth grade, I got off the school bus at her house after being introduced to 4-H one day. Per usual, she wanted to know what happened at school. I told her about the 4-H representative coming to school, how raising chickens and pigs and showing horses and cows sounded like fun but that I was going to pass on the public speaking contest. I did not raise one chicken, nor did I show a single cow, but by the time I graduated from high school, I had given about fifty speeches. Memaw formed me according to her will at least as much as my parents did theirs.

In May of 1999, my senior year of high school, Memaw lost her skirmish with cancer but realized her victory over death and the grave. I was not there at her passing. I went to see her in the hospital only once. The same is true when she came home under hospice care. I was at her funeral service for about two hours. To say I did not honor her in that season is an understatement. As an eighteen-year-old, I was entirely too consumed "doing my thing" to have to remember the life she poured into me.

Application for the Day: Today I will ask my Father, who is in heaven, to grant me the willingness to hallow His name, serve His kingdom, and pursue His will, under His reign wherever He reigns, not the other way around.

Monday, September 2, 2024

Give Us This Day Our Daily Bread – Part 4

Kevin Turbeville

Today's Scripture: Exodus 20:12

Our word create originally comes from the ancient term ker-, which means "to grow." This same term was used to create words like accrue, cereal, creature, recruit, and sincere. I find the creation of language fascinating because at some point someone somewhere needed to convey a concept for which there was no word, so that person sat down and drew on what was available to produce a single word describing a person, place, or thing which beforehand likely required at least a sentence, if not an entire paragraph.

One of the most intriguing words ever created was the name God gave Himself when Moses asked who he was supposed to tell Pharaoh had sent him to demand the release of the Israelites from slavery. God simply told Moses to inform Pharaoh he had been sent by "I AM." In essence, God wanted Pharaoh to know that Pharaoh's will began and ended with his Creator.

Almost every day my eyes open from a rest that has prepared my physical body for the tasks that lie ahead of me, and I take a deep breath of oxygen which has involuntarily passed into my body through the night without thinking. Not only did I not consciously decide to wake up or breathe all night long, but I did not even choose to be a part of this human economy. My parents did that for me. I merely serve at the pleasure of the I AM in His economy. Some days I manage to squeeze in a thank you for all of this before my feet hit the floor and I make my way to the kitchen to prepare the bread for which I exchanged a few sheets of cotton at the grocery store.

Application for the Day: Today I will ask my Father, who is in heaven, to grant me the willingness to hallow His name, serve His kingdom, and pursue His will, under His reign wherever He reigns, in faith that all is His to give and take away, not the other way around.

Tuesday, September 3, 2024

Forgive Us and Deliver Us – Part 5
Kevin Turbeville

Today's Scripture: Exodus 20:13-17

To what extent is grace to be extended? The extent to which I wish to receive this same grace. Unfortunately, I often read the "Thou shalt nots" and think, "That's right! Y'ALL shalt not!" Most of the time I make up my own "Thou shalt nots" and apply them arbitrarily as I move throughout my day, depending on whether the person or task in front of me is of personal interest.

This is most evident behind the wheel of my car here in Dickson. I live downtown. I have lived downtown for five years. I know the lane shifts, speed limits, and one-way streets. So not only do I know what I am supposed to do behind the wheel, but I know what you are supposed to be doing also. For example, since I spend 99.999% of my week traveling the same path I've traveled for the past five years, I know that the westbound right lane on College Street in Dickson ends at the middle school, so the mindful thing to do is to be in the left lane before getting to the middle school.

I try to make this point with everyone traveling this route anytime I see the driver in error, except when I am trying to impress my wife by how early I've made it home from work or the traffic at the light on Hwy. 46 is too much for me and that right lane is wide open. When these situations arise, I use the right lane to speed past the other cars and cut sharply into the left lane right before the stop sign in front of the middle school, but anyone else doing this should have his license revoked.

Application for the Day: Today I will ask my Father, who is in heaven, to grant me the willingness to hallow His name, serve His kingdom, and pursue His will under His reign wherever He reigns, in faith that all is His to give and take away. All grace is His, not the other way around.

Wednesday, September 4, 2024

Are We Listening?

Kyle Dickerson

Today's Scripture: Mark 1:35

Ever asked someone something and really not stuck around (metaphorically) to hear the answer? Listening is a skill most of us would like to think we pull off well, but reality is probably closer to selective hearing. When we come before God, seeking His counsel, it is imperative that we stick around for what He has to say. I wonder how many times I have missed His answer and guidance because I was not listening. Sometimes it is because the mood-boosting jolt of having asked for help is enough to stave off the feeling of uncertainty that pushed me there—I can be honest about that. Sometimes it's because I desire His counsel, but I am unwilling to let go of the illusion that I can fix it on my own. And through all of it, it is because I have failed to stop and be silent before Him.

Scripture speaks to us from Genesis through Revelation regarding the power of quieting the mind, being silent, and removing distractions. Even Jesus gave the example of retreating to a place without distraction. Mark 1:35 and Luke 5:16 describe this in quite literal terms. Still, it is no newsflash that we can be physically alone and still completely distracted with the noise of life. Our schedules run through our heads, our phones ding, stress pulls our minds back to work, and the list goes on.

I won't be so bold as to suggest I have the answer to how we do this, but I will suggest that God gives us a playbook to follow, and that's where it seems we should start, spending time reading the Word of God and listening for what He tells us through it. It is our charge to search our hearts and come before the Lord with honesty and prayers of humility and to strive to be silent and listen for His reply.

Application for the Day: Today I will strive to limit the distractions I have control over, make room for God's voice to be heard in my life, and pray for wisdom in seeking His will.

Thursday, September 5, 2024

Be All About It

Kyle Dickerson

Today's Scripture: James 1:22

"So, you know this is going to kill you, but you're going to do it regardless?" Smoke hung heavily in the air as the man gave a nod of confirmation. He had been consuming tobacco at record rates his entire adult life, could repeat every word of why that was not a great idea, but openly professed that he had no intention of changing the habit. Might it be that he had the knowledge, but lacked belief in what he knew, which would otherwise lead him to action?

James, in his writing to the scattered tribes, talked about many things, and one concept that hits at the heart of them all is that the Word cannot simply be heard, but must be put into action. There is a time for taking in the teachings and building a base of knowledge, but if that is where we stop, James tells us we are deceiving ourselves.

Being able to search and discern the application to our lives so that we might act upon that knowledge is paramount. James goes on to say that acting, along with "doing" with what we "know," leads to blessing. Keep in mind that the audience he was speaking to saw and knew the law and placed great value on the outward appearance of checking the boxes. Part of their charge to put the Word into action involved their hearts.

Our relationship with Jesus takes on a different look when our hearts become involved. It is the idea that the knowledge we have spent time acquiring becomes more than trivia answers, but instead comes forth as an expression of faith because it is foundationally believed to be true. There is an outward expression that others see, experience, and benefit from, but there is an internal matter of the heart that alters how we interact with the Word and Spirit and how our motivations drive our behavior.

Application of the Day: Today I will pray for wisdom and discernment in understanding the application of the Word for my life and the courage to put the Word into action in truth.

Pour Freely

Kyle Dickerson

Today's Scripture: 1 Timothy 1:14

"There is no possible way I can pay that." Grad school was a few months away, and that charge on that young man's account was a big hurdle standing in his path. It's not important what brought him to that moment, but rather that he found himself in need of mercy and grace, and he knew the people from whom he needed it were the very ones who had no obligation to give it. Our existence as sinners in this world places us at the feet of Christ, also seeking undeserved mercy and grace and needing it from the perfect Savior whom our sins wound.

Paul gives testimony in 1 Timothy 1:13-15 to the magnitude of the Lord's grace, referring to it as "abundant." He proclaims that he was shown mercy even though he professed that he was the worst of sinners. And is that not the essence of Christ—the pouring out of mercy and grace so that ALL might know the Father and receive the gift of salvation? Paul professed to believe that one of the reasons his life was used to reveal the mercy and patience of Jesus was the result of the sin in which he had lived.

His point is that if God would send Jesus and if Jesus would abundantly cover him in grace and mercy, even during his sin, why would He not do the same for everyone who would believe in Him? That is a powerful reminder of the value we have in our Lord and His desire that we should all be saved and not be held by the bonds of sin and death, even a death that our lives suggest we deserve. May we let our choices in those moments where our compassion is needed by others reflect the example of mercy and grace that has been poured out upon us.

Application for the Day: Today I will pray for wisdom to see the moments when I can offer grace and mercy to those around me and strive to express my gratitude for the gift of the same from our Lord.

Monday, September 9, 2024

Pray in Faith

Kyle Dickerson

Today's Scripture: Romans 8:26

"The answer may be packing up everything you own and moving halfway around the world. You ready for that?" Those were the words my friend so boldly and lovingly said as we stood on the side of Ring Road in Kathmandu. We were waiting for our Tandoori chicken order, and the conversation drifted to life, family, careers, and God's will. Proudly I boasted I had been praying vulnerably that God's will be done (specifically for the next step in my career), rather than mine, and that I was willing to follow His plan regardless of where or what that meant. My friend was driving the point of whether I was praying that from the heart or if I was just running over some words that sounded good in concept. In truth, that's a scary prayer to offer up.

We have this illusion of having control over our lives, so acknowledging that we do not—and actively asking God to do His thing—is a place of honest vulnerability that can be very uncomfortable when we first encounter it. But are we not called to that—laying down of ourselves and walking in trusting faith that He is the Almighty? Romans 8:26 tells us that the Holy Spirit intercedes on our behalf, even when we are unsure of what to pray. Then, in Matthew 21:22, we are told that our prayers will be heard and answered—if we pray in faith.

It seems that points to honesty in prayer, which calls us to vulnerability, because how can we submit ourselves to the Lord through prayer if we are being reserved in our faith or deceptive in our motives? We are often frightened by the idea of full release of control because we understand at some level that His will may not lead us where our plans would prefer. Yet His will is perfect, and in faith we can fully trust His love for us, His provision, and the future He has uniquely crafted for each of us.

Application for the Day: Today I will strive to pray with raw and honest vulnerability.

Tuesday, September 10, 2024

Heartburn

Written by Larry Snow
Published Here In His Loving Memory (March 3, 1954 – February 12, 2022)

Today's Scripture: Luke 24:32

Consider the subject of "fire." A fast-food restaurant sign advertised that the burgers there were "fire grilled" and that the "fire" was ready. That was good because I was hungry. Fortunately, I didn't get heartburn.

On the surface of the sun was a solar flare. Possibly it would damage satellites or interrupt radio and TV transmission, and those flying at high altitude might receive radiation equal to a chest x-ray. I didn't need an x-ray, so I was glad I wasn't flying that week. No heartburn either!

Who could miss the wildfires in California reminding us of the power of uncontrolled fire? The media has shown us what fire, wind, and fuel can do. These events testify to the devastation of these powerful forces. Lives are lost and property is destroyed. The power of fire can be devastating. While there is heartache, there is no heartburn.

As I thought about fire, I reflected on fire in the Bible. Fire was used to give answers and as an instrument of judgment, as a purifier, and as a symbol of divine presence. In fact, some of the most important commandments given by God concerned the fire that burned upon the altar in the tabernacle.

When the tabernacle was dedicated, the Lord sent special fire from heaven, and thereafter the priests were to keep it burning. Not only is there a special inference to those in ministry, but to every Christian as well.
> 1. Luke 12: 49 - "I have come to bring fire on the earth, and how I wish it were already kindled." The fire Jesus is referring to is the gospel. The preaching of the word would bring pain, sorrow, and division, as well as joy, peace, and salvation.
> 2. Luke 24:32 - "Were not our hearts burning within us while he talked with us. . . .?" If you don't have heartburn, you have a problem. You need to re-light the fire, prepare the fuel, and fan the flame.

Application for Today: Today I will have HEARTBURN. I can't live without it.

Wednesday, September 11, 2024

Two Promises

Lisa Cooper

Today's Scripture: Isaiah 41:10 - "Fear not, for I am with you; be not dismayed, for I am your God; I will strengthen you, I will help you, I will uphold you with My righteous right hand."

"Why did this happen to me?" Often after a tragedy, these words will be expressed by those who suffer loss. While we cannot know why everything happens, we can find comfort in our Heavenly Father. He does not promise to protect us from all harm, but He does make two amazing promises to us:

1. He will be with us.
2. He will give us the strength to endure.

These two promises from God are evidenced in Scripture through the life of King David. David suffered the loss of an infant son and the death of a rebellious adult son. Although he was a man after God's own heart (1 Sam. 13:14), God did not protect David from the devastating loss of his children. He was with David, and He provided him with the strength to live with his grief and endure through all the trials that beset him (2 Sam. 22:2-3). David said, "Even though I walk through the valley of the shadow of death, I will fear no evil, for you are with me" (Psa. 23:4a).

We will face troubles in this life—perhaps financial losses, divorce, addiction, health problems, death of loved ones. But God is with us. He loves us through those difficult times, and He will give us the strength to endure. We can be uplifted by knowing that David endured after devastating losses and that he continued to look to God for guidance. Indeed, David's first act after the death of his infant son was to cleanse and anoint himself, and then he proceeded to go into the house of the Lord and worship Him (2 Sam. 12:20).

Application for the Day: Today I will pray to God and thank Him for His continual presence and the strength He gives me to endure the hardships I face.

Thursday, September 12, 2024

Not of This World

Mark Gooch

Today's Scripture: John 17:9-15

Do you believe that God is actively working in the world today? Or, better yet, do you believe that God is actively working in your life today? Many believe in God, but as far as His involvement with man is concerned, some people believe that God created the earth and all that is in it, got the ball rolling, and then stepped back to see what happened. The Bible is clear in its teaching that God is, always has been, and will continue to be with us as we journey through this world.

In John 17, Jesus prayed that His followers would remain in Him. He prayed specifically for their protection from the evil one as we remain in the world.

> 9 "I pray for them. I do not pray for the world but for those whom You have given Me, for they are Yours. 10 And all Mine are Yours, and Yours are Mine, and I am glorified in them. 11 Now I am no longer in the world, but these are in the world, and I come to You. Holy Father, keep through Your name those whom You have given Me, that they may be one as We are. 12 While I was with them in the world, I kept them in Your name. Those whom You gave Me I have kept; and none of them is lost except the son of perdition, that the Scripture might be fulfilled. 13 But now I come to You, and these things I speak in the world, that they may have My joy fulfilled in themselves. 14 I have given them Your word; and the world has hated them because they are not of the world, just as I am not of the world. 15 I do not pray that You should take them out of the world, but that You should keep them from the evil one.

Application for the Day: Today I will remember that I am in this world, but I am not of this world.

Friday, September 13, 2024

Submission Honors God

Mark Holland

Today's Scripture: 1 Peter 2:13-16

" Be subject for the Lord's sake to every human institution, whether it be to the emperor as supreme, or to governors as sent by him to punish those who do evil and to praise those who do good. For this is the will of God, that by doing good you should put to silence the ignorance of foolish people. Live as people who are free, not using your freedom as a cover-up for evil, but living as servants of God."

Have you ever been told to do something with which you completely disagreed? I must admit that I have not always wanted to do what I was told. When I was a young man, I remember hearing about a new rule at work. I am ashamed of the attitude I had when reading about it on our bulletin board. I said to myself, "I am not going to do that." Again, it was not my best day. I realize now (and, really, I did the day I read it) that my employer had every right to require me to do what he wanted. It was not unreasonable, and it was best for our company. Looking back, I know it was best for me.

No matter how old you are, you do not always agree with what you are told to do. I was taught from a young age that if you are not being told to break God's will, then you should follow the laws created by those who are placed over you. Hopefully, they have our best interests in mind when making laws. We should always be prayerful for those in decision-making positions. Submission is not an easy thing. Submission is not a popular thing. But to Christians it is a wonderful privilege and opportunity to bring glory to our Father in heaven.

Application for Today: Today I will give thought to where I should submit to God and to those in authority over me to bring glory to Him.

Monday, September 16, 2024

Faith Is Our Victory

Mary Beth Peery

Today's Scripture: Hebrews 11:1

Faith is a common theme throughout the Bible. We are told of the great faith in the Old Testament shown by men such as Noah, Abraham, David, and Daniel.

We all struggle with various situations in our daily lives. Remember Mark 5:28: the woman with a twelve-year-long health issue. By faith she was healed when she touched Jesus' cloak. She was hurting, and all she had to offer was faith. The same can be said of us. We have nothing to offer but our hurts and faith.

Deaths, illness, family problems, betrayals, and job loss—the list is endless. Who can we turn to but to the Lord? Faith is a choice to believe that God will send healing powers in times of our deepest needs. He alone can pull us out of the despair, hurt, and pain. God may not always do what we want when we expect it. Faith is believing that God will do what is right for us when the time is right. Faith is believing that God is real and that God is good all the time. Recall Paul in the jail cell. He had nothing to offer, but he had kept the faith. Faith is trusting what the eyes can't see. When we come home at night, we turn on the lights. We can't see the electricity, but it is there. If we turn on a computer, TV, or phone, we can't see the signals being sent, but they are there. We assume it's all working. Do we assume that everything is working as it should on a daily basis and that God is looking over us?

Through daily struggles, pray for God to use these opportunities to help you grow a more committed faith. Pray for the grace to see God moving in your life to strengthen your personal relationship with Him.

One of my favorite hymns is "Faith is the Victory." It ends with "Oh glorious victory that overcomes the world."

Application for the Day: Today I will pray for a greater faith to strengthen me to overcome the world.

Tuesday, September 17, 2024

In the Subtle

Meagan Spencer

Today's Scripture: I Kings 19

How do we keep a pure mind when we are in distress and loss of hope?

In I Kings 19, we find Elijah fleeing to escape the death raid of Jezebel (19:3). While fleeing, he became weary and hopeless and quite frankly "edgy" in his hunger and fatigue, like many of us get in our "hangryness." Elijah still had purity of mind because he wanted to be with God and even asked God to take him in death. "But he himself went a day's journey into the wilderness, and came and sat down under a broom tree. And he prayed that he might die, and said, 'It is enough! Now, Lord, take my life, for I am no better than my fathers!'" (19:4).

But God wanted to make the point with Elijah that He is present in the subtle, not necessarily the extravagant. So what did God do? He had an angel to tell Elijah twice to eat something (19:5-8). Pretty simple, pretty subtle. Then Elijah asked God to show Himself, and a series of geological events occurred, such as an earthquake and a fire, all demonstrating God's might (19:9-12a). However, God chose not to show up in those demonstrations, but rather to show up in a whisper, in the subtle: "And after the earthquake a fire, but the Lord was not in the fire; and after the fire a still small voice. So it was, when Elijah heard it, that he wrapped his face in his mantle and went out and stood in the entrance of the cave. Suddenly a voice came to him" (19:12-13a). God appeared to and spoke with Elijah in that still small voice. Purity of mind often needs reflection to look at and see all the little, subtle ways in which God reveals His presence. Are we reflecting on the subtle?

Application for the Day: Today I will take five to ten minutes of reflective meditation to find the small whispers of God's presence.

Wednesday, September 18, 2024

Our Calling to Live Blamelessly Through Christ

Meagan Spencer

Today's Scripture: 1 John 3

"For this is the message that you heard from the beginning, that we should love one another.... We know that we have passed from death to life, because we love the brethren. He who does not love his brother abides in death" (1 John 3:11,14).

Who is our brother or sister? As Jesus walked the earth, we can easily see His inclusive nature of invitation. Jesus invited and continues to invite all into His fold (John 14:1-4). Now the action of accepting a relationship is exclusive because one ultimately must make a choice regarding whom he is going to serve. But the invitation to consider is very inclusive: "For God so loved the world that He gave His only begotten Son, that whoever believes in Him should not perish but have everlasting life" (John 3:16).

How does our purity show our love for others? We are to keep our eyes open to the needs of others and blamelessly serve such that we are free from condemnation: "Beloved, if our heart does not condemn us, we have confidence toward God" (1 John 3:21). Thus, we can be pleasing to the Father. We all suffer through different trials in life, we all have varying experiences, and we all have unique personalities. But, despite our differences, we are all called to the same thing: to love God and love others in purity. "And this is His commandment; that we should believe on the name of His Son Jesus Christ and love one another, as He gave us commandment" (1 John 3:23). How does loving God and loving others change how we live?

Application for the Day: Today I will think of how I can seek others outside of my friend and family group in inclusivity.

Thursday, September 19, 2024

Search Me, God, and Know My Heart

Meagan Spencer

Today's Scriptures: Psalm 139; Psalm 51

How do we feel about the reality of God's knowing our every thought? What emotions run through that thought? Guilt? Grief? Embarrassment? Yet in Psalms, we find David singing to God such that he wants God to search out his heart for the sake of making him pure so that God can better lead him. "O Lord, You have searched me and known me. . . . For there is not a word on my tongue, but behold, O Lord, You know it altogether" (Psalm 139:1,4). "Search me, O God, and know my heart; try me, and know my anxieties; and see if there is any wicked way in me" (Psalm 139:23-24a). We often see emotion as one-sided humanness, but God is an emotional being as well. He gets hurt, angry, grieved, and joyful by our thoughts and actions towards others and ourselves.

Psalms is a beautiful journey into what building a relationship with God in pureness of mind looks like. David messes up, is victorious, is grieved, and experiences a whole range of emotions, and he comes to God in Psalms to talk with Him. "Have mercy upon me, O God, according to Your lovingkindness, according to the multitude of Your tender mercies, blot out my transgressions. . . . For I acknowledge my transgressions, and my sin is always before me. . . . Create in me a clean heart, O God, and renew a steadfast spirit within me" (Psalm 51:1,3,10). Isn't the first step in building a relationship to talk? We can be reverent to God with pureness of mind and bring our emotions to Him at the same time when we ask God to search us out.

Application for the Day: Today I will start building a better relationship with God by speaking with Him through my emotions and understanding that He feels emotion too.

Friday, September 20, 2024

The Woman and the Oil

Meagan Spencer

Today's Scripture: John 12:1–8

Six days before the Passover, Jesus went to the house of Mary, Martha, and Lazarus. While there, in an elaborate display of love and respect for Jesus, Mary did something amazing. "Then Mary took a pound of very costly oil of spikenard, anointed the feet of Jesus, and wiped his feet with her hair. And the house was filled with the fragrance of the oil" (John 12:3). The disciples looked on and were appalled! What a waste of something so valuable! In fact, Judas said, "Why was this fragrant oil not sold for three hundred denarii and given for the poor" (John 12:5). John referred to Judas as a thief and stated that he had been stealing money from their money box. However, Jesus stopped to spend a moment explaining the humility of the situation. "Let her alone; she has kept this for the day of My burial. For the poor you have with you always, but Me you do not have always" (John 12:7). He praised the purity of mind that led Mary to anoint him. She had her eyes on the Savior and could only consider Him how much she Jesus had done for her. There are many other parallels of this moment in scripture that perhaps Jesus hoped HIs disciples would reflect upon and pick up on.

Mary wanted to be in Jesus' presence so much that in purity of mind she used the most expensive thing that she had to anoint Him. Consider how we need to constantly remember the purity to which we are called and that we should put ourselves in the Mary's shoes as we seek to be pure again through the sacrificial blood of Christ. Even after our baptism, we will make mistakes, but are we coming back to the purity of the grace of Jesus?

Application for the Day: Today, I will take a few minutes to reflect on my baptism into Christ or my need to humble myself before Him and be baptized into Him.

Monday, September 23, 2024

Whatever Is Pure

Meagan Spencer

Today's Scripture: Genesis 3:6; Romans 6:23

In the beginning there was grace…

How do we understand right from wrong? As we go back to Genesis, we read the story of the first humans, Adam and Eve, and get an understanding of what they knew about right and wrong and how it connects to God's instruction. Genesis 3:6 states, "So when the woman saw that the tree was good for food, that it was pleasant to the eyes, and a tree desirable to make one wise, she took of its fruit and ate. She also gave to her husband with her, and he ate." So why do we have this concept of sin? Sin resulted from their disobeying God. God holds true to His word and is not going to go against Himself, so something had to be done. In Romans 6:23a, we see the link to this payment of sin: "For the wages of sin is death." However, we have a gracious God, who, while keeping to His word, made another way—the sacrifice of Jesus—to be that payment. The rest of verse 23 states, "But the gift of God is eternal life in Christ Jesus our Lord."

What caused Adam and Eve to go through with this temptation? They were not thinking of staying pure, but were thinking of their own desires. Purity as discussed in the Bible is mindfulness and dedication towards God, putting God first above self. We are inevitably human and are going to sin, but where does our heart go when these things happen? Is our heart pure? Does it go back to God and His grace, or do we give up and give in to self?

Application for the Day: Today I will think on things that are pure by going to God when I make mistakes.

Tuesday, September 24, 2024

God Goals
Megan Lampley

Today's Scripture: Luke 9:24

As a college student, I spend a lot of time thinking about my future. I imagine the way I will develop into the person I want to be due to the work I have done and the decisions I have made. Some days this vision includes a successful job, sometimes a new town, sometimes the ability to buy two hundred dollars' worth of groceries in one trip.

While I don't believe that these aspirations are inherently sinful, I always wonder who I am following in these moments. Why do I want the things that I want? The things I desire are not wrong, but my motivation is tainted. This is where Luke 9:24 speaks loudly to me: "For whoever desires to save his life will lose it, but whoever loses his life for My sake will save it."

Every goal I set for my life is due to some standard I have set for myself. I want to be someone other people respect and the type of person I would look up to. But to follow Jesus, I need to shift my entire mindset. I need to make decisions, not through the lens of my own desires, but through what I know about God. Then, with a heart focused on God, I can consider my wants. I must let go of (lose) the life I have dreamed of so I can follow Jesus' plans for me.

I think anyone can benefit from taking time to consider what is driving them to make a specific choice—from deciding what job to take to choosing where to spend their disposable income on a Saturday. In situations where sin does not seem to be relevant, do you continue to keep God at the forefront of your mind? We must let go of the life that we can sometimes idolize in pursuit of allowing God to lead our lives in every way.

Application for Today: Today I will let God lead my vision and goal for my life, trusting that He has a plan that is above my human understanding.

Wednesday, September 25, 2024

God's Special People

Pat Berry

Today's Scripture: Deut.26:16,18a – "This day the Lord your God commands you to observe these statutes and judgments; therefore you shall be careful to observe them with all your heart and with all your soul. . . . Also today the Lord proclaimed you to be His special people just as He promised you."

After the Israelites were told that they were God's special people, Moses and the Levite priests told them that they must do everything that God told them to do. Moses told them that, after they crossed the Jordan River, they would be told the blessings and curses. The blessings would be received by those who obeyed the laws, and many curses would go to the disobedient.

Moses refocused on the promise to Abraham, Isaac, and Jacob of a land filled with many good things. The Lord told Moses to go up on Mount Nebo to view the Land of Canaan that God was giving the Israelites. He told Moses that he would die on that mountain. He was allowed to see the land, but he couldn't go in because of his disobedience: breaking the stones containing the 10 commandments and striking the rock instead of speaking to it in the miracle to produce water.

The Israelites mourned for thirty days. Israel never had another prophet like Moses. The Lord knew him face to face. In Egypt Moses had done powerful miracles for Pharoah, as well as all his officers and the Egyptian people, to see. No other prophet did as many amazing things as Moses did.

Joshua (who, along with Caleb, gave a positive report when they were sent to spy out the Promised Land) was chosen by Moses to take his place. Moses told Joshua: "Be strong and of good courage, for you must go with this people to the land which the Lord has sworn to their fathers" (Deut. 31:7).

Application for the Day: Today I will remember that Christians are God's special people and that if we are sacrificial with our time, our talents, our money, and our love for each other, we can inherit our eternal home.

Thursday, September 26, 2024

Jesus, Lamb of God

Pat Berry

Today's Scripture: Hebrews 5:8-10

In this Scripture we read, "Though He was a Son, yet He learned obedience by the things which He suffered. And having been perfected, He became the author of eternal salvation to all who obey Him, called by God as High Priest 'according to the order of Melchizedek.'"

Perhaps sacrifices started because of man's instinct to be aware of his sins and his desire to restore communion with God. Moses gave his brother Aaron and his sons the huge task of making certain that sacrifices would be handled correctly. Over and over the Jews were told that the lambs that were offered must be perfect---no blemishes, no illnesses, etc. They were told to offer the very best that they had.

God always had planned to sacrifice His only son as a sin offering for the world. The Apostle Paul, in 2 Corinthians 5:21 says, "For He made Him who had no sin to be sin for us that we might become the righteousness of God in Him." Jesus became God's sacrificial lamb. He abandoned His heavenly home, took up residence in a physical human body, and lived a sinlessly perfect life! "For we do not have a High Priest who cannot sympathize with our weaknesses, but was in all points tempted as we are, yet without sin" (Hebrews 4:15).Thus, only He was qualified to be the perfect lamb of God.

Twila Paris wrote, "Your only Son no sin to hide, But You have sent Him from Your side, To walk upon this guilty sod And to become the Lamb of God. Your gift of love they crucified, They laughed and scorned Him as He died, The humble King they named a fraud And sacrificed the Lamb of God. O Lamb of God, sweet Lamb of God, I love the holy Lamb of God. O wash me in His precious blood, My Jesus Christ, the Lamb of God."

Application for Today: Today I will "not forget to do good and to share, for with such sacrifices God is well pleased" (Heb. 13:16).

Friday, September 27, 2024

King of Kings, Lord of Lords

Pat Berry

Today's Scripture: Revelations 19:16

In 1953 the world was enthralled by the coronation of a new monarch in England. It was an unusual event because a woman in her twenties was becoming Queen of England. Queen Elizabeth reigned for <u>seventy years</u>. At her death in 2023 the increased ability of newspapers and television to report events made it possible for many millions to focus on the Queen's funeral. Shortly after, the British Empire held the attention of the world when Queen Elizabeth's son, Charles, became King Charles. The coronation was awesome with the millions in attendance, the huge number of soldiers on well trained horses, musicians in perfect harmony, etc. It was inspiring to see hordes of citizens who walked many miles to honor their King. The gold on carriages, crowns and in the cathedral spoke loudly of the wealth of the Kingdom. The possession of many castles was another indication of wealth.

We are part of God's Kingdom, but there are a lot of contrasts with earthly kingdoms. Our King was born in a stable because there was no room in the inn. He said of Himself, "I have no place to lay my head." He had no desire to accumulate wealth, but He used His time to heal the sick, feed the hungry, and provide the way for His people to obtain forgiveness of sins. Mark 16:14-16 states, "And He said to them, 'Go into all the world and preach the gospel to every creature. He who believes and is baptized will be saved: but he who does not believe will be condemned.'" Those who are saved will get to live forever with the King. One of our responsibilities to our King is to share His message of salvation! We can do so by financially to support our missionaries. We can also send the gospel by giving to World Christian Broadcasting who delivers the gospel message in many languages to millions every day.

Application for the Day: I will pray for missionaries and consider financially supporting the sending of the King's message to the world.

Monday, September 30, 2024

I Am on the Lord's Side!

Patty Givens

Today's Scripture: Judges 7

Do you ever wonder if God is on your side? The question we ought to be asking ourselves is, "Are we on God's side?"

In Judges 7:9-15, the Bible tells us about a man named Gideon and his interaction with God. God asked Gideon to lead a fight against the Midianites. He agreed to go into battle against the enemy, although he had doubts like many do today. Gideon had faith that God would be with him; however, he wondered if that was enough.

Gideon rounded up his army of only 300 men. He gave them each a trumpet, a pitcher, and a torch. The scripture tells us that the Midianites were lying in the valley as numerous as locusts. The Midianite army had swords. I love how God gave Gideon's men pitchers, torches, and trumpets to fight with, then gave the enemy dangerous weapons. The Israelites surrounded the camp. They broke the pitchers and shouted. They held the trumpets in their left hands and blew them with gusto. The Midianites ran and cried out as they fled. The Lord caused them to turn on themselves with their own swords. Judges 7: 14b states, "Into his hand God has delivered Midian and the whole camp." God promised Gideon that He would deliver the Midianites into his hands, and that is exactly what happened.

According to the Bible, we do not need a real sword to do God's will. We simply need the full armor of God. Ephesians 6: 13-17 explains that to defeat our adversary, the devil, we need the helmet of salvation, the breastplate of righteousness, the shield of faith, the belt of truth buckled around our waist, the sword of the spirit (the Word of God), and the gospel of peace strapped on our feet so that we can spread the gospel.

Application for the Day: Today I will have faith in my Creator, knowing that God, who led the battle against the Midianites, is the same God I serve today.

Tuesday, October 1, 2024

Valley of Tears

Peggy Berry

Today's Scripture: Ecclesiastes 3:4

The writer of the book of Ecclesiastes said that there is "a time to weep, and a time to laugh; a time to mourn, and a time to dance."

Of all the creatures created by God, only man can laugh and cry. The animals were not formed with these abilities. We are made in the image of God, and the ability of our hearts to be touched, to feel sorrow, is a part of our kinship to God.

Often, laughter and tears speak better than words. The sound of weeping spreads over the earth—weeping of saints and sinners, the rich and the poor, the young and the old. How terrible it would be if we could not cry! We know that tears serve good purposes, or God would not have created us with this ability.

Since the COVID-19 pandemic was brought into our country, we have lost many family members and friends. Social distancing required many changes in the normal order of our lives. Church attendance was deemed impossible for months. Families were told to refrain from getting together. Masks were required to be worn to prevent the transmission of the virus. Funerals were attended by only the family members. Many tears have been and are still being shed due to the pandemic.

Many examples of weeping are found in the Bible. In biblical times people wept because of fear, pain, guilt, sorrow, persecution, love, etc.

- Exodus 2:6 – "And behold, the baby [Moses] wept."
- Job 16:16 – "My [Job] face is flushed from weeping."
- Matthew 26:75 – "So he [Peter] went out and wept bitterly."
- Psalm 6:6 – "I [David] drench my couch with my tears."
- Acts 20:19 – [Paul] "serving the Lord with all humility, with many tears."
- Isaiah 38:3 – "And Hezekiah wept bitterly."
- Genesis 43:30 – "And he [Joseph] went into his chamber and wept there."
- John 11:35 – "Jesus wept."

Application for Today: Today I will remember that there is victory in tears. John wrote in Revelation 7:17, "And God will wipe away every tear."

Wednesday, October 2, 2024

Gemstones

Rachel Corlew

Today's Scripture: 1 John 1:7

A few years ago, Joe and I thought we would go out West during fall break. But just saying "somewhere out West" hardly narrowed down the destination! Needing to decide soon, we said, "Let's just pick the place with the cheapest flight." And that year it was Portland, Oregon.

Part of the itinerary for this trip was to drive a stretch of road on the Pacific Ocean where we could stop for some scenic beach walks. I envisioned picking up a few seashells to bring home like on other vacations. On our first stop to put our feet in the Pacific, I was stunned by not seeing any seashells, not even one! I was surprised, but not disappointed, because the beach was scattered with palm-sized stones of jewel-toned colors, gorgeous colors only God could create—deep royal blues, shades of aquas, reds, coral oranges, emerald greens, and gleaming stones of speckled black and white. Of course, I took pictures, but pictures were not necessary to remember such breathtaking beauty at our feet.

I hurried to pick up at least one of every color and wondered why no one else was out there, beating me to this treasure of color. When I stopped to check my jacket pockets, to be sure I had a good representation of all that beauty, I discovered that when the stones were dry, they no longer held the luster they had in the wash of the Pacific waters. Apart from their constant cleansing in the surf, they were no longer beautiful, just rocks. I returned them all to the sand, to the water they needed to stay beautiful.

I thought about how we constantly need the washing of Jesus's blood to stay beautiful in God's sight, to remain lustrous in this world. 1 John 1:7 says, "But if we walk in the light as He is in the light, we have fellowship with one another, and the blood of Jesus Christ His Son cleanses us from all sin."

Application for Today: Today I will walk in the light, singing "O Thou Fount of Every Blessing."

Thursday, October 3, 2024

Lessons from a Tree
Rachel Hedge

Today's Scripture: Jeremiah 17:7-8

Why are we so drawn to trees? As we have added decorations to our home over the years, we have unintentionally chosen trees as our theme. From paintings to metal wall art, we have accumulated trees in the living room, dining area, kitchen, and hallway. You can also look out of the windows in any direction, and guess what you will see? That's right—trees! While we may simply enjoy the way they look, I believe we have many lessons to learn from trees.

Trees never stop growing outward and upward. Their roots continue to spread underground, anchoring them to the earth and seeking nourishment while their branches reach up higher to the heavens each year. Trees provide many precious services and commodities, such as shelter from rain and food in the form of fruits, seeds, and leaves. They provide clean fresh air and shade from the hot sun. They encounter many seasons and storms but stand firm and endure. They change over time, leaves growing and falling, but returning fresh and new in the warmth of spring.

As Christians, our lives should be somewhat modeled after the trees. We should be "rooted and built up in him [Christ]," as Paul wrote in Colossians 2:7. We should never cease to dig deeper in the word so that we may "grow in the grace and knowledge of our Lord and Savior Jesus Christ" (2 Pet. 3:18). We should always be willing to reach out our branches in love to provide for those in need, whether it be food, shelter, or comfort. We must stand firm throughout the seasons and storms of life, and we must continue to plant seeds that may grow the kingdom. Finally, like the trees looking forward to the newness of spring, so should we look forward to a new home prepared for us in Heaven.

Application for the Day: Today I will look for lessons in the immense wonders of nature that the Lord has provided all around me.

Friday, October 4, 2024

Drawing a Line in the Sand

Regina Cathey

Today's Scripture: Matthew 25:34-36

Drawing a line in the sand is usually a challenge—just cross this line! Are you the aggressor, or are you the one ready to run? It is time for us to draw a line in the sand and cross. How far do I go in being compassionate, in being kind, in loving my neighbor? Am I in the game or on the bench? Am I the cheerleader or the fan in the stands, or am I so apathetic that I don't show up for the game?

Honestly, I've been the player, the benchwarmer, the cheerleader, and the observer, and sometimes I haven't been concerned enough to show up! It's great to be in the stands encouraging the players. It's even better to be a cheerleader on the line cheering every play and encouraging each player. It's important for the players to know that there are people who are there to push them to meet their goals. It is also important to be the person to fill in when needed. However, the most rewarding position is the player—the person who shows up and takes a chance, knowing that he might get hurt or disappointed. That player also knows that the taste of victory is the ultimate reward.

When was the last time you showed up and got in the game? When did you take time to visit someone in the nursing home or the hospital? When was the last time you comforted someone in grief or took food to someone sick? When was the last time you gave a smile to a stranger, a child, or even a friend? When did you give a sandwich or a few dollars to a homeless man? There is so much to be done if you just get in the game. Taste Victory!

Application for the Day: Today, I will draw a line in the sand for myself and get in the game. I will pray that God will put someone in my path that needs a friend, and I will be that friend in whatever capacity I can.

In All Things Be Thankful

Regina Cathey

Today's Scripture: Psalm 118:24

In today's scripture, the author says, "This is the day the Lord has made; we will rejoice and be glad in it."

In America, we celebrate Thanksgiving once a year on the last Thursday in November. It is a day that families gather together and enjoy being a family and being with each other. We eat a huge meal, and we are thankful for our family and the blessings of the past year.

Thanksgiving is modeled after a 1621 harvest feast shared by the English colonists and the Native Americans. As time has passed, Thanksgiving Day has been filled with traditions, such as football games and parades. Traditions are good, right?

There is another day of Thanksgiving celebrated by Christians all over the world. It is celebrated on the first day of the week—every week, every month, every year. This day God established as the day we come together to have a different kind of feast. We break the bread of Jesus's body and drink the cup of Jesus's blood in remembrance of our Lord's death, burial, and resurrection, looking to the day that Jesus will come again.

1 Corinthians 11:23-26 says, "The Lord Jesus on the same night in which He was betrayed took bread; and when He had given thanks, He broke it. . . . In the same manner He also took the cup after supper. . . . For as often as you eat this bread and drink this cup, you proclaim the Lord's death till He comes."

God has given us so much for which to be thankful. I am thankful for those Pilgrims and Indians who ate the first Thanksgiving feast, and I am thankful for my family, who gather on each Thanksgiving Day to eat turkey and watch football. But mostly, I'm thankful for the gift of salvation given by Jesus Christ when He died on the cross, and I celebrate that gift every Sunday when I partake of the Lord's Supper.

Application for the Day: Today I will be thankful and rejoice in the blessings and goodness of God.

Tuesday, October 8, 2024

Destroying Our Joy
Richard Jones

Today's Scripture: Matthew 6:25-34

Worry destroys our joy. At the very moment we stop to ask, "Do I have joy? Am I happy?" we may begin to destroy our joy. Joy is not a feeling as much as it is a decision. God must be our "chosen portion" (Psalm 16:5).

When we give the wrong things too much priority in our lives, then those priorities control our joy. If the priority is recognition, then recognition controls our joy. If the priority is convenience, then convenience controls our joy.

Charles Swindoll said, "Worry pulls tomorrow's cloud over today's sunshine." To avoid worry, we must reorder our priorities. Nothing destroys joy like comparison, especially with what others have and we don't. Don't look back or ahead. Focus on what God is doing in your life at this moment. Our joy is not tied to emotions of the moment. What is our source of joy? We have some backseat things that control our joy: feelings, finances, status, and standing. When we reset our priorities, we are setting joy before us.

Joy is something deeper than how we feel about it. Joy is something deeper than how it feels right now. We must set our joy before us; then we are resetting our priorities. When we do that, our joy flows not from what it is, but from what God is to us. This is the duration of joy. When our joy runs out, the reason is that our joy is coming from the wrong place. Our priorities control our joy. Have we let our joy be controlled by something other than the priority of God's presence in our lives? Have we let our joy be controlled by things that cannot sustain it?

Application for the Day: Today I will make my priority God's presence in my life.

Wednesday, October 9, 2024

Forgiveness Is Better

Richard Jones

Today's Scripture: Matthew 18:21-35

While forgiveness is something we seek, it is also something we must extend. Here is a story from the annals of Standard Oil and John D. Rockefeller. Unimaginably rich and successful, Rockefeller demanded high performance from his company executives. One day an executive made an error, costing Standard Oil $2 million. News of the error spread rapidly throughout the executive offices, and the employees feared Rockefeller's reaction. Later that day, when a young executive with a scheduled appointment shakily approached Rockefeller's desk, Rockefeller said, "I guess you've heard about the $2 million mistake our friend made." "Yes, sir," said the young man, expecting Rockefeller to explode. "Well, I've been listing all his good qualities, and I've discovered that in the past he has made this company many more times the amount he lost today. His good points far outweigh this one error. So, I think we ought to forgive him, don't you?" And that is what happened. The man who made the mistake was forgiven the entire amount.

Imagine that the man who made the mistake went home and discovered that a friend of his had forgotten to repay him a thousand dollars. He called the friend and demanded repayment immediately. His friend had just incurred some severe medical expenses, lost his job, and didn't have the money. Enraged, the executive who had been forgiven sued the man for the money.

Now, let's say Rockefeller heard what his executive had done. What do you think Rockefeller would do? We can be certain Rockefeller would call the executive into his office, possibly saying: "You wicked man! I forgave you, and yet you would not forgive a man for a much smaller amount. For that, I will now force you to pay back the $2 million you owe me."

Does this story sound familiar? It should because it is an updated version of one right out of Matthew 18 with Jesus' instructions regarding forgiveness. Jesus stated that if we do not forgive others, we will not be forgiven by God.

Application for the Day: Today I will forgive someone who has wronged me.

Thursday, October 10, 2024

On Searching

Richard Jones

Today's Scripture: Matthew 13:45-46

When I hear people say, "I have found the Lord," I usually smile and accept it because I think I know what they mean. But in my gently twisted mind, I'm thinking, "I didn't know **He** was lost." On the contrary, I was lost, and **He** found me—and **He** saved me.

Almost every other religion in the world calls for its adherents to search for God in some way. But with Christianity, before anyone could begin to search for God, God had to come to us through His Son—through His earthly birth, His teaching, His crucifixion, and His resurrection. Therefore, God had to come to us <u>before</u> we could come to Him.

Here's the way I see it. God holds a great rope—a strong rope, perhaps the strongest rope in the universe. His grasp is so strong that He will not, and cannot, let go. His Son and His Son's sacrifice form the actual rope. God will then draw the rope toward Himself and the Eternal. We search until we find the rope. All we have to do is grab hold and never let go. Remember: we are sinners clinging to a Savior.

The meaning of the rope analogy reminds me of another one. The proper seeking for salvation is like the conduct of Matthew's merchant. In his searches, this wise merchant found one pearl of great price and sold all his possessions to obtain it. So, says the Savior, people seeking for happiness and finding the Gospel (the pearl of great price) should be willing to sacrifice all other things for it.

And I respectfully submit that, even though it may not be Christmas, wise men still seek Him.

Application for the Day: Today I will seek the Lord and will be willing to sacrifice everything.

Friday, October 11, 2024

A Secret of Contentment

Richard Jones

Today's Scripture: Philippians 4:8-13

An old Chinese proverb says, "If you want happiness for an hour, take a nap; if you want

happiness for a day, go fishing; if you want happiness for a year, go inherit a fortune; but if you want happiness for a lifetime, go help someone."

Whether we call it *joy, happiness, gladness, contentment,* or *being blessed*, it is something almost all want. In many ways it is a journey, and for many people the journey lasts a lifetime, and they never seem to find it. We may look at others and think, "They sure look happy. Why do they seem to get all the breaks in life? What are they doing that I am not doing?" And sometimes, if we really get to a low place, we start thinking that everyone is happy and content except poor old me.

Why is it that we sometimes pray for happiness, but then look for it in the wrong place? Two of the most obvious places we turn to are money and things. We have been made to believe by TV ads or billboards that money will buy happiness. If we have money, then we can buy products to make us happier. One of Coca-Cola's new advertising schemes is, "When you open a coke, you are opening a bottle of happiness." Volkswagen tells us, "Get in—Get happy." The Bible puts all this into perspective: we are told that if we put Christ first, then all these other things will fall into place. The answer will not be found in things.

Here is the difference between happiness and contentment. Happiness is based on feelings; contentment is based on faith. Happiness depends on the actions of other people; contentment

is finding joy no matter the circumstances. Happiness is temporary; contentment is allowing others to live their lives. In short, happiness is based on things that are external, while contentment is based on things that are eternal.

Application for the Day: Today I will put my trust in things that are eternal.

Monday, October 14, 2024

A Gift of God

Robby Harmon

Today's Scripture: Ephesians 2:8-9

I was in the right place, at the right time, with the right question from someone who cared about my salvation. Forty years ago, this coming October 5th, I sat in a parking lot of Alabama Christian College with Buddy Bell, the campus minister of the Landmark Church of Christ.

As we were sitting there talking about everything under the sun, Buddy asked me a critical question: "Robby do you understand what Jesus did for you?" I said yes. "What did he do for you?" he asked. "He died for me," I responded. "I am glad you believe. Why did he die for you?" "Because I am a sinner." "Do you understand that God knows no sin, and because he knows no sin, he cannot accept us to himself with sin? We are dirty and unclean in his sight, but with Christ, we are made clean. Do you know how he makes us clean?" "Through baptism," I responded. "Why are you waiting to be baptized?" I did not have an excuse and was immediately baptized.

Here are my questions to you: Are you saved? Have you accepted Christ? These are questions we all must answer for ourselves or answer later in judgment before God. I feel confident I am saved. I am not perfect. I am not sinless, but I am saved because of God's gift of grace. With Him and His saving grace, I have this hope. I feel obligated to share my story. Why? Because someone was courageous enough to ask me about my salvation.

If you were given a great earthly gift what would you do? Would you talk about it and share it with others? Do you feel obligated to share your faith? If not, why not? If you are in Christ, you have been given a gift. Because of that gift, if you continue to read in Ephesians 2, "We (you)… are created in Christ Jesus for good works." Part of that work is introducing others to Jesus.

Application for the Day: Today I will try to introduce someone to Jesus.

Tuesday, October 15, 2024

A Masterpiece

Robby Harmon

Today's Scripture: Ephesians 2:10

There are several people in my past who have made an impact on me. One of them is Gene Stallings. Coach Stallings, former coach of the University of Alabama, Texas A&M, and several NFL teams, is now in his late 80s. Over the last few years, his health has been a challenge. However, he continues to support several volunteer organizations. I first met Coach Stallings in 1991. The occasion was an event in Montgomery, AL, celebrating volunteerism. The sold-out event was filled with anticipation of hearing Stallings possibly talk about playing for Bear Bryant; or his Super Bowl coaching days with the Dallas Cowboys; or numerous players, coaches, or games from his past. To everyone's surprise, the coach said very little about football and much more about impacting other people's lives.

What made this good man have this perspective? In 1962, John Mark Stallings, his only son, was born with Down syndrome. An unanticipated event like this is always a challenge, but even more so since most kids during this time who had this condition were institutionalized. Coach Stallings and his wife refused to do so. From 1962 to 2008, the Stallings never let John's Down syndrome limit them from making a difference in others' lives.

Here is a personal experience I can share. We were living in Dickson and received news of friends from church who had a child born with Down syndrome. This news came as a shock. The child was not doing well at birth and sadly died shortly after. Knowing what I learned about Coach Stallings over the years, I called the Alabama football office and asked the secretary if the coach would mind calling this couple to comfort them. The next day he called and spoke to this couple with gentle words. This phone call was not something he had to make, nor did he do it for attention. He did it because he wanted to. God molded his life during difficult times to serve others.

Application for the Day: Today I will allow God to mold me to be His service masterpiece.

Cave of Despair

Robby Harmon

Today's Scriptures: 1 Samuel 22:1-5; Psalm 142

Have you ever felt like quitting? Have you ever been beaten down? I am not talking about a physical beating like a wrestler, UFC fighter, or boxer in a competition. I am talking about being beaten down mentally. In the story of David and the cave of Adullam, we see a tired man. David was anointed to be king of Israel by the prophet Samuel years earlier. However, all he has done since then is fight and run for his life. This short story in five verses does not give a complete picture of what is going on in David's life. However, reading Psalm 142 gives a sense of David's mindset.

David starts this psalm by saying, "With my voice, I cry out to the Lord: with my voice I plead for mercy to the Lord. I pour out my complaint before him; I tell my trouble before him. When my spirit faints within me, you know my way!" I want to focus on that last statement. When everything seems to be going wrong (and it is for David), it is a comfort to know that someone understands. David is at his wit's end. David is surrounded, hungry, and tired, and he does not know what to do. He has no one to turn to except God.

Life is a series of frustrations. The prophet Job said, "Man who is born of a woman is few of days and full of trouble." Life is full of trouble, heartache, and unfairness, and sometimes, it seems, overwhelming odds. We are no different than David, the man who chased after God's heart. God is the only resource of strength and comfort we have in these times of trouble. We see in this story that God does ultimately help David. There is power in prayer through faith. God is our refuge and our strength in a time of storm.

Application for the Day: Today I will remember that people may let me down, but God is faithful to help me make it through challenging times.

Thursday, October 17, 2024

Fear

Robby Harmon

Today's Scripture: 2 Timothy 1:7

The late, great Zig Ziglar, motivational speaker and salesman extraordinaire, had many memorable sayings during his years of motivational speaking. This quote is one of my favorites: "FEAR has two meanings: Forget Everything and Run, or Face Everything and Rise. The choice is ours to make." This is the daily dilemma of humankind. For some, fear is real and is very difficult because of anxiety and depression. Others find facing life's challenges too difficult, so they try to numb themselves with drugs or alcohol—you fill in the blank. None of us can run from our fear forever. Sooner or later, we must face it.

Are you in a state of fear? From our scripture today, we can all gain confidence that God has not given us the spirit of fear but has equipped us through Jesus Christ to face our fears. With God, all things are possible. All things! How did David kill a lion? How did Shadrach, Meshach, and Abednego walk into a fiery furnace? How did Peter walk on water? On and on we go, but each of these men faced his fears, knowing that God was on his side.

You and I have the same power. No matter what happens, God is with us. God can help with depression and anxiety. God can help with mountains of debt. God can help you face the demons from past mistakes, decisions, and lifestyles. However, it takes trust. Just like the individuals from scripture, the most significant decision we can make is to believe in His ability to do these things.

Do you believe in the words of 2 Timothy 1:7, "For God has not given us a spirit of fear, but of power and of love and of a sound mind"? In this scripture, Paul instructs Timothy not to buy into the fear of time and circumstances surrounding him. What is holding you back today? Of what fear can you let go?

Application for the Day: Today I will reflect on the words of Paul and embrace the powerful spirit that God wants me to have.

Friday, October 18, 2024

"Goose"

Robby Harmon

Today's Scripture: Romans 8:35

The tragedy of the unexpected loss of a pet is painful. Recently my daughter lost her furry friend named Goose. The pain associated with this loss has been gut wrenching. We all have been there, or maybe not? That statement assumes that you are a dog lover. I realize that not everyone loves dogs. I guess I don't understand that, but God made us all different. However, whether you love them or not, you must admire some of their traits. I have always had a strong love for dogs. It has been a great blessing for me to have owned several throughout my life.

When I think about my past pet dogs, or even Goose, it reminds me of many of the same traits of God. God is consistent in love, justice, patience, kindness, and joy. Now compare that to one of his creations. I have seen very few dogs who do not love with unconditional love. I want to hone in on that statement. If you own a dog or have owned one in the past, you know how much they love and want to be with their owners. When your day is terrible, their day is spent in anticipation to greet you, love you, and spend time with you.

Since the beginning of time, God has wanted a close relationship with his children. God provided for man from the start, and even when his sin separated him, God was loyal and unwavering in His love for humankind. God told the prophet Jeremiah, "I have loved you with an everlasting love" (Jer. 31:3).

I am thankful that God created an animal that reminds us of His love. I am not sure if there are going to be dogs in heaven. I want to think that dogs are there because of their nature to love and cherish their owners. If so, one day I will see Tar, Aubie, Bama, and Goose —great dogs who loved me and reminded me of God's amazing love.

Application for the Day: Today I will remember that God is faithful and that His love is everlasting.

Monday, October 21, 2024

Is Your Bucket Full?

Robby Harmon

Today's Scripture: John 4:1-30

No Jew wanted to go to Samaria. Jesus wanted to go. The ESV says, "And he had to pass through Samaria" (John 4:4). Our story begins with this travel completed. Jesus was resting by a well. The text says it was the sixth hour of the day, and he was tired from his journey. Jesus was on a mission.

Side note, have you ever been in the right place at the right time? As you reflect, you say, "Wow, I was meant to be here!" Jesus knew what he was doing. He was here for a reason. Jesus had a reason to talk with this woman. He was in the right place at the right time.

Perhaps we could say the woman's life represents us all too well. This woman was coming to the well for water, but it was more than water she sought. This woman had unmet needs. You could say that the bucket she carried that day was not filled. Have you seen the homeless holding out jars at an intersection or street corner? They are saying, "Please help me; I have an

unmet need." The woman at the well was saying the same thing. Five times she tried for happiness with different men, and now she was living with a sixth.

People carry different buckets of needs. All of us have them. Perhaps it is a bucket of religion that has not been filled with a deep relationship with God. Maybe it is a bucket for bigger,

better things: houses, cars, etc. Perhaps it is a bucket of relationships. A bucket for a better job.

None of these buckets being filled will give you true happiness. Just like the woman at the well,

we sometimes seek, search, and desire more peace, love, comfort, and security in our lives.

Jesus said, in John 14:6, "I am the way, and the truth, and the life. No one comes to the father except through me." Jesus is the only answer.

Application for the Day: Today I will remember that only in Jesus can I find contentment.

Tuesday, October 22, 2024

The Devil Cannot Control You

Bob Spencer

Today's Scripture: 1 Corinthians 10:13

The devil does not have power *over* us in this world. While the devil has power in this world, he can only influence us, but he cannot control us.

In 1 Corinthians 10:13 (ESV) the Apostle Paul writes, "No temptation has overtaken you that is not common to man. God is faithful, and He will not let you be tempted beyond your strength, but with the temptation will also provide the way of escape, that you may be able to endure it."

C. S. Lewis, the great essayist, observed that "Satan, the leader and dictator of devils, is the opposite, not of God, but of Michael the Archangel." God reigns supreme over all celestial and earthly beings, including Satan. Satan works in this world because God allows it. Satan cannot control us, but merely influence us.

In Revelation 12:9 the Apostle John writes, "And the great dragon was thrown down, that ancient serpent, who is called the Devil and Satan, the deceiver of the whole world—he was thrown down to the earth, and his angels were thrown down with him."

We generally think of the devil as less powerful, but the equal of God. This is not true; the devil was created by God and was an angel until he challenged God and was expelled from Heaven along with his angels. Scripture is clear that Hell was created for Satan and his angels.

There is no doubt that Satan is persuasive and can know and exploit our weaknesses. God will give us the strength to overcome the lies of Satan if we choose.

In James 4:6-8, the solution to the problem of overcoming the devil is given to us: "But he gives more grace. Therefore, it says, 'God opposes the proud but gives grace to the humble.' Submit yourselves therefore to God. Resist the devil, and he will flee from you. Draw near to God, and he will draw near to you. Cleanse your hands, you sinners, and purify your hearts, you double-minded."

Application for Today: Today I will focus on God and His love for me.

Wednesday, October 23, 2024

Whom Does God Love?

Bob Spencer

Today's Scripture: Joshua 5:13

The Israelites had crossed the Red Sea and were encamped at Gilboa near the city of Jericho. God had given Joshua very specific instructions on how the city was to be approached and the battle conducted. Before the battle, the king closed Jericho, and visitors and residents were not allowed to go in or out of the city. Before the battle, Joshua walked around the outside walls of Jericho.

Joshua 5:13-14a (ESV) states, "When Joshua was by Jericho, he lifted up his eyes and looked, and behold, a man was standing before him with his drawn sword in his hand. And Joshua went to him and said to him, 'Are you for us, or for our adversaries?' And he said, 'No; but I am the commander of the army of the LORD. Now I have come.'"

In reply to the question "Are you for us or against us?" the commander of the Lord's army said, "No." We like to believe that God is on our side and holds all others in disdain, that somehow we have achieved a favored status in His eyes.

This verse reminds us that God loves all His children whether they are obedient or disobedient. God loves those who follow Christ, and it pleases Him and He loves us. God also loves those who do not believe, and He continues to be willing to accept them if they will turn toward Him. Paul writes in 1 Timothy 2:3-4 (RSV), "This is good, and it is acceptable in the sight of God our Savior, who desires all men to be saved and to come to the knowledge of the truth."

God loves the people who have offended us, He loves the people who hate us, and He loves the people whom we hate. As you go about in this world and see people who do not look like us, act like us, talk like us, or think like us, remember that God loves them in their sin just as He loves you in your sin.

Application for Today: Today I will do good and love everyone I see.

Thursday, October 24, 2024

A Gift from God

Robin Nelson

Today's Scripture: Romans 12: 6-8

I would like you to consider 2 truths: you *are* a gift, and you *have* a gift!

A Gift I will show to you this day,
one that will bless you, in this I pray.
A Gift you can have, given by God,
one that you carry, one that is odd.
A Gift of Joy, of Peace, and of Love,
one that guarantees us a home up above.
A Gift you take and carry each day,
one that you have, and one to give away.
A Gift you must find, it IS within you,
one that gives hope and makes you anew.
A Gift that began from God's perfect plan,
one that He had before creating man!
A Gift so precious, so great, and so grand,
one that He bought you with His mighty hand.
Let's discover this Gift as we open it wide.
Take out what's there and see inside.
The perfect fit, the perfect size!
God picked this Gift for you with His perfect eyes!
We will wear it well and we'll wear it proud,
to Glorify God, Let us live it out loud!
We need others to see from where our
Gift came to share with those who are sorrowful and lame!
So, let's begin to unwrap our special Gift,
to stir it up and give us a lift!

Our gift from God is special and unique to each of us, and though we may not always recognize our gift, that doesn't mean we did not get one. Our unique way of touching the lives of others in a positive way allows each of us to carry an aspect of God's goodness and love.

Always consider that your gift from the Father is perfect; although we may not be perfect, His gift to us is perfect (James 1:17). We need to use our gifts to glorify Him, whether in service or as an example (1 Tim. 4:14).

Application for the Day: Today I pray that I will share the special gift in me and that others will see the goodness and love of God!

214

Friday, October 25, 2024

A Prayer of Songs

Robin Nelson

Today's Scripture: 1 Thessalonians 5:17

There is always room for prayer and praise to God each day. I recall a quote from Chris McCurley's podcast, "Prayer is a lifestyle, not an event." Some days I am lacking, and it is a constant challenge for me. If there are others having the same struggle, I hope that this prayer of songs I wrote for Ladies' Day several years ago will inspire your day to pray and praise.

Dear Lord and Father of Mankind, I Exalt Thee! How Great Thou Art! Oh, Thank you Lord!

Father, I Adore You & Glorify Thy Name, for Earth Holds No Treasures. I am Redeemed!

Jesus Is Lord, and He Bore It All. Jesus Saves! He Paid a Debt, and by his gift, He Has Made Me Glad.

Sing Hallelujah to the Lord! As you Count Your Blessings, Praise Him, Praise Him! To God Be the Glory! I will Trust and Obey.

I Need Thee Every Hour; Jesus Hold My Hand! For my Heart Bowed Down with Sorrow, give me Peace in the Valley, and Be with Me, Lord. You are a Shelter in the Time of Storm!

Nearer Still Nearer, O Master, Let Me Walk with Thee. Purer in Heart, Oh God, Let Me Live Close to Thee Each Day. Day by Day I Stand in Awe. Each Step I Take, may I Be Still and Know that Great Is Thy Faithfulness and that Jesus Loves Me!

I have Blessed Assurance that Anywhere with Jesus, There is a Place of Quiet Rest. As long as I Lean on the Everlasting Arms and follow the Footsteps of Jesus, I can have Victory in Jesus!

Amazing Grace! I will Shout the Victory, and as I reach my Home of the Soul, My Hope is Built on Nothing Less than that Heaven's Really Gonna Shine!

Holy Father, How Beautiful is Your Heavenly Sunlight. O Happy Day! In all gladness I will Sing Hallelujah to the Lord!

In Jesus, Name Above All Names, Amen.

Application for the Day: Today I will pray without ceasing and carry a song of praise in my heart.

Monday, October 28, 2024

"No Guts, No Glory"

Robin Nelson

Today's Scriptures: Matthew 5:16; Proverbs 25:27

In 1955, Major General Fredrick Corbin Blesse wrote an air-to-air combat manual titled "No Guts, No Glory." It is still considered a primer on air combat. As a quote, its meaning suggests that if you do not have courage to take a risk, you will not be able to achieve a goal or be successful. In consideration of Christian living, being a follower of God is much the same way.

1 Corinthians 10:31 says, "So, whether you eat or drink, or whatever you do, do all to the glory of God." How often do we go about our day, meeting goals, living successfully, and forget that we did not do that alone? In our own self-minded glory, we forget who really should get the glory.

Confusing our goodness with the goodness that comes from God is a consideration for me at times. As I serve the Lord, I want my heart and mind to serve for Him and not for my own glory. I try to be mindful that any good I can do is not from the human me but because God is in me.

The Pharisees were guilty of glorifying self (John 12:43). They frequently belittled others to gain the appearance of their own glory. Their measures were neither brave nor courageous. Godly glory involves sacrifice and denial of self. The "guts" to turn our lives and wills over to God is our glory in Him.

To whom do you give credit for your success? Be courageous to ask yourself: Will I give Him glory? Give thought to how Jesus responded so many times as He walked among the crowds and taught the apostles that the Father was His reason and His cause (John 5: 43-44). Jesus gave the ultimate sacrifice to glorify His Father, so we too being joint heirs must sacrifice self in this world to glorify our Lord.

Application for the Day: Today I will consider how Paul prayed in Philippians 4: 19-20, that God will supply every need, and pray for the "guts" to give God the glory in all things.

Tuesday, October 29, 2024

The Bottom Line

Robyn Lampley

Today's Scripture: Psalm 15

A lawyer once asked Jesus, "Who is my neighbor?" His intent was to challenge Jesus to see how this teacher would answer him. But Jesus took advantage of the situation to inform His audience then, and us today, that all members of the human race are our neighbors with no regard to race, gender, ethnicity, or socio-economic level. Jesus spoke of The Bottom Line—the sum of the matter.

Often in life, we seek broad information and varying viewpoints when exploring a topic or issue. When we are merely curious, we throw a wide net. When we are searching for truth, however, we are critical of information and test it for credibility and integrity. When a crucial decision is necessary, we seek the recognized experts, the proven research—and rather than a broad perspective, we hone in on The Bottom Line. We desire simple, yet profound, summation.

In my decades of exposure to God's word, I have found broad truths and depths of considerations of how to live, how to love, how to serve, and how to be pleasing to God. At some point, I came across Psalm 15, and, for me, this is The Bottom Line.

1 LORD, who may dwell in your sanctuary? Who may live on your holy hill? 2 He whose walk is blameless and who does what is righteous, who speaks the truth from his heart 3 and has no slander on his tongue, who does his neighbor no wrong and casts no slur on his fellowman, 4 who despises a vile man but honors those who fear the LORD, who keeps his oath even when it hurts, 5 who lends his money without usury and does not accept a bribe against the innocent. He who does these things will never be shaken.

Application for the Day: Today I will meditate on these characteristics—goodness, honesty, kindness, discernment, constancy, generosity—and consider how I can make them my own, preparing myself for His holy hill.

Wednesday, October 30, 2024

Let There Be Light

Roger Chester

Today's Scripture: Genesis 1:3 – "Then God said, 'Let there be light,' and there was light."

> In black before night darkness surrounds;
> void of all only Three abound.
> The universe expands no limits could be;
> no human around only Three could see.
> The earth placed there no form to behold,
> waiting for orders by God to be told.
> Over the waters, His Spirit did hover,
> speaking the words soon to be seen by others.
> "LET THERE BE LIGHT." The order was given,
> the universe obeyed, and the darkness was riven.
> The curtain was torn; the day rejoiced in light;
> the darkness took its place but only in the night.
> The One who made all was pleased at the sight,
> the good that He did when He made light.
>
> Now God made man to rule the land;
> over all the creatures he has the upper hand.
> But man follows his path and struggles his way;
> life's full of troubles till the very last day.
> With arrogance and pride man is covered with sin;
> God in His mercy must give light again.
> From the beginning of time, the Father has shown,
> sin overwhelms; there's only one way home.
> As the Father takes pity on man below,
> He sent His only Son with the path to show.
> As darkness veiled the cross, His blood did flow;
> the curtain was torn; it's Christ we must know!
> The light of the world, salvation to all,
> the light of God's Son to halt man's fall.

God gave up His Son for the world to be known; with the death of His Son the greatest love is shown, and there is eternal light to guide us home.

Application for the Day: Today I will look to the author, creator, and source of light, who gave His life for me on Calvary's cross.

218

Thursday, October 31, 2024

True Beauty

Roger Chester

Today's Scripture: Philippians 4:7

What is true beauty? When we walk in the woods or stare out across the ocean, why is it beautiful? When we look into the eyes of the one whom we love the most, why do we see beauty? It has often been said, "Beauty is in the eye of the beholder." How do we see the same thing, and to one it is beautiful and to another a burden?

We need to understand where beauty comes from. It does not come from outward things, but from the spirit who is seeing it. The wrinkly newborn is the most beautiful thing in the world to the loving mother. We are given a spirit by God to guide us through life. That spirit will guide our souls to God, to the One who made us, who knows us better than we know ourselves. God, the Perfect Spirit, looks at us with perfect love.

When we see something soothing to our spirit, it is beautiful. When we see something that produces turmoil in our spirit, we have feelings of uneasiness. When we see snow-capped mountains, we are in awe of their majesty and beauty, but if we are lost in the snow-capped mountains, we see danger and discomfort.

God gives us the ability to change our perspective on what we see—whether good or bad. When we look at people with the love of God, our perspective changes. We can then see that they are created in God's image. They may look ugly at the present time for the way they are living, but they are still from our God. Circumstances in which we find ourselves may be very ugly at times, but we have the opportunity to grow out of pain and leave a very beautiful image to remember. So remember: "Beauty is in the spirit of the beholder."

Application for Today: Today I will, through the peace I find in my spirit, which comes from God, see the beauty around me in everything and everyone.

Friday, November 1, 2024

I Know Things

Sherrie Spencer

Today's Scripture: Acts 4: 23-31

I know things. I know that:

God is Sovereign. He has absolute power. He made all things. God is the ruler with absolute power. "Sovereign Lord, who made the heaven and the earth and the sea and everything in them" (Acts 4:24).

God is Love. He sent His only Son into the world to take our place in eternal damnation (I John 4:7-21).

God is the Creator. As the Creator (Gen. 1:1), He is omniscient (all-knowing), omnipotent (all-powerful), and omnibenevolent (supremely good—no evil).

God is ALWAYS. He is Yahweh, the I AM. He was revealed to Moses (Ex. 3:14-15) with God's covenant name in a covenant made with Abraham, Isaac, and Jacob. Just as Yahweh made a covenant to be their God, He made a covenant to be our God. God is always and un-changing through all generations.

God is El Shaddai. He is Almighty (El Shaddai). He revealed His name to Abraham, who was 99, when he made a covenant with Him. This is the first time in Scripture God refers to Himself as El Shaddai, "God Almighty." El Shaddai establishes His power on earth, over na-ture, and over Abram and Sarai's lives. This covenant is a two-way contract. God's promise is dependent on Abram's reciprocal contract with El Shaddai to walk before Him faithfully and blamelessly. Thus, Abram is to live in a covenant relationship with God. It is a dual con-tract. God will provide and Abram will serve God (Gen. 17:1-2).

God is Adonai. Adonai means "Lord and Master." The name Adonai is found more than 400 times in the Bible The use of Adonai throughout Scripture is significant. God, who is LORD and Master (Adonai) and God is Always (Yahweh), is demonstrated throughout the Word of God. David said to the Lord, "You are my Master! Every good thing I have comes from you" (Psa. 16:2).

Application for the Day: Today I will say, "LORD God Almighty, I know you knew me before I was formed in my mother's womb, and I know you love me sacrificially. I LOVE YOU, my LORD and Master."

Monday, November 4, 2024

What Would Jesus Say?
Think on These Things

Sherrie Spencer

Today's Scripture: Hebrew 4:15-16

What would Jesus do? He would and has done it ALL. He came to earth in a human body and lived as all of us do. He got cold and hot, He became hungry, He felt isolated from His Father, and He bled and experienced death. He was humiliated, grief-stricken, beaten, mocked, tempted, and the list goes on and on. Because He lived through human experiences, we have assurance that He loves us and that His love is sufficient to get us through all the trials and tribulations we face on this earth.

Jesus is the Word, and we have been given the Word in written form to read, study, and apply to all our daily fears, tears, joys, and tribulations. And not only were we given the written Word of God, but we are also given the Holy Spirit to guide us, give us counsel, and comfort us.

We are like newborn babies requiring sufficient nourishment, consolation, and guidance. God planned and purposed all things even before He created mankind. The Godhead Three—God the Father, Jesus our Redeemer, and the Holy Spirit—determined to create mankind, fully knowing we would disobey and fall from His perfect plan.

"Parents-to-be" know their precious children will be born needing total care only to grow up to be rebellious teenagers and independent adults. They grow up to be rebellious against the very beings who brought them into this world. Does that sound familiar? Have you read this very thing in the Bible or heard it from a pulpit? God created, loved, and sacrificed for His creation, knowing full well that His creation would rebel against His plan and His will for us.

Our daily prayers and actions should demonstrate our acceptance of His perfect plan of love for His creation. We do have a high priest who empathizes with our weaknesses.

Application for the Day: Today I will "approach God's throne of grace with confidence" so that I "may receive mercy and find grace to help" me in my time(s) of need (Heb. 4:15-16).

Tuesday, November 5, 2024

Be a Barnabas

Steve Baggett

Today's Scripture: 1 Thessalonians 5:11

One of the really neat blessings in life is being in the presence of an encourager: someone who builds you up, smiles, gives you a pat on the back, and says things to you that make you feel energized and ready to conquer the world. Do you know people like this? Better yet, are you a person who encourages?

Barnabas was just such a person.

- Acts 4:36-37 – His name means "Son of Encouragement," and he generously gave to others.
- Acts 9:27 – After Saul met Jesus on the road to Damascus and was baptized into Christ, Barnabas brought the newly converted Saul (formerly a persecutor of Christians) to Jerusalem and testified on his behalf to the apostles.
- Acts 11:20-30 – He was sent by the apostles to Antioch to work with and encourage new Christians. He found Saul and together they preached the gospel for three years. He delivered funds for famine relief to Christians in Jerusalem.
- Acts 12:25; 15:37-39 – He was a great encourager of John Mark.
- Acts 13:1 – He, along with Saul, was selected by the Holy Spirit and sent out by the church at Antioch on a major preaching tour.
- Acts 15 – When there was disagreement over the acceptance of Gentiles as Christians, Barnabas was one of the men chosen to meet with brethren in Jerusalem and determine a solution.

While there are many other references to Barnabas in the New Testament, these are sufficient to emphasize his role as an encourager!

Christians, more than any others, should be encouragers. We have been saved by grace (Eph. 2:8-9), have been adopted into the family of God (Eph. 1:5), have every spiritual blessing in Christ (Eph. 1:3), and are part of a congregation of people who love us. Consequently, we are encouraged to "comfort each other and edify one another, just as you also are doing" (1 Thess. 5:11).

Application for the Day: Today I will strive to rejoice in the Lord (Phil. 4:4), build others up in the faith (Eph. 4:12), and be a positive influence on others (1 Cor. 11:1).

Wednesday, November 6, 2024

Born Again

Steve Baggett

Today's Scripture: John 3:5

In John 3:3 Jesus said to Nicodemus "Truly, truly, I say to you, unless one is born again, he cannot see the kingdom of God." Nicodemus did not understand what Jesus meant so he asked, "How can a man be born when he is old? Can he enter again a second time into his mother's womb and be born?" (John 3:4). Jesus answered, "Most assuredly, I say to you, unless one is born of water and the Spirit, he cannot enter the kingdom of God" (John 3:5).

That statement begs the question, "How and when is one born of "water and the Spirit?" The Holy Spirit did not leave us to figure this out for ourselves. The Bible says that following the death, burial, and resurrection of Jesus, Peter, on the Day of Pentecost, preached the gospel in the city of Jerusalem. When asked by those present, "what shall we do," (Acts 2:37), Peter (through the inspiration of the Holy Spirit) responded "Repent and let every one of you be baptized in the name of Jesus Christ for the remission of sins; and you shall receive the gift of the Holy Spirit" (Acts 2:38). As a further explanation, the Holy Spirit led Paul, in writing to the Romans to say, "Therefore we were buried with Him through baptism into death, that just as Christ was raised from the dead by the glory of the Father, even so we also should walk in newness of life" (Romans 6:4). In both instances we are taught that people were born again of water (baptism) and the Holy Spirit.

When I read these verses, I am reminded of the night I was "born again." Batsell Baxter had just concluded a sermon entitled "What Must I Do to Be Saved?" in a gospel meeting in Clarksville, TN. I responded to the invitation, and Hugh Fulford baptized me into Christ. I had been born again, born of the water and the Spirit!

Application for Today: If I have not been born again, I will seek to do so today.

Thursday, November 7, 2024

Choose to Be Happy

Steve Baggett

Today's Scripture: Philippians 4:4 – "Rejoice in the Lord always; again I will say, rejoice!"

"Open to me the gates of righteousness, that I may enter through them and give thanks to the Lord. This is the gate of the Lord; the righteous shall enter through it. I thank you that you have answered me and have become my salvation. The stone that the builders rejected has become the cornerstone. This is the Lord's doing; it is marvelous in our eyes. This is the day that the Lord has made; let us rejoice and be glad in it" (Psa. 118:19-24).

This passage reminds us that today is a blessing from God! In order to serve others and be a blessing to them, let us then choose to be happy today! While joy comes from the relationship we have with the Lord, happiness is a choice! In Philippians 4:4, Paul wrote, "Rejoice in the Lord always; again I will say, rejoice!" Circumstances in life are not always pleasant! In fact, sometimes they can cause sickness, pain, betrayal, death, etc. Those circumstances seem to be anything but joyful. But, according to Paul, our joy is not tied to circumstances; it is tied to the Lord and being in Him. Whatever is happening in life, those who are in Christ can always rejoice because they ARE in Christ!

We often sing with our kids, "If you're happy and you know it, clap your hands . . . stomp your feet . . . say amen. If you're happy and you know it, then your face will surely show it." What does your face say to others? What do your actions say to others?

As you go through your day today, do a little clapping, stomping, and saying amen! And, by the way, be sure to inform your face that you have made the decision to be happy. The Bible says, "A glad heart makes a cheerful face" (Prov. 15:13a) and "A joyful heart is good medicine" (Prov. 17: 22a).

Application for the Day: Today I will choose to have a happy day!

Friday, November 8, 2024

Do You See Him?

Steve Baggett

Today's Scripture: Numbers 23:8-9

The Old Testament prophet Balaam is one of the more interesting characters in the Bible. When bribed by Balak, king of Moab, to place a curse on God's people so he would be able to defeat them, amazingly Balaam:

- Asked God if he could curse Israel, and God told him no (Num. 22:8-12).
- Asked God again, and God told him to do only what He prescribed (Num. 22:20).
- Argued with a donkey (Num. 22:22-30).
- Blessed Israel three times instead of cursing them (Num. 23:1-24:13).
- Predicted the downfall of many nations, beginning with Moab (Num. 24:14-25).
- Induced the Midianite women to seduce Israel (Num. 31:16).
- Was killed along with the Midianites when Israel defeated them (Num. 31:8).

Though it appears that Balaam wanted to accept Balak's bribe and curse Israel, three times he did as God said and blessed Israel. When God first sent him to speak with Balak, Balaam made this inspiring statement, "How shall I curse whom God has not cursed? And how shall I denounce whom the Lord has not denounced? For from the top of the rocks I see him, And from the hills I behold him" (Num. 23:8-9a). Sadly, Balaam ended up disobeying God, but this statement about seeing God is significant.

Scripture teaches that God can be seen in many ways. The apostle Paul stated that He can be seen in creation (Rom. 1:20). The Psalmist stated that He can be seen in His word (Psa. 119:18). The prophet Isaiah stated that He can be seen throughout the earth (Isa. 6:3). Paul stated that He can be seen in the lives of God's faithful children (Col. 1:27). And the Hebrew author stated that He can be seen in His suffering and death (Heb. 2:9).

Are you looking for the Lord? Can you see Him? Look around you; look in His word; look at His creation; look at His death and resurrection! He can always be seen by those who are looking.

Application for the Day: Today I will look for God in every area of my life.

Monday, November 11, 2024

Doing Good

Steve Baggett

Today's Scripture: James 4:17

Several years ago, when performing a wedding, I stood with the wedding party at the front of the auditorium, awaiting the bride's entrance. When the doors at the back of the auditorium opened and the groom saw his beautiful bride, he leaned over to me and said, "I did good, didn't I?" "Yes, Justin," I said. "Yes, you did!" "Doing good" applies not only in the selection of a future mate, but in every area of the Christian's life!

The five-chapter book of James has much to say about "doing good." Many believe, and I concur, that James is the most practical book in the New Testament and has more specific instruction for living as a Christian than any other source. In chapter four, following a discussion where he emphasizes that we are not to be friends with the world (4:1-6), James gives some specific examples of what "doing good" looks like:

- Submitting to God and resisting the devil (4:7)
- Drawing near to God (4:8)
- Weeping over sins (4:9)
- Humbling oneself before God (4:10)
- Refusing to speak evil of another (4:11)
- Refusing to be judgmental (4:12)

Following these instructions, James gives a specific example of doing good. "Come now, you who say, 'Today or tomorrow we will go into such and such a town and spend a year there and trade and make a profit'— yet you do not know what tomorrow will bring. What is your life? For you are a mist that appears for a little time and then vanishes. Instead you ought to say, 'If the Lord wills, we will live and do this or that.' As it is, you boast in your arrogance. All such boasting is evil" (4:13-16). In other words, talk is cheap. Do something good! James' concluding statement is, "So whoever knows the right thing to do and fails to do it, for him it is sin" (4:17). So "doing good" is both refraining from doing what is bad and proactively doing what is good.

Application for the Day: Today I will seek ways to do good!

Tuesday, November 12, 2024

Give Me This Mountain

Steve Baggett

Today's Scripture: Joshua 14:10-12

He was eighty-five years old. Years earlier he had faithfully served as one of the spies God had sent into the land of Canaan. His positive report that, with God's help, Israel could take the land, was remembered and appreciated by the Almighty. Throughout the years of wandering in the wilderness, his faithfulness to God had remained strong.

Israel now possessed the land of Canaan. Kings had been defeated, land had been taken, and it was time to divide the land among the tribes. Caleb, this eighty-five-year-old warrior, approached Joshua and said, "I am this day eighty-five years old. I am still as strong today as I was in the day that Moses sent me; my strength now is as my strength was then, for war and for going and coming. So now give me this hill country of which the Lord spoke on that day..." (Joshua 14:10-12). Verses 13-15 indicate that Joshua gave Caleb the hill country he requested, and Hebron became his inheritance.

What if Caleb had taken the approach of many seniors in the church today? "I taught classes when I was younger. Now it is someone else's turn." "I can't do what I used to do." "They don't really want me to volunteer, they want someone younger." Admittedly, age does catch up with us, strength does wane, eyesight does begin to fail, and our ability to function does diminish.

However, God can use all who make themselves available to Him. One of the beautiful blessings of age is the ability to serve God unhindered by the responsibilities of youth! Another blessing of age is wisdom gained from a lifetime of studying God's Word and serving Him faithfully! How thankful the church needs to be for the "Calebs" of our day who are still wanting to take their "hill country," and faithfully use their talent to serve God and others.

Application for Today: Today I will thank God for preserving the story of Caleb's faithful service through the ages and will strive to be more like him.

Wednesday, November 13, 2024

Golden Deeds

Steve Baggett

Today's Scripture: Galatians 6:9-10

"Each day I'll do a golden deed, by helping those who are in need; my life on earth is but a span, and so I'll do the best I can." That dearly loved song was written by William Golden in 1918 and is said to have been inspired by the parable of the Good Samaritan. That parable is about a despised Samaritan helping a Jew who had been beaten and left for dead. When he saw a person in need, nationality didn't matter, social equity didn't matter, and a lack of acceptance didn't matter. What mattered was doing what was right!

Doing good deeds is the byproduct of a life lived in Christ. Paul put it this way, "And let us not grow weary of doing good, for in due season we will reap, if we do not give up. So then, as we have opportunity, let us do good to everyone, and especially to those who are of the household of faith" (Gal. 6:9-10). James said, "What good is it, my brothers, if someone says he has faith but does not have works? Can that faith save him? If a brother or sister is poorly clothed and lacking in daily food, and one of you says to them, 'Go in peace, be warmed and filled,' without giving them the things needed for the body, what good is that? So also faith by itself, if it does not have works, is dead" (James 2:14-17).

Imagine the lives you can bless by doing "golden deeds": a phone call, a text message, a card or letter, a brief visit, a gentle hug, a firm handshake, a warm meal, a ride to the doctor, a ride to worship or Bible study, or a visit to the hospital or nursing home! These are things we all can do by developing a mindset of service, by following the example of Jesus of loving and serving others.

Application for the Day: Because of whose I am, I will look for opportunities to do "golden deeds" today!

228

Thursday, November 14, 2024

Peacemakers

Steve Baggett

Today's Scripture: Matthew 5:9

The word "peace" is a beautiful word and describes a beautiful state of being! It involves eliminating bitterness, pursuing what is best for others, and uniting with others to accomplish God's will. In fact, Jesus said, "Blessed are the peacemakers, For they shall be called sons of God" (Matt. 5:9). So much could be said about the need for having peace with God and living in peace within the church, as well as enjoying peace among nations, between races, and in families. But today's thought centers on being at peace with and striving for the right relationship with all people.

Notice that Jesus used the word "blessed." Some translations use the word "happy," which is a good word. But Jesus' use of the word means so much more than just being happy. It refers to the ultimate state of spiritual joy and happiness one can experience. Thus, the one who is a peacemaker experiences a state of spiritual joy and happiness that others will never experience.

Being a peacemaker does not happen accidentally. It requires constant prayer and effort. It must be part of who we are deep within our core. What are some valuable keys for peaceful relationships with others?
1. Remember that all people are created in the image of God (Gen. 1:26).
2. Remember that all people, including you, have sinned (Rom. 3:23).
3. Remember that all people have difficult days and that you probably have no idea regarding the depth of their struggles (Phil. 1:23-24).
4. Treat others as you wish to be treated (Luke 6:31).
5. Be kind to others (Eph. 4:32).
6. Use only words that will edify and encourage others (Eph. 4:29).
7. Let your light shine in a world of darkness (Matt. 5:16).
8. Be an example to others (Titus 2:1-8).
9. Love your neighbor as yourself (Matt. 22:39).
10. Tell others of God's love for them (John 3:16).

Application for the Day: Today I will do all within my power to enjoy a peaceful relationship with others.

Friday, November 15, 2024

Repentance Leads to Salvation

Steve Baggett

Today's Scripture: Luke 13:3 - "I tell you, no; but unless you repent you will all likewise perish."

How does one repent of sin and accept God's gracious gift of salvation?

1. *Know the difference between right and wrong.* The Old Testament prophet Jonah was able to repent of his refusal to preach to the people of Nineveh because he knew that his actions were wrong. That knowledge of right and wrong comes through an understanding of God's Word (John 12:48).
2. *Understand the consequences of sin.* We are all sinners (Rom. 3:23). And the Bible clearly states the consequences of sin: "For the wages of sin is death" (Rom. 6:23a).
3. *Desire to serve God.* Without a desire to serve God, one will never make the necessary changes in life to overcome sin.
4. *Be filled with godly sorrow.* "For godly sorrow produces repentance leading to salvation, not to be regretted; but the sorrow of the world produces death" (2 Cor. 7:10). While sorrow for sin is not repentance, it does lead one to repent.
5. *Be courageous.* The courageous will be strong enough to break sinful habits and remain steadfast in the presence of those against whom they sinned (1 Cor.15:58).
6. *Sincerely act.* Repentance requires action. "Therefore, bear fruits worthy of repentance" (Luke 3:8a). Repentance involves knowledge, understanding, desire, godly sorrow, and courage. But if one does not act upon what he knows and does not follow through with his desire to serve the Lord, he has not repented.

Lest we be left with the wrong conclusion, these actions will not earn forgiveness. Salvation from sins is a gift of God (Eph. 2:8-9). We do not deserve it; we cannot earn it; all we can do is happily and thankfully receive it. Repenting of sin is one of the very important steps in accepting God's gracious gift of salvation. That gift is received when one, following repentance, is baptized into Christ (Acts 2:38).

Application for the Day: Today I will be filled with the desire to turn my back on sin and serve God!

Monday, November 18, 2024

The Cost of Salvation

Steve Baggett

Today's Scripture: Philippians 2:5-11

⁵ Have this mind among yourselves, which is yours in Christ Jesus, ⁶ who, though he was in the form of God, did not count equality with God a thing to be grasped, ⁷ but emptied himself, by taking the form of a servant, being born in the likeness of men. ⁸ And being found in human form, he humbled himself by becoming obedient to the point of death, even death on a cross. ⁹ Therefore God has highly exalted him and bestowed on him the name that is above every name, ¹⁰ so that at the name of Jesus every knee should bow, in heaven and on earth and under the earth, ¹¹ and every tongue confess that Jesus Christ is Lord, to the glory of God the Father (Philippians 2:5-11).

Have you considered the personal sacrifices Jesus endured in order to be our sin offering?   Certainly, His excruciating death on the cross was the crowning point of His suffering for us, but His personal sacrifices began long before that day.

- He sacrificed being in the form of God.
- He gave up His being equal with God.
- He emptied himself (poured himself out) of His heavenly existence.
- He voluntarily assigned Himself residence in a lowly human body.
- All of this was prior to allowing man to crucify Him.

All of this was part of God's plan to save those who would turn to Him.   The apostle Paul in 2 Corinthians 5:21 said, "For He made Him who knew no sin *to be* sin for us, that we might become the righteousness of God in Him."   Peter said in 1 Peter 3:18 "For Christ also suffered once for sins, the just for the unjust, that He might bring us to God, being put to death in the flesh but made alive by the Spirit. And in 1 John 4:10, John said "In this is love, not that we loved God, but that He loved us and sent His Son *to be* the propitiation for our sins.

"Why did the Savior heaven leave and come to earth below where men His grace would not receive? Because He loves me so!"

Application for Today: Today I will thank God for the gift of salvation.

Tuesday, November 19, 2024

What Do You Have in Your Pockets?

Steve Baggett

Today's Scripture: Colossians 3:17

My good friend, David Swanger, in his blog *Building a Better You,* shared the following story:

> In his book <u>Undistracted</u>, Bob Goff talks about a class he taught at San Quentin prison. One day he received a call from one of the guys who had been in his class and his first words were "Bob, I'm on the other side of the wall." Bob envisioned bed sheets being tied together and a daring escape, but there was a simpler explanation. He continued, "I'm out. They just released me." Ever the searcher for a story to share, Bob asked, "Kevin, what was your first thought when you stepped outside?" Keven didn't hesitate and replied, "I realized I've got pockets." A bit disappointed, Bob first thought that this was not the deep insight he was expecting, but upon further thought he replied to Kevin, "Be really careful what you put in them." Bob then made the observation that we all have pockets, and it is what we put or keep in them that determines so much in our lives. It is what we allow into our lives and carry each day that determines our future.

When writing to the Colossians Paul said, "Therefore put to death your members which are on the earth: fornication, uncleanness, passion, evil desire, and covetousness, which is idolatry" (Col. 3:5). In contrast, he said, "Therefore, as the elect of God, holy and beloved, put on tender mercies, kindness, humility, meekness, long-suffering; bearing with one another, and forgiving one another" (Col. 3:12-13a). Tying the statements together he said, "And whatever you do in word or deed, do all in the name of the Lord Jesus, giving thanks to God the Father through Him" (Col. 3:17).

What do you have in your pockets? Things which destroy or things which build up? Things which tear down or things which encourage? Things which distract your mind from that which is pure and holy or things which instruct your mind in the way of God?

Application for the Day: Today I will seek to fill my pockets with things of God.

Wednesday, November 20, 2024

Behold: A Monument

Steve Moore

Today's Scripture: 1 Samuel 15:10-16

Saul was the first king of Israel. God chose him and had him anointed, and things started out pretty well. But by the time of the Scripture above, things had gone terribly wrong with Saul. In this particular account, he had his orders from God to destroy Amalek, and King Saul did not exactly do as he was told.

Was it disobedience? Yes. But based on what? One clue is found in today's reading: as Samuel went to find the king, he was told, "Saul came to Carmel, and behold, he set up a monument for himself" (v. 12). I perceive that what is in our Bible is there because our loving Creator wants it to be there. He knows our weaknesses and desires that we live an abundant life (John 10:10); those common human weaknesses keep us from the best life.

The best (and abundant) life is when we walk closely with our Lord and join Him in His work. It is a walk of trust—our obedience says to God that we know that He knows best, even if we cannot see the end result. The Spirit often leads us into places where we cannot see the end of a matter.

On the other hand, our disobedience says something altogether different. In effect, when we disobey, might we be building a monument to our own greatness, just as Saul did? In other words, the first king of Israel rationalized an adaptation of the plan God told him. No doubt Saul's plan seemed sound and better than the plan God delivered to him, and it did not seem as though he was disobeying; rather, he was improving upon what God intended. A monument to the superior (to God) intellect and wisdom of Saul. How tragic!

To whom are you building a monument? Is your life concerned with making much of yourself by rationalizing deviance from what God has clearly taught?

Application for the Day: Today I will know and trust the Lord so strongly that I will simply go and do as He says.

Thursday, November 21, 2024

Big Me?

Steve Moore

Today's Scripture: John 6:1-15

So there was this kid. For some reason his parents or someone in his life sent him out for the day going somewhere with five loaves of bread and two fish. Whoever did that had a purpose for that food. Maybe it was to feed the boy, or perhaps he was taking food to his grandparents. Who knows? Scripture doesn't specifically tell us— except that it does.

God in heaven (or God on earth at that time, the Son) orchestrated the whole event. The boy did not know this, nor did his parents or whoever gave him the food. But God needed the boy to cross the path of Jesus at a particular time and place for one grand purpose: to show the unlimited power and love of the God-man Jesus.

Jesus was going to feed more than 5,000 people and have more left over than what started the meal. The boy with the fish and bread just needed to show up and be willing to consider that this rabbi was worthy of fish and bread—a pretty small part in the scheme of things.

We live in an age where narcissism is common; making a name for yourself and being well known is highly desired. This young boy— we know *of* him, but we do not know his name. He had a small part to play in the big plan of the Messiah.

We sing that great hymn "Our God, He Is Alive"; may we learn to live as though we believe it. In this proud age, may we embody the words of the Apostle Paul, "For by the grace given me I say to everyone among you not to think of himself more highly than he ought to think" (Rom. 12:3a).

Application for the Day: Today I will learn to walk in expectancy with humility, believing that my Lord is active all around me and that each day He will put people and situations in which He needs me to be His hands, feet, and heart.

Friday, November 22, 2024

Big Person or Big God?

Steve Moore

Today's Scripture: 1 Samuel 17:41-47

Surveys from the 1950s found that young people wanted to be firemen, policemen, doctors, lawyers, mothers, fathers, husbands, and wives. A recent survey found that young people of today, about 80 percent of them, simply desire to be famous. The desire for the approval of man is a trap. Dante noted in his Divine Comedy:

"A breath of wind is all there is to fame

Here upon earth: it blows this way and that,

And when it changes quarter it changes name.

Though loosed from flesh in old age, you will have in, say, a thousand years, more reputation than if you went from a child's play to the grave" (Dante Alighieri, Purgatorio).

This wisdom of the ages has been all but lost today. So how should we live? We should live in view of the truest reality. We are spiritual beings, every single one of us, housed in a temporary physical body. Our lives are a precious gift given to us by our loving Creator. Jesus said that unless we "abide in me [Jesus]" we can "do nothing" (John 15:5). He also told us that He came in order that we may "have life and have it abundantly" (John 10:10). His servant and brother Paul even stressed the pure truth, "He who did not spare his own Son but gave Him up for us all, how will he not also with him graciously give us all things?" (Rom. 8:32).

In view of all of that, what exactly does the approval of man— "fame"—do for us?

Exactly. When we consider the ultimate spiritual reality of life, man's approval does nothing of value for us. It pales in comparison to the glorious koinonia (intimate fellowship) we can have daily with our Savior.

As Dante noted (and he struggled with pride, the desire to be well known), fame is just a "breath of wind."

Application for the Day: Today I will dwell in the beauty of the grace lavished upon me daily and let the person of the Christ be my food, my portion.

Monday, November 25, 2024

Enduring Faith

Steve Moore

Today's Scripture: 2 Chronicles 16:12

King Asa of Judah came out of the starting gate like a stallion. He took the throne and immediately began cleaning the land of idols and high places, even removing his mother from her place for making a detestable idol. He had the foresight and courage to know that when the Lord grants peace, we should use that time to grow in strength. He fortified the cities of Judah and trained the fighting men.

Asa faced Zerah, the Ethiopian, found himself greatly outnumbered, yet drew up his fighting men (with him being right in the middle) and prayed to God: "O LORD, there is none like you to help, between the mighty and the weak. Help us, O LORD our God, for we rely on you, and in your name we have come against this multitude. O LORD, you are our God; let not man prevail against you" (2 Chron. 14:11).

Wow! This guy, as I read this, was the ultimate King. Total reliance on the LORD! This guy was living his faith to the point of putting himself in a situation where, if his God didn't show up, he was going to be dead.

Perfect King. Except for the verse that started this devotional. Somewhere in the later years when things got rough, instead of trusting the God who delivered him when outnumbered two to one, he relied on his own social and political skills. As the prophet Azariah warned Asa: "The LORD is with you while you are with him. If you seek him, he will be found by you, but if you forsake him, he will forsake you" (2 Chron. 15:2). Starting strong is great, but shouldn't finishing strong be our goal?

Application for the Day: Today I will make a resolute covenant to forever hold on to the robes of Yeshua the Messiah; even if He has to drag me through the dirt, I will live to finish well, to live in the abundance that my Savior intended (John 10:10).

Tuesday, November 26, 2024

God of "Meh" People...

Steve Moore

Scripture for today: 1 Samuel 13:1-12

King Abijah and his troops were in a standoff against King Jeroboam. Outnumbered two to one, Abijah used some strong spiritual words to attempt to prevent the conflict, the words in the Scripture above. They all sound so holy and righteous—Abijah seems like a stand-up man-of-faith.

There is a problem, though. The story above of the battle between the two kings is from 2 Chronicles 3. The account of Abijah in 1 Kings 15 gives an important detail the chronicler *leaves out:* " ...he [Abijah, called *Abijam* in Kings] walked in all the sins that his father did before him, and his heart was not wholly true to the LORD his God...". Here's this guy proclaiming how good his side is and as far as his devotion to God it is just sort of "meh." Does God hear and help the mediocre believer?

Let us allow Scripture to answer that. While Abijah was trash-talking his enemy something big was happening. "Jeroboam had sent an ambush around to come upon them from behind" (13:13). Outnumbered two-to-one, now surrounded by an enemy force, and really just a "sort-of-believer" in God, not doing everything right in spite of his religious trash talking—will the LORD allow him to be defeated? Here's the skinny:

"And they [Abijah's forces] cried to the LORD, and the priests blew the trumpets. Then the men of Judah raised the battle shout. And when the men of Judah shouted, God defeated Jeroboam and all Israel before Abijah and Judah" (13:14, 15). The great news about our great God is that He hears us in our weak and uncertain faith! He will come storming in and save the day at times even for a marginal believer.

Application for today: Given the big heart of the One who gave us life, we can count on Him even in our "meh" moments. But why be "meh?" Our God is worth our all, and what might we see Him do if we went *all-in* for God every day?

Wednesday, November 27, 2024

Mid-Course Correction? Yes

Steve Moore

Today's Scripture: 2 Chronicles 19:1-7

King Jehoshaphat's early years were stunning. He educated, sanctified, and purified Judah. He followed much of the early pattern of his king-father Asa, fortifying the cities while peace was upon the land. It's great to see how *good* a king he was.

But at some point, in his middle-aged years, perhaps, after all the initial goodness and the blessings of wealth and success from the Lord—the prophet Jehu says *this* to Jehoshaphat:

"Should you help the wicked and love those who hate the LORD? Because of this, wrath has gone out against you from the LORD. Nevertheless, some good is found in you" (2 Chron. 19:2,3a).

In the Scripture for today, you see something important about this king—he was willing to take criticism. He put pride aside and humbled himself again before the God that he and we serve.

But if Jehoshaphat, as on fire as he was to begin with, could become a "some good in you" kind of guy—can it happen to us?

What does our Lord want us to know about the nature of our long walk with Him? Do you have strong relationships with other believers in which you *seek* negative feedback, rebuke, and reproof? Do you come to the Word with a heart willing to change if it challenges you?

In *The Screwtape Letters*, C.S. Lewis pointed out about the devil, "The long, dull, monotonous years of middle-aged prosperity or middle-aged adversity are excellent campaigning weather." Indeed, they are. It's easy to get psyched up to serve God when we are young and bursting with idealism and energy. But as we slog through the years and even decades of daily life, maintaining zeal is very difficult.

But we must. Are you willing to make a mid-course correction? Can you take some reproof or a rebuke if you've drifted from your zealous pursuit of our Holy God?

Application for the Day: Today I will think hard about *why* God saw to it that we would have stories such as that of Jehoshaphat where he gets called on his drift from zeal.

Thursday, November 28, 2024

Most Better

Steve Moore

Today's Scripture: 1 Kings 12:25-27

Jeroboam was a "very able" (1 Kings 11:28) servant of Solomon who was told by a prophet of God that he would become the king of ten of the twelve tribes of Israel. In working for Solomon, Jeroboam may have desired to move up in the rank structure—but did he want to be a king? Scripture doesn't say, but that was quite a promotion by God himself!

After the death of Solomon, it happened. Rehoboam, one of Solomon's sons, took some unwise counsel, and the nation of Israel became two: Israel and Judah. Not long after Jeroboam became king, the thoughts in the verse above occur—he suddenly realized that everyone was supposed to go to Jerusalem to sacrifice, and in his heart there was fear. Fear of losing his power as a king. Fear of being killed by his own people. Fear of people not looking up to him as a great man.

So he hatched a plan. He made some golden calves, erected high places, and appointed priests who are not from the tribe of Levi. His plan to stay on the throne was an affront to the One who put him on the throne. Fear, based on his lack of knowledge of our completely trustworthy God, was at the root. Perhaps that was the problem all along, though. While Jeroboam was "very able" and a go-getter to better himself, perhaps he forsook doing the "most-better" of all: getting to know God intimately. After all, if the Creator and Ruler of the Universe puts you on the throne, doesn't He have the power to keep you there? And if He needs to remove you from power, are you strong enough to stop Him?

Application for the Day: Today I will not get lost in my daily efforts to do what is urgent and fail to sit quietly with God in His word, to perceive His voice as I go through the day, and to reflect upon what He has always done in my life.

No One's Regret

Steve Moore

Today's Scripture: 2 Chronicles 21

It is a very sad statement at the end of our Scripture for today: "And he [Jehoram] departed with no one's regret." The son of Jehoshaphat and grandson of Asa, it was not the case that King Jehoram had no good examples of godliness—Jehoram just chose a path of absolute evil. When he died, no one was sorry.

The king of Judah was supposed to represent the presence and precepts of God Himself. His rule was to be contained within the Law handed down to Israel, and he was to be obedient to God. As such, what was it supposed to be like to live under a king of Israel?

Of course, when we think of the Law, we often think of the very specific 600+ commands, preceded by the overarching Ten Commandments—the principles that undergirded the whole of the Law. Of a truth, the typical person from Judah who was honest before God couldn't keep ten commandments, much less 600 or more. If the king of Judah, or Israel, were to represent and keep the Law—what would it be like to live under his reign? Impossible? No. For with the Law came the sacrifices. With the Law came the tacit recognition that God's people could not keep the Ten Commandments, much less the 600+, without an atoning sacrifice.

The grace and mercy of atonement through the ever-available sacrificial system came with the commandments given to Moses. As a representative of the Law, which represents the beautiful heart of our magnificent and ultimate King, living under a godly king should have reflected what God revealed of Himself in Exodus 34:6b: "The LORD, the LORD, a God merciful and gracious, slow to anger, and abounding in steadfast love and faithfulness." As we go into the world to represent our Savior, do we ooze mercy, grace, calmness, and steadfast love for all?

Application for the Day: Today I will prayerfully seek to be the refreshing and life-giving representative that our loving Father is.

Monday, December 2, 2024

The Counselors of Our Undoing

Steve Moore

Today's Scripture: 2 Chronicles 22:1-9

Ahaziah became king and was executed only one year into his reign. The LORD arranged for his execution. He was that bad. The recorder of his reign notes in two places that his downfall was due to those he was listening to: his mother (vv. 2-3) and the house of Ahab (v. 4), who were his advisers.

We live in a time of both isolation and illiteracy. We are, though supposedly electronically connected, the loneliest generation of people in history. We surround ourselves with amusement in the forms of electronic devices and streaming content, shut off our brains, and waste our lives being programmed by stimulating messages.

We have become, as a whole, a people overly concerned with our image, rather than the image of God—and so we do not bear our burdens (Gal. 6:2) because admitting our struggles would harm our carefully crafted appearance and perceived strength before others. We are also, although capable of reading, not likely to do so. We make excuses for our lack of discipline in reading and reflecting, but in truth it is just our choice to be amused, rather than edified. It is spiritual sloth justified by our claiming to be incapable for some psychological or physiological reason.

Our counsel comes from our chosen entertainment: our streaming content and the pleasing sound of our favored speaker at church or in Bible class. We do not make the choice to allow Scripture personally to penetrate our hearts, nor do we trust one another to speak into one another's lives as we strive to keep our curated image intact. We are following the path of Ahaziah. Will our great God do for us as he did for Ahaziah? Shouldn't he? We have the revelation of God and the abiding presence of the Lord who desires to "lavish" (Eph. 1:8) his grace upon us. Can we really afford to go on walking alongside Ahaziah?

Application for the Day: Today I will begin the hard, but good, path of seeking the counsel of the Lord through the written word and intimate fellowship with His people.

Tuesday, December 3, 2024

What Shall We Instruct God?

Steve Moore

Today's Scripture: Job 37:14-20

A few of my best friends and I have been reading Dante's Divine Comedy lately, and some of it seems a bit shocking. As one of my co-readers puts it, their "potty-language" is pretty crude by current Christian standards. Written in Italian, the more faithful translators make it clear that the chosen words are the more vulgar forms, much as our "four-letter-word" varieties. You get the picture.

On the other hand, when our God is spoken of, there is only reverence—with one exception.

Those who are in the inferno (eternal hell) are the only ones who speak ill of God or make accusations against Him. Strange, isn't it, how so often we question God's goodness—much as Job did! We obliquely make accusations that His goodness is not that good or even unfair. Much as Job did, for example, when he said the following: "Though he slay me, I will hope in him; yet I will argue my ways to his face" (Job 13:15). "My ways!" You see, Job's friends thought he was suffering because he had done something wrong. After all, only sinful people suffer.

Job knew better: God had made a mistake. He was ready to argue his "ways" to God's face.

So in today's reading is the beautiful truth—and the attitude I pray I will have every day. This guy Elihu, who is so unimportant that he is not even introduced early in the story, is young and not as respected as Job's other companions. But he knows what people of Dante's time at least tried to respect: God is always good, right, and holy. If you perceive that God has made a mistake in your life, you are mistaken.

When God shows up in the whirlwind around Job and his friends, only one person in that group receives no condemnation. It is the young Elihu, the one who says, "Shall it be told him [God Almighty] that I would speak?" (Job 37:20a).

Application for the Day: Today I will remember that, when all else seems confusing, God is always good and right.

Final Viewing

Originally written by Larry Snow
Submitted in his memory by Susan Snow

Today's Scripture: Luke 9:25 "For what profit is it to a man if he gains the whole world, and is himself destroyed or lost?"

Have you seen Fredric Baur lately? Recognize the name? How about his product? (Pringles). Mr. Baur died in Cincinnati, OH at the age of 89. As an organic chemist and food packaging tech., he was the man who designed the Pringles packaging system. He was so proud of his invention that he had a portion of his cremated remains buried in a Pringles can. Don't ask me if they just used the resealable lid or had it vacuum sealed at the factory – I don't know.

In the same article was referenced a man that had custom designed his coffin to look just like his favorite beverage can. He is using it as a cooler until needed for its final purpose. "Scottie" from Star Trek had his ashes launched into space in 2005, and the family of Frank Sinatra say they buried everything from tootsie rolls to a bottle of his favorite beverage with him.

All these references to people being buried with what they were known for in life caused me to think. What if that were the norm instead of the quirky exception that it is? What would you be buried in (or with)? What if at your final viewing, the true emphasis of your life was as evident as a Pringles can? Right there for all to see. What would it be?
- A bank account?
- Deeds of all the property you own?
- A picture of your house?
- Golf clubs, fishing boat, the purchases of your latest shopping spree?
- A TV, video game, a duck blind, your new wardrobe?
- A car?
- A Bible, a lesson, the difference made in the lives of people, a crowd of Christians taught the gospel by you, a sea of faces changed by your example?

There it is for all to see…The object of my being…the fruit of my labor…the meaning of my life…for all to see.

Application for the Day: What is your final view?

Thursday, December 5, 2024

At the Right Time

Suzanne Gillson

Today's Scripture: I Peter 3:15-16

I marvel at the timing of Jesus' arrival on earth. It was a simple time and space in which He chose to spend His earthly ministry. The only means to spread His message was through word of mouth and His own two feet. He carried no suitcase and made no plans for meals and lodging. He chose twelve common men to accompany Him. His message was often rejected, and He often commanded silence about Himself (Matt. 16:20, Mark 5:43, Luke 5:14).

In John 7:1-8, Jesus' brothers challenge him to *publicly* pronounce His message if He "seeks to be known openly," and His reply is, "My time has not yet come." God's covenant with us is all about timing. From the beginning, God set a plan in motion to redeem mankind in "the fullness of time" (Gal. 4:4). As a result of God's right timing, 3000 souls were added to the church following Peter's sermon at Pentecost (Acts 2:41).

With today's busy schedules, we are often ruled by time. We set alarms for when to wake up, when to meet up, and when to pack up. We have appointed times to eat, exercise, and engage, but do we have scheduled time to talk about Jesus? You might say, well, of course—Sunday and Wednesday. Ouch!

When is the right time to spread the Gospel? With our advantages of technology and resources, we have more than the early church could have imagined. So what are we waiting for? Just the right time? We are living in the right time on this side of the cross! Peter instructs, "But in your hearts honor Christ the Lord as holy, always being prepared to make a defense to anyone who asks you for a reason for the hope that is in you; yet do it with gentleness and respect" (I Pet. 3:15). Plan today to appoint a time of study, prayer, and evangelism because now is the right time.

Application for the Day: Today I will schedule a time to study, pray, and reach out to a friend about Jesus.

Friday, December 6, 2024

Taking Matters into Our Own Hands

Suzanne Gillson

Today's Scripture: Romans 12:12

Have you ever become impatient when waiting for something and decided to take matters into your own hands? If you have taken a scenic route instead of looking at a map or wound up with too many screws left over from a project, then you know what I'm talking about.

People have always been people, and as such we are an impatient lot. We can blame this trait on our technology or our genes, but all we need to do is look back to the beginning of man's story in Genesis to find an early example and ongoing instances of impatience. Sarai, in Genesis 16, decided to hurry God's plan along, and Naaman, in 2 Kings 5, wanted to be cured of his leprosy instantly. James and John, in Luke 9:54, were ready to bring fire down from heaven to punish the Samaritans immediately for rejecting Jesus. Impatience: it is a human flaw that requires godly intervention—prayer.

Praying for patience while learning to be patient can be challenging, yet the lessons we learn are invaluable. Learning to wait on God's timing allows us space to grow in our faith. It produces within us both character and hope (Rom. 5:3-5). One of my favorite people in the Bible to learn from is Joseph. He waited in the pit, he waited in prison, and he waited patiently when he discovered his brothers and realized God's plan for the preservation of his family (Gen. 45:5). At the end of his life, Joseph reassured his brothers that God's plan was always at work (Gen. 50:20). In our present trials, we may not see God's plan, but we can rest assured that He is working for our good.

"And we know that for those who love God all things work together for good, for those who are called according to his purpose" (Rom. 8:28).

Application for the Day: Today I will reflect on the things God has done for me in the past in order to see the good that He is working for me today.

Monday, December 9, 2024

The In Between

Suzanne Gillson

Today's Scripture: Philippians 2:7-8

Lately, I have been thinking about transitions in life. Along our journey there are forks in the road where decisions must be made. We make decisions about college, careers, relationships, and family journeys. We find ourselves at a point of transition where we are leaving one role and migrating into another area of life. It can be a point in life that causes us to pause and feel anxious, excited, and nervous all at once. Leaving the safety and security of the known to step into the unknown takes courage and faith. As roles in life change, our identities are molded and restructured. Throughout a lifetime, we may be called children, students, sons and daughters, and husbands and wives, along with our professional roles. We are constantly changing and adapting.

When you feel overwhelmed during inevitable transitions, remember that Jesus is our constant reference for life. Hebrews 2:17 reminds us, "Therefore he had to be made like his brothers in every respect, so that he might become a merciful and faithful high priest, in the service of God to make propitiation for the sins of the people." Every word in the Bible has a purpose for our edification (Acts 20:32). We can rely on its truth for our lives. In every respect, Jesus knows the full extent of the human experience. He transitioned from a place of glory for us. He came to the earth when there was no running water, ease of transportation, or comfort of technology. He was a son, a friend, and the Messiah. He walked the road between heaven and earth and fulfilled God's plan for salvation. Every step He took led Him closer to the cross. He knew the plan, He subjected himself to the plan, but His humanity dreaded the pain it would bring.

When you are anxious about the roles you are stepping into, remember that your Savior has walked the road ahead of you and is able to sympathize with you.

Application for the Day: Today I will pray for peace during the transitions in life.

Tuesday, December 10, 2024

The Missing Peace

Suzanne Gillson

Today's Scripture: John 14:27a – "Peace I leave with you; my peace I give to you."

Sitting there on the table was a half-done puzzle. The pieces were strewn about the table with some still in the box. Someone had started it and then just walked away. I sat down at the table with mindless ambition. I started picking up the pieces and just moved them around. I didn't really want to put the puzzle together, but it gave my hands something to do. Before I knew it, a part of the puzzle's picture had appeared. Soon I found myself engaged in finding and fitting together the pieces. Finally, the last piece was in place, but there was still a hole in the picture. A missing piece! How frustrating! Then I heard the voice, "Miss, your mother is done with her exam."

I sat in countless waiting rooms while my mother endured endless testing and exams in search of a cure for her cancer. In the hospital waiting rooms were puzzles for those who were waiting. Piece by piece the time passed, yet it was the peace that only God can offer for which I was searching.

During times of great trials, we can find ourselves lost in the storm. We are like the disciples who cried to Jesus, "Do you not care that we are perishing?" (Mark 4:38). And like the disciples, Jesus is there to remind us that He is the master of the storm. He is the only One who can offer the peace that we need (John 14:27).

In the end, my mother's cure was a heavenly one, but as I reflect on the experience, my mind settles on the puzzles. How often do we spend countless hours trying to fit all the pieces of our lives together only to find that there is a piece missing? We search and search for the missing piece when what we are really missing is God's peace.

Application for the Day: Today I will pray for the peace that only God can give.

Wednesday, December 11, 2024

The Road to Grace

Suzanne Gillson

Today's Scripture: 2 Corinthians 12:9

Incest, murder, adultery, pride, dishonesty, idolatry! When Matthew wrote the genealogy of Jesus in chapter one of his gospel account, we often hurry through until we get to verse 16, where we recognize Joseph, Mary, and Jesus. I'm making this assumption based on how I typically read this passage. However, when we stop to place these verses in the context of grace and realize that no words are ever wasted in God's inspired Word, it should cause us to ask why Matthew took the time to tediously inform us of Jesus' relatives. Matthew was writing to a Jewish audience, and it was important that His roots be traced back to the "father of the Jews," Abraham. However, when we broaden our lens and focus on grace, do we think about the people He used to deliver Jesus to the earth? It's a list of imperfect people, to say the least.

Our gift of grace entered this world as each of us did—naked and in need of care. The miraculous birth was not without worries, as we read about in Matthew 1:19, when Joseph thought to divorce Mary, or in Luke 1:29, when we are told about Mary's initial fear of the angel's visit to her. David, a man after God's own heart (Acts 13:22), had his share of problems with adultery and managing his own household. Rahab had no idea that she would be listed in the genealogy of Jesus (Matthew 1:5)! I don't how that affects you, but it gives me reassurance. God provides grace because we are imperfect people, but He loves us anyway. What we can take from this, though, is that the grace of God makes a way. It cuts its own path through our world, and it will cut its own path through yours if you let it. God's grace is "made perfect in weakness" (2 Cor. 12:9).

Application for the Day: Today I will thank God for the grace that He gives and realize that, while I am imperfect, I am made perfect through Him.

248

Thursday, December 12, 2024

Reaching for His Power – Part 1

Ted Williams

Today's Scripture: Ephesians 3:20-21

Have you ever experienced an electronic rolling blackout? Power companies occasionally use these breaks in local services when the power grid cannot provide enough power to cover the demand of the entire region. This phenomenon has not happened very often in my lifetime in Middle Tennessee, thanks to our TVA Power Grid, but it did happen a few months ago for just a few hours one day.

During the rolling blackout, I found myself repeatedly going to the light switch on the wall and requesting the power. I knew for several days in advance that the rolling blackout would occur, and when the power went off, I knew exactly what was happening. However, after a few minutes, I forgot. When I went into a different room, I naturally wanted the light to come on and, out of habit, reached for the switch to turn the light on. The light did not come on, however, because the power source was not supplying our house.

When you are accustomed to having power so accessible and reliable, it is so easy to take it for granted or use it and not even realize it. Electricity is a blessing that most Americans accept as a right instead of a privilege. It is understood to be a privilege, however, by people in the world globally.

In considering the blessing of our physical power grid, notice what the apostle Paul said about God's spiritual power grid. Ephesians 3:20-21 says, "Now to Him who by His power working in us is able to do far beyond anything we can ask or imagine, to Him be glory in the church and in Christ Jesus from generation to generation forever. Amen." (Complete Jewish Bible version)

Application for the Day: Today I will remember God's promise of abundant power to those who reach for it.

Reaching for His Power – Part 2
Ted Williams

Today's Scripture: Ephesians 3:20-21 – "Now to Him who by His power working in us is able to do far beyond anything we can ask or imagine, to Him be glory in the church and in Christ Jesus from generation to generation forever. Amen." (Complete Jewish Bible version)

Note the words in verse 20: "His power working in us." The Creator of the universe has given His power to His children. And that power "is able to do far beyond anything we can ask or imagine." God's power grid never has a break in service. Romans 8:34 describes Christ at the right hand of God working for us all the time, and Jesus himself committed to never leave us. In Matthew 28:20, He said, "And behold, I am with you always, to the end of the age." Scripture plainly teaches us that, for the child of God, His power supply is always with us and available to us.

When I try to accomplish things on my own, in my pride I seek to act independently. I then realize that I should have begun working on an issue by engaging God's power first. In some ways, the independence of our American culture works against us when we seek to prove to ourselves that "I have this." We really have nothing without God and His power.

Here is my prayer for today: "As I strive to live in this physical world, may I remember this day that I can do anything that God allows and helps me to do." Only negative things happen outside of His blessings.

Reach for His power today. It is within your grasp and is always available to His children. He has put His power within us to do His will. Blessings for your spiritual power-filled day!

Application for the Day: Today I will remember that I can do anything that God allows and helps me to do.

Monday, December 16, 2024

Comfort Zone

Tim Hogue

Today's Scripture: Genesis 12:1-3 – "Now the Lord said to Abram, 'Go from your country and your kindred and your father's house to the land that I will show you. And I will make of you a great nation, and I will bless you and make your name great, so that you will be a blessing. I will bless those who bless you, and him who dishonors you I will curse, and in you all the families of the earth shall be blessed.'"

In our den, there is a spot. It's "my spot." It is the spot in the house where I feel most comfortable. I'm not sure if it is the chair that occupies that spot or the angle it sits to the TV. Maybe it is because it is right by the fireplace. I love "my spot." I will occasionally sit somewhere other than "my spot," and it feels uncomfortable. I don't like it.

We have comfortable spots in our spiritual lives as well. I know I do. I am happy to do *this*, but I don't want to do *that*. Sometimes what God has planned for me is the thing that makes me the most uncomfortable.

When I feel that way, I think of Abram. If anyone had a valid reason for telling God that He was asking too much, it would be Abram. God asked Abram to move away from everyone he knew and go to a land that he did not know, with no more incentive than that God promised him he would be blessed.

Abram might have thought, *I'm good. I am already blessed.* We sometimes think that way. God has promised us blessing beyond compare, but we have to be prepared to move from our place of comfort to receive it. We might have to do that thing that seems hard. Uncomfortable. Despite the fears, Abram heard the call, and he obeyed.

Application for the Day: Today I will be open to the Lord's call and allow God to turn me into the person He desires me to be, knowing that embracing the discomfort helps me to grow.

251

Tuesday, December 17, 2024

God's Love

Tim Hogue

Today's Scripture: Zephaniah 3:17 – "The Lord your God is in your midst, The Mighty One, will save; He will rejoice over you with gladness, He will quiet you with His love, He will rejoice over you with singing."

Life can be very noisy. Constant demands of our time, combined with the hustle and bustle of daily living, take their toll on each of us. If we are not careful, this busy life we lead can shape our image of God's love to the point that we limit God's love, and the noise consumes us.

Scripture helps us to see beyond the clutter. God's love, though without measure, is high, wide, long, and deep (Eph. 3:17-19). It is bigger than the noise of our lives.

Witness the love of God in Scripture:

1 John 3:1a: "Behold what manner of love the Father has bestowed on us, that we should be called children of God!"

Eph. 3:17-19: "That Christ may dwell in your hearts through faith; that you, being rooted and grounded in love, may be able to comprehend with all the saints what is the width and length and depth and height— to know the love of Christ which passes knowledge; that you may be filled with all the fullness of God."

1 John 4:9: "In this the love of God was manifested toward us, that God has sent His only begotten Son into the world, that we might live through Him."

Romans 5:8: "But God demonstrates His own love toward us, in that while we were still sinners, Christ died for us."

Romans 8:35: "Who shall separate us from the love of Christ? Shall tribulation, or distress, or persecution, or famine, or nakedness, or peril, or sword?"

Finally consider John 3:16: "For God so loved the world that He gave His only begotten Son, that whoever believes in Him should not perish but have everlasting life."

Application for the Day: Today I will allow God's loving presence to be a comfort in this chaotic world.

Passion

Tim Hogue

Today's Scripture: Mark 12:30 – "And you shall love the Lord your God with all your heart and with all your soul and with all your mind and with all your strength."

I think we all have a desire to be passionate. We all pull for the hero in movies and cheer for the athlete on the field. We admire and hope to emulate the passion that makes them great. We are passionate because God created us that way. He created us with a desire to be passionate so that He can use that passion to accomplish His plans.

The Bible is the ultimate story of passion. It speaks the passionate love of Jesus that caused Him to leave His place of status and live among ordinary people ultimately giving His life, providing hope for otherwise hopeless people (people like me).

We were made to be passionate people. Is your passion out of whack? It happens.

Passion is a very hot term in our contemporary culture. People are always asking, "What's your passion?" What they're really asking you is, "what is it that really gets your heart racing"?

What is it that makes you excited to get up each day? For some the answer would be, the job – making money, maybe football, baseball… or some hobby. For some it is simply doing nothing.

I think that for most of us when we were first baptized and became children of God, we had a hunger to learn more about God. We were quick to talk about God. There was a real spiritual passion. A passion for God.

So, where are you right now? Has your passion moved from the spiritual to the recreational? Have you lost your passion all together?

Jesus reminds us that when you give your heart to God, you want to maintain that passion and love Him with all your heart.

Application for Today: Today, I will with purpose center on God and rekindle my spiritual passion and allow Him to use my passion for His purpose.

Thursday, December 19, 2024

God's Word – Part 1

Tim Spann

Today's Scripture: 2 Peter 1:3

In today's text Peter said, "His divine power has given to us all things that pertain to life and godliness, through the knowledge of Him who called us by glory and virtue." With this verse in mind, I would like for us to think about how God spoke to His people in the Old Testament compared to now. Close your eyes and try to think about standing at the base of Mt. Sinai with the Israelites. There's a dark cloud with fire over the mountain. Thunder and lightning. Loud trumpet blasts. The very ground under you is trembling. You hear a voice that rattles your liver. So strong and powerful, you actually fear for your life! (Ex. 19:18-20)

Now place yourself at the feet of Jesus as He gives the Sermon on the Mount. Calm and peaceful. A voice that draws you in, yet still just as strong and powerful (Matt. 5-7).

Today we have the written Word of God given to us from forty different men over a period of 1500 years. Everything fits together perfectly, and even now it is strong and powerful. God's Word is the only offensive weapon we are given in our battle against Satan. His Word is compared to a sword that has the ability to bring the biggest, toughest man to his knees.

Through the Word of God, we have everything we need to communicate with the Creator of the Universe. His Word is so much more than history, laws, and rules. It's a story of complete love. It's a story of redemption. It's the story of Jesus, our Lord and Savior.

I'm thankful for His Word, for the connection it gives us to God, as well as the spiritual connection we have with each other. I'm thankful that I have everything needed to defeat Satan.

Application for the Day: Today I will say a prayer of thanksgiving for the wonderful story of love and redemption found in the true and living Word of God.

Friday, December 20, 2024

God's Word – Part 2

Tim Spann

Today's Scripture: Isaiah 55:11

"So shall my word be that goes out from my mouth; it shall not return to me empty, but it shall accomplish that which I purpose, and shall succeed in the thing for which I sent it" (Isa. 55:11). "All scripture is breathed out by God and profitable for teaching, for reproof, for correction, and for training in righteousness, that the man of God may be complete, equipped for every good work" (2 Tim. 3:16-17). "For the word of God is living and active, sharper than any two-edged sword, piercing to the division of soul and of spirit, of joints and of marrow, and discerning the thoughts and intentions of the heart" (Heb. 4:12).

Isaiah 55:11 is very powerful in my mind. What God speaks is going to happen. What does that look like? I have trouble wrapping my mind around it. But I can grasp the other two verses. A sword does a lot of damage when it goes in. God's sword goes in and cuts you all the way to your spirit and soul. What does it do? It teaches what is right. It rebukes what is not right. It corrects so that we know how to get it right. And it trains so that we can stay right.

Because God's Word is alive, it is always applicable to us. It never goes out of date or needs improvement. We can always trust what it says. Since it is "at work," it is able to discipline us and allow us to know about His amazing love, grace, and mercy. As we read and study with an open heart, it affects how we think and feel, shaping us to be more Christlike and strengthening our relationship with our eternal Father.

God's Word is active and alive in our lives working through the Holy Spirit. It gives us hope, strength, peace, and joy!

Application for the Day: Today I will allow God's Word to shape me and transform me into being more like Him; I will feel His presence and allow the Holy Spirit to work in me.

Monday, December 23, 2024

God's Word – Part 3

Tim Spann

Today's Scripture: Matthew 28:19-20

Have you ever thought about the question, "What does God's Word say about God's Word?" It is a very important question. Jesus said, "Go therefore and make disciples of all nations, baptizing them in the name of the Father and of the Son and of the Holy Spirit, teaching them to observe all that I have commanded you. And behold, I am with you always, to the end of the age" (Matt. 28:19-20).

If we truly believe in God, then we have to believe His Word. You can't have one and not the other. We are given His Word so that we can be ready to work. We are given His Word so that we can share it. It's not meant for us to hold on to, but rather slosh it around freely to everyone. Kevin Turbeville once made a powerful statement: "If you get this gift and you try to hoard it, it will sour. Then you don't want it, and neither will anyone else."

Think about that and let it really sink in deeply. His Word should be a fire in our belly that has to come out! And yet we go to "church" and read our Bible and pray but never share, and soon we become apathetic to all of it. We are commanded to be disciple makers, but, in reality, we should be eager and willing and excited to tell everyone the Good News about our Lord and Savior and the wonderful love He has for each one of us! But let's not forget that last sentence in Matthew because that's extra good. No matter what happens, no matter how dark a place we find ourselves, no matter what life brings our way—no matter what, Jesus is always with us!

Application for the Day: Today I will make a new commitment to be better at sharing my faith and His Word with everyone I meet.

Tuesday, December 24, 2024

Going to Church in the Navy – Part 1
Tommy Davidson

Today's Scripture: Hebrews 10:24-25

When I was thinking about joining the Navy, it never entered my mind about where I would go to church. Mother and Daddy always took all six of us to the Pomona Church of Christ every Sunday morning and evening and most Wednesdays. My first two Sundays in basic training were busy with our company. There were about 65 per company and about 50 companies. The third week all the recruits had to go to church. There were about 50 of us who went to the Church of Christ service. It was a joy and blessing to go to a church service like I attended back home.

When I went aboard the USS Passumpsic in Long Beach, I had duty the first weekend. The next Sunday I put on my dress uniform (you could not wear civilian clothes aboard ship). I caught the liberty boat across the harbor, found a phone booth, and looked up the Church of Christ. The closest one was about five or six blocks away, so I walked to the church building. It was a nice older brick building with more seniors than younger people. It was a very nice service just like we have in Tennessee.

Back home after church there was always something to do on Sunday afternoon. Sometimes Mother had a good dinner, and someone usually came home with us from church. Daddy never worked in the field on a Sunday. Sunday was my time, and I always had a friend or cousin over, or I would go to their house. It was never boring. I was walking back toward the ship and had this hollow, lonesome feeling in my gut. It was a nice sunny day, and I had been to church. There is a line in an old country song which says, "When you're young, a long way from home, there is nothing like a Sunday that makes a person feel alone." I thought to myself, "Welcome to the world, Davidson."

Application for the Day: Today I will remember those who nurtured my faith and prepared me for difficult times.

Wednesday, December 25, 2024

Going to Church in the Navy – Part 2

Tommy Davidson

Today's Scripture: Acts 1:8

On the three trips I made to the Far East, the only Church of Christ I attended was in Subic Bay, Philippines. The Subic Bay Naval Base was a great place to be. It was tropical and clean; there were a nice swimming pool, tennis court, exercise club, ballfield, eating places, movie theaters, and a nice beach. The base had everything.

I was aboard ship one Saturday afternoon, and up on a hill I saw a building that had the words "Church of Christ" painted on the roof. What a surprise! I worshiped there several times.

One Sunday afternoon two of the male members invited me to go with them out in the bush to have a church service. We rode a "jeepney" several miles out and walked about thirty minutes to a small group of thatched houses on stilts, six to seven feet above the ground, where members held a service in one of the houses. The house was very clean and neat, and I was thankful to be there. Everyone sat on the floor. It was a regular service with communion.

During the ten days I spent in Saigon, I came by a large residential house with a sign that read "Church of Christ." I took note of the times for worship, and the next Sunday I went to that house. There were about fifty people. The preacher was Maurice Hall, an American civilian. He would talk about five minutes, and then a Vietnamese interpreter would speak. It would go back and forth. After the service, I shook the preacher's hand and told him I was from Dickson, Tennessee. He asked if I knew of the Pomona Church of Christ. I informed him that it was where I went to church most of my life. I enjoyed dinner at his house the next evening.

Here I was halfway around the world in a country at war, and I met someone who had attended my hometown church.

Application for the Day: Today I will thank God for my home church and the church worldwide.

Thursday, December 26, 2024

E. Winston Burton
1922- 2012
Tommy Nicks

Today's Scripture: Proverbs 3:1 - "My son, do not forget my teaching, but keep my commands in your heart."

One of the great blessings I have experienced in my life has been the influence of E. Winston Burton during his tenure as the preaching minister here at Walnut Street during the 1960s. Brother Burton began preaching at the age of fifteen and served churches in Alabama, Tennessee, and Arkansas. During those days he wrote profusely and conducted popular radio programs. He was a wonderful pulpit preacher, an even better teacher, and over the years he became a good friend. Brother Burton passed away on September 19, 2012. To the end, he loved, he taught, and he served. I am grateful for having known him, and as Solomon instructed his son, I want to remember Brother's Burton' teachings and keep his commandments in my heart.

I offer the following from his *Pine Knot Kindling* articles in his memory:
*   Old age is like a bank account. You withdraw from what you have already put in.
*   I believe that our background and circumstances may have influenced who we are, but we are responsible for who we become.
*   I believe that true friendship continues to grow, even over the longest distance. Same goes for true love.
*   I believe that you should always leave loved ones with loving words. It may be the last time you see them.
*   I believe that you can keep going, long after you can't.
*   I believe that no matter how good a friend is, he is going to hurt you every once in a while and you must forgive him for that.
*   I believe that we are responsible for what we do, no matter how we feel.
*   I believe that either you control your attitude or it controls you.
*   I believe that it is taking me a long time to become the person I want to be.

Application for the Day: Today I will strive to remember the wise "teachings" and "commandments" of those who positively influenced me early in life.

259

Friday, December 27, 2024

Joy and Peace

Tommy Nicks

Today's Scripture: Romans 15:13 – "Now may the God of hope fill you with all joy and peace in believing, that you may abound in hope by the power of the Holy Spirit."

Paul desired that Christians live in a delightful state of mind filled with joy and peace and that this state of mind would lead to an abundance of hope in our lives. Paul desired that we not only be comforted by joy but that we also dwell in peace and enjoy an abundance of it.

It is not through our own strength that we obtain this condition of joy and peace. This blessing is accomplished only through our faith in God. Every privilege obtainable in this life and in eternity comes from the God of hope. We cannot first ask for joy and then base our faith upon it. Our joy must grow out of our faith in God. Trusting in God fills us with hope.

Joy is a state as safe as it is pleasant. Joy is provided by God to man for man's enjoyment; however, the best of joy in this world is but for a season. Even while we are enjoying it, we live in fear that it will soon be gone.

The state of mind that is most pleasant is filled not only with joy but also peace in believing. The thing that makes this condition both pleasant and profitable is the addition of peace.

Joy is active and expressive; it sparkles and flashes like a diamond; it is delicious excitement. However, the human flesh is weak and cannot endure continuous delight. Relief comes in the lovely form of peace.

Peace arrives in a calm and quiet manner. Peace comes to give us rest. During trials, it may be hard for us to rejoice. It is through our faith that we have the hope of peace. While we work with joy, we rest with peace.

Application for the Day: Today I will strive for both joy and the solid assurance of peace.

Monday, December 30, 2024

The Wings of Eagles

Tommy Nicks

Today's Scripture: Isaiah 40:31 – "But those who wait on the Lord shall renew their strength; they shall mount up with wings like eagles, they shall run and not be weary, they shall walk and not faint."

A man may sometimes soar on eagle's wings or run without becoming weary, but most of the time he will only walk. In this life, the mounting up with wings as eagles will always be temporary. The real test of our faith comes not when we fly or run, but when we must plod along. It is the tedious walk of everyday life that reveals our true character and our enduring faith in God.

While it is a grand thing to be able to fly, it is a better thing to be able to walk. It is more like a man, involves less danger, and is practically more useful. While it may sometimes be better to run, it is not the best pace for a long journey.

The most sustainable pace for a long journey is to walk. It is a steady, persevering pace that we are better equipped to maintain. In the Scriptures, we read of the walk of faith (Romans 4:12) and the walk of holiness (1 Peter 1:15-16). God desires us to walk in unity with our brethren (Ephesians 4:3). We are instructed to walk worthily with God (Ephesians 4:1). Walking is more practical and designed for everyday living.

God wants our walk with Him to be humble, gentle—with patience and love (Galatians 5:22-23). Our walk is to be according to His will, not ours (Matthew 6:10). We are always to be in obedience to Him (Romans 1:5). In this life, we are not eagles and cannot always be on the wing. But if we wait, we will soar like eagles when God's promise of everlasting life becomes our eternal destiny through our Lord and Savior Jesus Christ.

Application for the Day: Today I will strive to "walk by faith" and "not by sight" (2 Cor.5:7).

Tuesday, December 31, 2024

Unity of the Spirit
Tommy Nicks

Today's Scripture: Ephesians 4:1-3 - "Therefore I, the prisoner of the Lord, urge you to walk in a manner worthy of the calling with which you have been called, with all humility and gentleness, with patience, bearing with one another in love, being diligent to keep the unity of the Spirit in the bond of peace."

Paul urged the Christians at Ephesus to walk in a manner worthy of the Lord while being diligent to keep the unity of the Spirit in the bond of peace. During all the issues and problems that the first century church faced, God never suggested that division was a solution. In fact, God expects us to do just the opposite by walking worthy of Him in unity and peace.

This walk that God wants us to take with Him requires a certain mindset on our part, and we must be engaged in love for Him and for our fellow man. John said, "If we walk in the Light as He Himself is in the Light, we have fellowship with one another, and the blood of Jesus His Son cleanses us from all sin" (1 John 1:7). This approach requires that we be humble, gentle, and patient.

We should bear with one another, granting to others the same right to belong that we claim for ourselves. This concept of bearing does not mean we simply tolerate each other; that would be patience. Bearing with one another is holding one another up, supporting each other, and adding strength to one another while being in obedience to His commands.

Paul said in 1 Corinthians 13:13, "But now faith, hope, and love remain, these three; but the greatest of these is love." Love is what prompts us to seek unity with our brethren. It leads us to forgive others and not to hold their actions against them. It reminds us to seek what is best and to serve our brethren whenever possible.

Application for the Day: Today I will pray for and promote the unity of the Spirit in the bond of peace.

Wednesday, January 1, 2025

Bear One Another's Burden

Troy Williams

Today's Scripture: Galatians 6:1-10; James 5:19-20

Christians are called the body of Christ. In a person's physical body, when one part hurts, it affects the entire body. We then look for the source of the pain and try to remedy it. This concept is true in Christ's spiritual body also.

As we look around the church, we can see many Christians hurting. We also see non-Christians suffering. As we look at some ways people suffer, let us think about how we can bear the burdens of those in the body of Christ and those outside the body of Christ.

Physical Burdens – People are hungry or lonely, have health struggles or money struggles, and are without hope.

Spiritual Burdens – People are being tempted by the evil one and are caught in worldly sins. He uses our selfish nature to pull us away from the Spiritual One.

Family Burdens – There are many people being pulled from their family responsibilities because of jobs, friends, entertainment, recreation, and selfishness.

How can we help ease the burdens of the world? If we share the burden, we have a better chance to bring others to Christ and repair the body of Christ.

In Galatians 6, the burden to be shared involves those who have been caught in transgressions. This passage talks to the one who wishes to restore them. How should we bear the burdens of those people?

    1. Be spiritual.
    2. Be gentle.
    3. Don't be selfish in your actions and feel you are better than the hurting.
    4. Verse 10 states that, as we have opportunity, we should do good to all, especially to those in the body of Christ.

Application for the Day: Today I will make a list of ways I can bear a burden of one in the body of Christ and a list of ways I can bear a burden for someone not a member of the body of Christ. I will pray that my eyes will be open to the opportunities to do both.

Thursday, January 2, 2025

Busy Bee
Troy Williams

Today's Scripture: Colossians 3:23

"I'm in a hurry to get things done. Oh, I rush and rush until life's no fun. . . . I'm in a hurry and don't know why." This was a song sung by the vocal group Alabama. What an accurate depiction of some in society and of our culture today! We are impressed by and praise people who are hard workers. It is a characteristic in someone that is greatly admired. There are even scriptures that back up this hard work attitude: Prov. 12:24, 13:4, 16:3; 2 Thess. 3:10-12. God admires people who work hard, but their work should be the Lord's work. "Whatever you do, work heartily, as for the Lord and not for men" (Col. 3:23).

Work is good, but when is it a problem? It is a problem when we put work before God, when making money or gaining status and power are more important to us than God and His people, when we look to our work to give us self-satisfaction. We can even be busy for a good cause and neglect the Lord, which makes it a bad cause. In the story of the Good Samaritan, the priest and the Levite did not love their fellowman because they would not take the time to help. Their own prejudice got in their way of pleasing God and helping their neighbor. Luke 9 57-62 discusses the cost of discipleship. Trying to gain prestige, position, salary, retirement, family, recreation, or power defeats us from being a faithful Christian. If we work our whole lives and gain all these things, what do we really have (Luke 9:25)?

We cannot serve two masters. We are to seek Him first. Beware of being like Martha and working so much to entertain Christ that we miss His presence. We are here to do the will of the father just as Christ did (Phil. 3:7-8).

Application for the Day: Today I will list all the things I am going to do and count how much time I spend doing God's will and how much time following my own.

Friday, January 3, 2025

Our March to the Promised Land

Troy Williams

Today's Scripture: Numbers 9:15-23; Matthew 16:24

It was God's plan to lead the Israelites to the promised land. He freed them from their bondage and destroyed the ones who persecuted them. God brought them to Mt. Sinai and taught them how to commune with Him. In Leviticus He taught them how to be spiritual. In Numbers He revealed His plans to lead them to the promised land. Fire at night and Cloud by day would be the light to lead the way. When the Fire or Cloud moved, the Israelites would follow and allow God to lead them.

Let us compare our march today to the one they had to the promised land:

- They were to follow the Cloud. We are to follow the Christ – Matt. 16:24.
- They were rescued from slavery and prepared for the journey to the promised land. We are to be prepared. – 1 Cor. 16:13 – Stand in the faith. Study, pray, and encourage each other. – Luke 12:35 – Be ready when the master returns.
- They trusted that God would fight their enemies. No matter how big our struggles, God will provide. – Eph. 6:11 – Put on the armor of God.
- Moses invited his father-in-law to go with them to the promise land. We should invite others. – Rom. 10:15 – We must have beautiful feet that go and tell others.
- When the Cloud moved, they kept their tabernacle in the light. As Christians, our bodies are the temple of God. When Christ moves, we move. We walk in the light as He is in the light – 1 John 1:7.

"We're marching to Zion." May God be with us in our march, and may we follow God.

Application for the Day: Today, I will pray for trust to follow, courage to convert, strength to stand, and perseverance to walk in the light. May this prayer be carried out in my march through the day with Christ.

Bonus Devotional

Stir Up One Another

Troy Williams

Today's Scripture: Hebrews 10:19-25

It is cool watching things get stirred up. I especially like watching my wife take ingredients for a pie and stir them up. I know that there is going to be a great smelling aroma and a tantalizing taste. Her pies are delicious. If she did not stir up all the ingredients, then the pie would not look or taste the same.

"Stir up" is an action term. God uses the same action term "stir up" when He is describing what we should do for each other. We are to stir each other up to good works. What does that look like in the body of Christ?

One ingredient we should stir up is found in Hebrews 10:22, which says that we are to draw near to God. Drawing near to God includes listening to His voice, talking to Him, and walking with Him. We insert these ingredients into our bowl.

Another ingredient is the hope that we have of salvation through Christ. If we do not put this ingredient into our batch, the evil one can pull it out of the bowl and lead people to fall away (Heb. 3:12-13).

When our relationship with God and the hope of salvation through Christ are in the bowl. we then can add the church. Hebrews 10:24-25 describes how we are to "consider" each other and be with each other. We can look people in the face and rejoice in God's mercy, take comfort in Christ's sacrifice, and be encouraged in our faith. We stir "as we have the opportunity" when all ingredients are in one bowl. When all our individual personalities and talents are mixed, the texture will be love and good works and become a sweet savor to the Lord.

Application for the Day: Today I will find a way to stir up a brother or sister in Christ through a kind word, a call, a letter, or a text. I will encourage a fellow ingredient to love and have good works in our Christian bowl.

Bonus Devotional

Heavenly Endurance
Zach Fuller

Today's Scripture: 1 Corinthians 10:13

Sin is a stain on the soul, but through Christ we have been washed clean of these stains. It is a matter of great distress, then, when one finds themselves committing more sins, adding more stains. Though we may rejoice that even these stains will be washed away, Jesus told us to repent of our sins and do them no more. That is the blessed path we have been set upon as Christians, but what of the temptations of the world which take us off this path, as a lamb strays from the herd? What if we find the temptations too great?

Even in this situation, God comforts us. "No temptation has overtaken you that is not common to man. God is faithful, and he will not let you be tempted beyond your ability, but with the temptation he will also provide the way of escape, that you may be able to endure it" (1 Cor. 10:13). Here it is made clear that whatever we may be tempted with, it is nothing that has not already been used by the devil to tempt those who came before us. No matter what may test you, God has given you the strength and faith to endure.

Not all temptations come as a promise of material pleasures but may arise out of fear of what may be brought against us. In today's world, Christians find themselves struggling against a tide of ill will from those who would "call evil good and good evil" (Isa. 5:20). As the apostle John wrote to the church of Smyrna, we must not fear what tribulation is to come for those who endure and hold fast to the faith shall be with God in heaven (Rev. 2:10). Jesus has shown the way; let no one turn you from his path! Be steadfast in your faith in God for "the righteous are bold as a lion" and bear no shame (Prov. 28:1).

Application for the Day: Today I will pray for God to help me endure temptations.

Index